... *Metamorphosis*, the photographic book *The Theatre of Steven Berkoff* and his autobiography *Free Association*. Among his film credits are *Octopussy, Beverly Hills Cop*, and his own production of *Decadence*. He lives in London.

STEVEN BERKOFF

Plays One

East

West

Greek

Sink the Belgrano!

Massage

Lunch

The Bow of Ulysses

Sturm und Drang

faber and faber

This collection first published in 1994 as *The Collected Plays* Volume I
by Faber and Faber Limited
3 Queen Square London WC1N 3AU
Reissued in 1996 as *Steven Berkoff: Plays One*
Reprinted in 2000 with revisions to *East* and *The Bow of Ulysses* and
Sturm und Drang included

East was first published in 1997 by John Calder (Publishers) Ltd, London
West was first published in *West and other plays* in 1985
by Faber and Faber Limited
Greek was first published privately by the author
1980 and then 1982 by John Calder (Publishers) Ltd, London
Sink the Belgrano! was first published in 1987
by Faber and Faber Limited
Lunch was first published in 1985 by Faber and Faber Limited

Photoset in Plantin by Parker Typesetting Service, Leicester
Printed in England by Mackays of Chatham PLC, Chatham, Kent

British Library Cataloguing in Publication data is available

ISBN 978-0-571-20721-3
ISBN 0-571-20721-9

6 8 10 9 7 5

CONTENTS

EAST

*Elegy for the East End
and its energetic waste*

CHARACTERS

DAD
MUM
SYLV
LES
MIKE

AUTHOR'S NOTE

This play was written to exorcize certain demons struggling within me to escape. *East* takes place within my personal memory and experience and is less a biographical text than an outburst or revolt against the sloth of my youth and a desire to turn a welter of undirected passion and frustration into a positive form. I wanted to liberate that time squandered and sometimes enjoyed into a testament to youth and energy. It is a scream or a shout of pain. It is revolt. There is no holding back or reserve in the East End of youth as I remember . . . you lived for the moment and vitally held it . . . you said what you thought and did what you felt. If something bothered you, you let it out as strongly as you could, as if the outburst could curse and therefore purge whatever it was that caused it. One strutted and posed down the Lyceum Strand, the Mecca of our world, performed a series of rituals that let people know who and what you were, and you would fight to the death to defend that particular life style that was your own. *East* could be the east side of any city where the unveneered blast off at each other in their own compounded argot as if the ordinary language of polite communication was as dead as the people who uttered it. I stylized the events further by some cross-fertilization with Shakespeare and threw in a few classical allusions – this seemed to help to take it out further into a ritual and yet defined it with a distinct edge. It still felt like *East* and could not have been done, I believe, in any other dialect or accent except perhaps East Side New York. The acting has to be loose and smacking of danger . . . it must smart and whip out like a fairy's wicked lash. There is no reserve and therefore no embarrassment. One critic described it as 'filthy beyond the call of duty' but in fact it is a loving appreciation of the male and female form. We played it in three theatres starting at the small Traverse, Edinburgh, and it was good to hear the kind of laughter that came not only from the belly but had that ring of familiarity, that sudden explosive yelp of identification, when they laughed hardest, the dirty beasts.

East was first performed at the Traverse Theatre by the London Theatre Group for the 1975 Edinburgh Festival which then transferred to the King's Head, London. The cast was as follows:

DAD	Barry Stanton
MUM	Robert Longden
SYLV	Anna Nygh
LES	Barry Philips
MIKE	Steven Berkoff
Music	John Prior
Producer	Steven Berkoff

This version of *East* was first performed at the Greenwich Theatre in July 1976. The cast was as follows:

DAD	Matthew Scurfield
MUM	David Delve
SYLV	Anna Nygh
LES	Barry Philips
MIKE	Steven Berkoff
Music	Neil Hansford
Producer	Steven Berkoff

A new production of *East* was presented at the Regent Theatre in August 1977.

SCENE I

The stage is bare but for five chairs in a line upstage whereby the cast act as chorus for the events that are spoken, mimed and acted. A piano just offstage creates mood, adds tension and introduces themes. A large screen upstage centre has projected on it a series of real East End images, commenting and reminding us of the actual world just outside the stage. The cast enter and sit on five chairs facing front – piano starts up and they sing 'My Old Man says Follow the Van' – out of order and in canons and descants. It comes suddenly to a stop, MIKE *and* LES *cross to two oblong spots – image of two prisoners photographed for the criminal hall of fame. They pose three times before speaking.* DAD, MUM *and* SYLV *speak as a chorus.*

LES: Donate a snout, Mike?

MIKE: OK I'll bung thee a snout, Les.

MIKE: ⎫
LES: ⎭ Now you know our names.

MIKE: Mike's OK. After the Holy Saint . . . Mike with a hard K. Like a kick . . . swift . . . not mad about Les.

LES: It's soft, it's gooey . . . but choose it I did not . . . in my mother's hot womb did she curse this name on me . . . it's my handle . . . under the soft – it's spiky, under the pillow it's sharp . . . concealed instrument . . . offensive weapon lies waiting.

MIKE: Oh, he doth bestride Commercial Road like a Colossus . . . that's my manor . . . where we two first set our minces on each other . . . and those Irish yobs walk under our huge legs and peep about for dishonourable bother . . . he's my mucker, china or mate.

LES: And he mine since those days at least twelve moons ago when sailing out the Black Raven pub in Whitechapel the selfsame street where blessed Jack did rip and tear in cold thick nights so long ago . . . those muffled screams and slicing flesh no more than sweetest memories of him that went so humble 'bout his nightly graft. Tell how it chanced that we sworn mates were once the deadly poison of each other's eye.

7

MIKE: He clocked the bird I happened to be fiancéd to, my darling Sylv (of legendary knockers) and I doth take it double strong that this short git in suede and rubber, pimples sprouting forth like buttercups on sunny days from off his greasy boat: that he should dare to lay upon her svelte and tidy form his horror leering jellies . . . so I said to him 'fuck off thou discharge from thy mother's womb before with honed and sweetened razor I do trouble to remove thy balls from thee.'

LES: Oh! Ho! I gushed. You fancied me around the back with boots and chains and knives, behind the super cinema it was then called afore it came a cut-price supermarket . . .

MIKE: Which we have well and truly robbed since then.

LES: So round the back we went that night . . . the fog was falling fast, our coat collars were up . . . our breath like dragon's steam did belch forth from our violent mouths . . . while at the selfsame time we uttered uncouth curses, thick with bloody and unholy violence of what we would most like to carve upon each other's skulls . . . the crowd of yobs that formed a ring of yellow faces in the lamplight.

MIKE: Right.

LES: . . . Hungry for the blood of creatures nobler and more daring than themselves.

MIKE: Right.

LES: With dribble down their loathsome mouths they leered and lusted for our broken bottles and cold steel to start the channels gouging in our white and precious cheeks.

MIKE: I thought now fuck this for a laugh.

LES: That's right.

MIKE: So what if sly old Sylv had led me on a touch by showing out to all the lads, provoking hard-ons and gang wars between opposing tribes from Hoxton to Tottenham . . .

LES: From Bethnal Green to Hornsey Town.

MIKE: From Poplar up to Islington. The clash of steel and crunch of boot on testicle has long disturbed the citizens of those battle-scarred manors and blue-bottles with truncheons hard as iron have had their helmets.

LES: And their heads.

MIKE: Sometimes removed by rude and lusty lads complete with knuckle-dusters and iron bars nicked from their dads.

CHORUS (*sing*): Any old iron, any old iron, any any any old iron . . .

MIKE: Honest and trusty trade upon the streets. We thought . . .

MIKE: ⎫
LES: ⎭ Now fuck this for a laugh!

LES: But we could hardly turn back now with five and fifty chinas egging us on there, with shouts of 'come on Les, cut off his cock', and 'punch the fucker's head in.'

CHORUS: Come on Les, cut off his cock and punch the fucker's head in.

LES: Or destroy him Mike . . . for fuck's sake don't just stand there . . .

CHORUS: Destroy him Mike . . . for fuck's sake don't just stand there. Nut him in the nose . . . and part his skull from him the greasy turd.

LES: And yaroo! Yarah!

MIKE: Use your iron . . . put the boot in with shrieks of 'bollocks'.

LES: 'Slerp!'

MIKE: 'Dog face.'

CHORUS: 'And fucking hell' . . .

MIKE: 'Smash.'

LES: 'Hit.'

MIKE: 'Shithead' . . .

SYLV: 'Anoint the cunt with death.'

MIKE: One cried (with voice so vehement). Oh Sylv, it was thee, yes, thy gentle voice did sway me finally to deal out pain, then in I went like paste. I flashed my raziory which danced about his face like fireflies, reflecting in the cold wet streets the little yellow gas light, till the sheet of red that splat from out his pipes did dull it . . . just felt that soft thud, thwat, as knife hits flesh . . . You know the feel? It's soft and hard at once and gives you collywobbles with thrilldoms of pure joy.

LES: My pure and angel face, my blessed boat did, on that sacred night receive his homage . . . red did flow – I knew my cheek

9

was gaping open like a flag . . . but never mind, to stop the Tiber, stop myself from kissing death flush on the lips I held it with my hand, held what I could while trickling through my fingers ran my juices sweet as life.

CHORUS (*murmurs*): 'Brave Les' . . . 'hard man', *etc.*

LES: And then I simply said 'you cunt'. Just that. 'You cunt . . . I'll shit down scorpions of pain upon thee . . . I'll eat you! Get it!!!' My iron found his skull where he had just begun to move but left enough for me to bang and crack a dash, enough bone there to bend and shift a bit . . . split off and splinter bits in brain . . . his brain . . . splatter . . . the lads said.'

DAD: Oink.

SYLV: And assholes.

CHORUS: Fucking hell!

LES: Too far thou'rt gone and really farted death on him . . .

CHORUS: Oh shit . . . swerp . . . ugh . . . AAAAAARH . . .

LES: Have it away, before the law doth mark us for accessory.

MIKE: So off they flew . . . left me for dead and Les near dying too in pools of his own blood he choked . . . the steel had bit too deep . . . I felt the silence creeping in . . . and found myself in an old movie, silent like . . . and flickering to its end . . . so what? What's it all about?

CHORUS: Alfie?

MIKE: Those cunts have left us, shit in pants (their own) while we slosh round in guts . . . they watched, were nicely freckled by our gore, and thought 'Let's scarper now, we had our fun, those cunts are done . . . let's piss off 'fore the law should stride with boots hobnailed in woe to grab us in their fat and gnarled claws.'

LES: We picked ourselves and all our bits from off the deck and fell into each other's arms . . . with 'What the fuck', and flashed a quirky red-soaked grin at our daft caper thinking what a bloody sight . . . we can't jump on the 19 bus in our condition looking like what they hang up in Smithfields . . . Those bloody sides of beef (for those of thee unversed in the geography of our fair state) so we did crawl and hop . . .

stagger and slide 'hold on Mike, nearly there . . . don't die in
Balls Pond Road you berk . . . grip hard' . . . I only had a pint
or two of rosy red in my tired veins myself . . .the rest I used
to paint the town with . . . would I have strength enough to
get there with my new-found mate, whose brains were
peeping out the top of his broke patch . . . would I not conk
out in the street at Aldgate East (untimely end dear Les of
youthful folly) our mums and dads with bellow, whine and
oily tears at our sad stones . . . we had those visions come
and go . . . they'd tell sad stories of the death of kids who
lived not wisely but too well.

MIKE: We were in love the time we stumbled into the casualty at
Charing Cross. And fell into the arms of white-gloved saints
who sewed a nifty stitch or ten . . . no questions asked and
when John Law did come and mum to visit us we pleaded we
were set upon by those vile cunts from Tottenham.

LES: Who picked on us.

MIKE: The innocent.

LES: To venge some deadly feud.

MIKE: From bygone days. The two of us got thick as tea leaves in
a pot that's stewed too long and hatched out in our white
and cosy starched beds a dozen saucy plots of murders,
armed assaults and robbery with harm.

LES: Bank raids so neatly planned in dead of night . . .

MIKE: Of rape's delight we'd chat . . .

LES: Exchange a tale or two of cold-blood deeds we done in
alleys dark as hell.

MIKE: And other heinous escapades

LES: Too heinous to retell.

MIKE: Yeah, that's how it happened . . . Yeah, that's it . . .

LES: She was a bitch.

MIKE: A slag of advanced vile.

LES: A pint of filth . . .

MIKE: But still . . . She was nice.

SCENE 2

Silent Film Sequence.
Piano.
A silent film now ensues performed in the staccato, jerky motion of an
old movie. It shows MIKE *calling on* SYLV *– meeting* MUM *and* DAD *–*
going for a night out – SYLV *is attracted to* LES *– a mock fight. They*
are separated and SYLV*'s long monologue comes from it. The movie*
sequence reinforces and fills in the events of scene 1.

SCENE 3

Sylv's long speech . . . She was there.

SYLV: At it they went . . . it weren't half fun at first it weren't my
    fault those jesting-jousting lads should want a tournament
    of hurt and crunch and blood and shriek . . . all on my dress
    it went . . . That's Micky's blood I thought . . . it seemed to
    shoot up from something that cracked . . . I saw him
    mimicking an oilwell . . . though he'd take off many things
    for a laugh this time I did not laugh so much . . . they fought
    for me . . . thy blood my royal Mick wast shed for me and
    never shall the suds of Persil or Daz remove that royal
    emblem from that skirt that many times you gently lifted in
    the Essoldo Bethnal Green. I was that monument of flesh
    thy wanton hands would smash and grab, I only clocked the
    other geezer Mike, and can I help if my proud tits should
    draw their leery eyes to feast on them . . . and now a hate
    doth sunder our strong love and never more will my soft
    thighs be prised apart by his fierce knees with 'open them
    thou bitch before I ram a knuckle sandwich in thy painted
    boat'. I miss him true in spite of all and did not wish to see
    him mashed and broken like a bloody doll . . . but now the
    bastard blameth me for all and seeks vile vengeance on my
    pretty head . . . which if he tries will sorely grieve my
    brothers Bert and George who will not hesitate to finish off
    the bits that Les did leave but all this chat of violence I hate

... is ultra horrible to me that thrives on love and tongue-wrenched kisses in the back of MG Sprites with a 'stop I'm not like that!' ... Oh just for now which doth ensure a second date, so hold a morsel back girls and he'll crave it all the more.

SCENE 4

MIKE *and* LES *commence* 'If You Were the Only Girl in the World' *which covers the bringing on of the only props - a table and chairs. On the table are toast, a teapot with steaming tea, a tureen of baked beans, a packet of margarine – in fact the normal tea-time scene. They sit around the table and eat. During* DAD*'s long speech he eventually destroys everything on the table in nostalgic fury. The table and contents become a metaphor for the battle of Cable Street – his rage becomes monstrous and gargantuan.*

Ma and Pa.
DAD: Mum?
MUM: What?
DAD: What time does *Hawaii Five-O* come on?
MUM: What time does it come on?
DAD: Yeah!
MUM: I don't know dear ...
DAD: She doesn't know, she watches it every night, and doesn't know.
MUM: (*Reading*) ... What's a proletariat?
DAD: A geezer who lassoes goats on the Siberian mountains.
MUM: In one word I mean. Six letters.
DAD: *Panorama*'s on first ... yeah that's worth an eyeful ... Then we can catch *Ironside*, turn over for *The Saint* and cop the last act of Schoenberg's *Moses and Aaron*.
MUM: Charlton Heston was in that.
DAD: Machinery has taken all the joy out of work ... the worker asks for more and more money until he breaks down the economy hand in hand with the unions who are

communist-dominated and make the country ripe for a takeover by the red hordes.

MUM: You haven't paid the licence.

DAD: She's a consumer on the market, that's all, not even a human being but a consumer who's analysed for what she buys and likes by a geezer offering her a questionnaire at the supermarket – makes her feel important . . . I try to educate it but 'tis like pouring wine into the proverbial leaking barrel.

MUM: Suppose they come round.

DAD: Nobody visits us any more.

MUM: They might then you'd go to court and it would be all over the *Hackney Gazette*.

DAD: You don't want to believe all that rubbish about detector vans. That's just to scare you . . . make you think that they're on your tail . . . anyway if anyone knocks on the door we can whip the telly out sharpish like and hide it in the lavatory until they're gone . . . simple . . . say . . . 'There's been a mistake . . . your radar must have been a few degrees out and picked out the hair dryer performing on her curlers.'

MUM: But anyone can knock on the door . . . you'll have to start running every time someone knocks.

DAD: When was the last time we had a visitor – especially since the lift's nearly always broken by those little black bastards who've been moving in, and who's going to climb twenty-four floors to see us except the geezer for the Christmas money – so if anyone knocks on the door it can only be one of two things – the law inquiring after Mike since they think he's just mugged some old lady for her purse, or the TV licence man – in either case I can shove it in the loo!

MUM: Mike doesn't do things like that – I won't have you uttering such dreadful libels – my son takes after me – you won't find him taking after you – he is kind to old ladies – helps them across the road on windy days.

DAD: That was only a subtle jest you hag, thou lump of foul deformity – untimely ripped from thy mother's womb – can't you take a flaming dash of humour – that I so flagrantly waste on you – eh? What then . . . what bleeding then – thank

God he's not a pooftah at least already so soon – Eh . . .
where would you put your face then – if he took after me the
country would rise to its feet – give itself an almighty shake –
and rid itself of all the fleas that are sucking it dry . . .
(*Wistful*) He could have . . . Ozzie.

LES: Who?

DAD: Ozzie Mosley, he had the right ideas – put them into
uniforms – into the brown shirts – gave people an identity.
Those meetings were a sight. All them flags. Then, they
knew what to do – take the law into your own hands when
you know it makes sense. That beautiful summer in '38 was
it? – When we marched six abreast to Whitechapel –
beautiful it were – healthy young British men and women –
a few wooden clubs – just in case they got stroppy down
there, just the thoughts of the people letting the nation know
it weren't stomaching any more of it – the drums banging
out a rhythm in the front and Ozzie marching at our head.
We get to Aldgate – if you didn't know it was Aldgate you
could smell it – and there were us few loyal English telling
the world that England is for us – and those long-nosed gits,
those evil-smelling greasy kikes had barricaded up – you,
couldn't even march through England's green and pleasant,
the land where Jesus set his foot – they had requisitioned
Aldgate and Commercial Road – our lads, what did they do,
not turn back – not be a snivelly turn-coat but let them have
it. They soon scuttered back into the tailors' shops stinking
of fried fish and dead foreskins – and with a bare fist, a few
bits of wood, we broke a skull or two that day – but Hebrew
gold had corrupted our fair law and we were outnumbered –
what could we do – the oppressed still living there under the
Semite claw sweating their balls out in those stinking sweat
shops – could only shout 'come on lads' – they had no
stomach for it, no strength. It were for them that we had to
get through. But we were outnumbered – the Christian
Soldiers could not get through this time – not then, and
what happened – I'll tell you what happened – by not getting
down Commercial Street . . . by not getting down

Whitechapel – Alie Street, Commercial Road and Cable
Street, Leman Street we opened the floodgates for the rest –
the Pandora's bleeding Box opened and the rest of the
horrors poured in. That's what happened mate. (*Suddenly*)
What's the time?!

MUM: Eight o'clock.

DAD: We've missed *Crossroads*!!?!
  (*Blackout.*)

SCENE 5

The table and its contents are splattered to the floor from prior speech.
MUM *wipes it up. The five chairs now become a row in a cinema – we
see the different films by the piano suggesting the theme from a
'Weepie', a 'Western' and the characters relating to them all –* MIKE
chats up SYLV *–* DAD *goes to the toilet offstage – much vomiting and
noise – people change seats –* SYLV *leaves and* MIKE *follows – chat is
improvised until we see the scene with* MIKE *and* SYLV *in 'How the
Two Fought for the Possession of'. During it* DAD *and* LES *become
chorus and mates of* MIKE.

SCENE 6

How the Two Fought for the Possession of.

SYLV: She were in ingredients of flesh-pack suavely fresh . . .
  deodorized and knicker white . . . lip-gleam and teethed . . .
  shoes thick-wedged with seam running up the back of her
  leg as if to point the way to tourists pruriently lost . . .

MIKE: 'Hallo darlin' . . . fancy thee a chat, a meal, a stroll, a drink
  in the Cock and Bull surrounding a Babycham or two and
  plethoras of witty verbiage spewing from my gutter mouth
  . . . with a larf or two . . . they say a laugh doth provide the
  key to open Pandora's Box of dirty tricks.

SYLV: Piss off thou lump. Though hast no style for me get lost
  . . . too old . . . too young . . . too slow . . . I'm too trim for

thee and move like what you dream about (on good nights)
I'm sheer unadulterated pure filth each square inch a
raincoat's fantasy – all there swelled full – I am the vision in
your head – the fire you use to stoke your old wife's familiar
stoves (you know what I mean) . . . sag not – pink tipped,
tight box, plumbing perfect – switches on and off to the
right touch . . . not thy think-fingered labourer's paws thou
slob and street-corner embellishment . . . thou pin-table
musician . . . thy flesh would ne'er move – would shrink
under my glare – so try.

MIKE: Tasty verily – so thou, bitch, seeks to distress my johnny
tool with psychological war, humiliating it into surrender-
shrink . . . I'll descend on thee like a moon probe, thou
planet of delights fleshy . . . advance my antennae, vibrating
back to the lust-computerizing cells the sanguine goodies
that do lie unmined . . . I'll chart thy surfaces until thou
criest from within thy depths, subterranean and murky and
foetid swamps, 'Mike oh Mike', fluting gurgled falsettos
from thy lips of coral, 'What dost thou dooo! . . .' I'll rip off
my clothes and gaberdine and make thee view the sight that
sent Penelope mad and wait ten years for that . . . the girth
of a Cyclops to stun to stab, screams like Attila, growls,
snarls, froths, foams and speaks to you in a thousand ways.
The length of an ass, the stamina of a Greek, the form of
Michelangelo's David, as solid as a rock, as tricky as a fox,
as lithe as a snake, as delicate as a rose, the speed of a
panther, reflexes match the piston power of the Flying
Scotsman, as hot as hell, as pretty as Paris, its helmet
matches the battering ram that felled the walls of Troy, *balls*
like the great cannon that Pompeii used to subdue the
barbarian, as rich in goodies as the Tiber bursting its banks,
its juices as sweet as the honey from the little wasps of
Lesbos that only live a day, as sweet as the dripping that
mum puts on the Sunday joint, and with the magic sceptre
that laser-like splits and cracks through walls, I'll fill you
full till thou'll not feel one shred of space not occupied by
flesh-blood-splech-filled-slurp . . . tongue tied, lava flow-

flesh eat. Where thy arse rises creamily mocking Bertorelli's
ice-cream, the trembling domes of the mosques of Omar
bounce, weave, bob, groan and whine. Oh, you're the
spring time after fierce winter ... buds sprout ... opening
... little whisper in the hawthorn ... Oh! I thought thy
planet shook then, caught thee then a word did it ...
Pandora's Box teases open, does it with a yes ... yes ... yes
... No! No!
YESYESYESYESYESYESYESYESYESYESYES
... (*Blackout.*)

SCENE 7

Syv's Longing Speech.

SYLV: I for once would like to be a fella, unwholesome both in
deed and word and lounge around one leg cocked up and
car keys tinkling on my pinky. Give a kick* at talent strolling
and impale them with an impertinent and fixed stare ...
hand in Levi-Strauss and teeth grinding, and that super
unworrisome flesh that toys between your thighs, that we
must genuflect and kneel to, that we are beaten across the
skull with. Wish I could cruise around and pull those tarts
and slags whose hearts would break as he swiftly chews us
up and spits us out again ... the almighty boot! Nay, not fair
that those pricks get all the fun – with their big raucous
voices and one dozen weekly fucks ... cave mouths, shout,
burp and Guinness soaked ... If I dare do that ... 'What an
old scrubber-slag-head' utter their fast and vicious lips ...
so I'd like to be a fella. Strolling down the front with the lads
and making minute and limited wars with knife-worn
splatter and invective splurge. And not have the emblem of
his scummy lust to Persil out with hectic scrub ... just my
johnny tool to keep from harm and out of mischief ... my
snarling beasty to water and feed from time to time to rotten

*eye up

time . . . to dip my wick into any old dark and hot with no
conscience or love groan . . . doth he possess the plague in
gangrened bliss to donate to me and not give a shit. I am
snarled beneath his bristly glass-edged jaw, beneath a
moving sack of leer and hard and be a waste-bin for his
excessives and embellishments and No . . . no . . . not
tonight my friend, a dangerous time is here in case your
tadpoles start a forest fire in my oven or just a bun . . . you
won't will you? . . . you will be careful! (Yes!) . . . you won't
. . . not inside (No!) Not tonight . . . ('Doth thou not love me
then') he quests ('nor feel my intense pain, then see me not
again, for you must sacrifice thy altar of lust-pink and
pornographia to my tempered sullen and purple swollen
flesh.') Oh Micky! Micky! Wait until tomorrow.
('Tomorrow I may be dead,' he chants in dirge of minor key
. . . 'by then my softly flesh may lie in shreds and curling on
the streets a victim of nuclear aggro from the powers that
deal out death on wholesale scale and liquidize your little
Mick to tar, and what was once a silken mass of moving
ecstasy programmed by filthy raunchy lust lay now a
charred and bitter heap.') Oh who can put it back again
those swivel hips/ball-bearing joints flicker spine and tongue
like a praying mantis . . . ('so listen', he adds 'dunk-head
and splatter-pull . . . seize the time before time doth seize
thee . . . you of the intricate wrist and juice imbiber from the
holy North and South.' . . . 'Give me all now or "it" may
with my balls explode, such things are known when
passion's smarting angels are defied and I may die in
loathsome sickness here upon this plastic and Formica
divan (mum and dad meanwhile in deathly lock of wrath
from heavy bingo economic loss) . . .') So wrench open
deflower unpeel, unzip . . . pull off . . . tear round knee tights
stuck . . . get your shoes off . . . Ow. Knickers (*caught on heel*)
. . . OOh, zip hurts . . . dive in and out . . . more a whip in,
like a visit – quick, can't stay just sheltering from the rain –
cup o'tea hot and fast . . . hot plunge-squirge and sklenge
mixed for a brief 'hallo'. A rash of oohs and aaahs quiver

and hummmmmmy . . . mmm . . . then hot and flushy he
climbs off (come in number four) and my tears those holy
relics of young love tracing mortal paths to elysium down
my cheeks . . . while the 'he' with fag choke and smoke . . .
tooth-grin-zip-up . . . me lying looking at the future flashing
across the ceiling. He, flashing his comb through his barnet
and reddened cheeks blood soaked (like a saucy cherub, so
lovable sometimes you know how boys have this lovely thing
about them, some little-boy habit that makes them
adorable, crushable-eatable-sweetable-dolly cuddly though
sometimes you could kill them) and me lying there a pile of
satiate bone and floppy tits flesh-pinched and crack-full of
his slop containing God only knows what other infernos but
thought I tasted something very strange on his straining
dangle which he is wont to offer to me sacrificial like . . . Oh
let me be a bloke and sit back curseless, nor forever join the
queue of curlered birds outside the loo for dire-emergency
. . . do we piss more than men or something . . . nor break
my heels in escalators and flash my ass, ascending stairs, to
the vile multitude who fantasize me in their quick sex-
lustered movies in which I am cast as the queen of slut and
yield . . . let me be a bloke and wear trousers stuffed and
have pectorals instead of boobs, abdominal and latissimus-
dorsi, a web of knotted muscular armature to whip my
angered fist into the flesh-pain of mouthy geezers who dare
to cast on me their leery cautious minces . . . stab them with
fear and have a dozen flesh-hot weekly . . . sleep well and
mum fussed, breakfast shoved, 'who's been a naughty boy
then', to this pasty wreck of skin and bone gasping in his bed
skiving work through riotous folly, bloodlet assault and all
night bang and 'our lad's a lad, and sown his wild then has
he and did you cut yourself a slice' . . . while 'get yourself to
the office Sylv or you'll be late,' and the sack in its bed is
parlering for another cup of rosy. He's lying in bed whiles
I'm on the Underground getting goosed in the rush hour
between Mile End and Tottenham Court Road by some
creepy asshole with dandruff, a wife and three accidental

kids and who's probably in the accounts department . . .
most perverts come from there.

SCENE 8

LES *comes down downstage and mimes office scene, says* 'Miss Smith
would you please take this to the accounts department.' *As she
complies he gooses her and shrieks with maniacal joy thus fulfilling the
prophecy in her last speech. His leaping up and down dissolves into a
seaside scene –* MIKE *bouncing a ball.* SYLV *skipping, etc.* DAD *and*
MUM *enter.*

DAD: Years ago things were good, you got value out of your
money, a dollar was five bob, a summer's day was hot and
sunny like a summer's day, you weren't short changed, you
got your full twelve hours' worth, then we'd take the train
from Liverpool Street to Leigh-on-Sea and walk to
Southend, go to the Kursaal Amusements . . .
(*On the words 'Kursaal Amusements' the cast become bumper-
cars – roller coasters. The ghost train. 'I've Got a Lovely Bunch
of Coconuts' is sung – What the Butler Saw. Ice-cream sellers.
The Carousel. Swimming in the sea.* MUM *gets out the
sandwiches and Tizer –* SYLV *takes a photo, then so does* MIKE.)
SYLV: Smile, Mum.
DAD: She is smiling.
(*The scene should be improvised and the mime accurate and
clear. The piano reinforces all the vignettes. It leaves* LES *alone
on stage at the end of the last photograph. The scenes of fun at
Southend delicately indicating* LES*'s sense of isolation.*)

SCENE 9

Les's Tale of Woe when he did Sup on Porridge.
LES: (*Start slow pianissimo and build*) I was lonely, you know what
I mean. Just lonesome basically I think, like is one born that

way, I always felt lonely as if it was something like a habit, or
the colour of your hair . . . like even a bit of clobbering now
and then, the taste of pain and blood, was like an act of love
to me: so when two nifty lads went round the back to
bundle, it could be like your bird that you pulled round for
stand-up charvers. And sometimes you would pull ('cause
you were lonely basically) anything that came along . . . so
she looked at me, I crossed the road and gave it a bit of chat,
just some bird of tender years or jail bait if you like. Maybe
fourteen or fifteen. I said meet me after work, she said OK
why not, with a tiny giggle and freckles leaping all over the
place, and I was working in this dump, impersonating
Frankenstein, a place where you stood round pretending to
be busy – one of those stores where you'd try to con people
into buying what they didn't want, a grimy little men's wear
shop, not a geary boutique but full of rotten little grotty
striped ties and collar studs, ('don't forget to dust the cuff-
links Les. Straighten out the ties Les') where you stood
around dying and acquiring bad breath, pop eyed for a
pathetic wet customer to bleed. Horrible beige pullovers
bought by the wives of Irish navvies who'd come back to
change it half a dozen times 'cause we always bunged them
whatever size we had in stock ('don't take a swap Les, get
their gelt, they can always change it') . . . incredibly crummy
blazers hanging in a rack like dead fish on parade, shirts with
drab little collars with a million pins, in two-tone checks
that hangmen and clerks would buy with shit-coloured ties
to go with them . . . and maybe a cardigan in maroon . . . this
month's colour . . . the wives trotting round the mirror
anxious for their fifty bob, the manager's loathsome mask
that he wears for a face creases like Fu Manchu. 'A nice tie
to go with it sir? How are you fixed for shirts . . . Okayee?'
His eyes look like two gobs of phlegm, he sits in the back
room where they kept those fucking horrible Y-front pants
that make you look like a rupture case – he'd sit there so
greasy you could fry him – in that dirty little back room he'd
be watching – having his crummy little tea break . . . ''ere

Les, go get us a cake will ya son . . . a chocolate éclair or
something' . . . 4.15 his looked-forward-to-tea break in a day
that poured down boredom like yellow piss . . . his frog's
eyes bulging in case you didn't sell the shop-soiled crew
neck six sizes too big to some innocent black cunt. 'Yeah it
fits you beeauutiful! Lovely shade, it goes with anything' . . .
he spits as he rushes out of the back room like a great huge
dirty spider with bits of éclair sticking to his revolting fat lips
. . . 'Fuck me! Les we got to top yesterday's figure,' he
squelched from the side of the mouth, a hiss like a rat's fart
. . . but the black is confused by being surrounded by faces
the colour of plague victims, all the retchy salesmen with
bent knees and worn-out grins. Yellow-teethed vultures
whose eyes vaguely send out a couple more volts every time
the shop door opens. 'Only take thirty minutes for lunch on
Saturday – busy day for shirts' . . . some slag says 'that one in
the window', 'Oh show me which one you mean love', any
excuse to escape and breathe some fresh air fumes from the
lorries and buses belching past which is as fresh as a Scottish
loch compared to the smell in the shop of rotten cancered
flesh laced by a few farts when everyone scatters. 'Oh fuck,
Harry's farted again' . . . chortle-burp . . . all the macabre
and twisted figures of humanity oozed through that
deceased testament to Beau Brummel, that charnel house of
gaberdine and worsted hell . . . the living corpses – slack
mouths and brains waiting for 6 p.m. or death, one of the
two or both – hands in pockets playing with anything that
reminded them that they had a tiny dot of feeling left –
standing there like it was a way of life. I was thinking of that
bird which was making me very anxious about the Hickory-
Dickory and impatient to act out a few skin scenarios
floating around in my skull. At 6 p.m. the morgue closed for
the night. I'd check the gelt I half-inched, not a bad day a
few ties wrapped round my waist – given a dozen pairs of
socks to my mate and watch Mr Greasy with fag hanging
out of his perpetual mouth check his cash. The cunt never
found out 'cause his brains were soaked in grease, his lungs

in cancer and phlegm and his jacket in dandruff . . . so I
escaped from that place wondering how I might burn it to
the ground with all of them frying in the manager's grease. I
saw her as planned and she was waiting for me like she said
she would, and that had kept me going for the day – had
stopped me from going insane, the idea of the two of us
hacking away at each other's goodies – that was something
real, alive . . . that would give a bit of meaning to my life – us
two locked away in a little cosy place, where I could crawl
out of my skin and get into hers, sweat, pant and shriek – so
she was standing there, happy like it was Xmas and she said
yes and I took her back to my pad all freckling and giggling
and then she delivers her history in a funny Irish – how she's
pissed off at home with a mad Irish dad who beats her and
whiles I pacify her with a quick, svelte and heroic in and out,
she says could she stay with me since she's bound to be
clobbered by her paddy daddy for being so late. I demur to
the riotous demand with full awareness of the Law's
nastiness to the souls who taste young flesh and instruct her
to the bus to take her back to evil Kilburn. Just one hour
later I was in the middle of some shrewd interpretations of
the theory of relativity and just getting into the quantum
theory and boggling how light would take 200 billion years
to get round the universe, when bang bang at the door and
two thick-eared brainless cops come yobbing in. Dressed in
the kind of clobber I'd been flogging all day, scaring the shit
out of me and the cats – the mad Irish had gone to the
johnny law with some mad tale of rape and kidnap to avoid
chastisement at the hands of dirt-head dad. Grabbing me in
their thick fingers (not made for Chopin's 'Etudes') while
they call me 'dirty bastard' and other unflattering epithets
while breathing their foul vomit breath in my face. 'I'll kill
thee' I spray (hair on end) 'not now, not tomorrow but one
day I'll eat your eyeballs, I'll bathe you in acid, I'll stab your
fat guts with icepicks when lying in your bed beer-soaked
bloated, thick with haze and swill like drunken pigs. I'll stab
and thrust until your tripe explodes,' which doubtless did

not go down very well, since they pounded all manner of horny fist into my soft and sweet flesh . . . those harbingers of death . . . those wholesale legal sadists . . . those lawmen did believe the slag, which got her off the hook, and rendered carte of blanche to them for fun and thump, and poor old Les before a graven magistrate is dragged who chides and moralizes 'bout snatch too young for me while thinking of his handicap in bed and golf and house in Esher, Surrey, his furtive weekly whore and sessions of paid lash, looking down at me from dizzy heights he says he would be lenient and I reply from the bottom of my black and lying soul, of 'heartfelt sorrow', and 'never again', and then he said, 'three years I curse on thee' and as he did I heard my mouth reply that he would die a death in fire so slow he'd rather be eaten by ants while bathed in honey . . . and as they dragged me screaming down some cold stone corridor my shouts sent curses ripping through his skull, and now my curse comes true.

MIKE: So ho did you kill him Les?

LES: I doubt if I should let on now, lest hungry ears attend, you do not know whose flappy lugs may bring a fate too horrible for verbs upon my lovely head. But content yourself I did.

MIKE: There's no one here but us and our rabid desires.

LES: I think I hear the beating of a hundred hearts.

MIKE: Only us and our imaginations, as foul as Vulcan's stithy.

LES: What are those sighs and murmurs, soft groans?

MIKE: The punters who paid for a seat to witness thy foul and cruel beauty, that will haunt them in their dreams.

LES: Do you mean we're in a play?

MIKE: Something of that kind.

LES: I am not, even if you may be.

MIKE: You mean to say . . .

LES: Exactly, you sussed it true, I am no player who struts and frets his hour upon the stage and then is heard no more.

MIKE: You guessed aright, I am that merry wanderer of the night.

LES: You've made a time slip into the wrong play.

MIKE: I'm caught in a time-space trajectory.

LES; Can you see me . . . I can only just see you.

MIKE: Yes, but you're fading fast. What's happening?

LES; Think you've hooked on to an errant radio wave from c56, your own waves are sacrificing themselves to its force until your anti-matter coalesces.

MIKE: Fuck! What can I do . . .

LES: Nothing, just go with it. I'll tell your mum and Sylv.

MIKE: OK. See ya around sometime . . . I've lost you now . . . can you hear me? . . .

LES: Only just . . . see ya . . .

(*The whole cast become involved in the latter part of the scene . . . floating slowly in space until* MUM *settles down with legs comfortably sprawled over* DAD *on two chairs stage left. The three other actors face offstage and* MUM *is lit in her own space. She takes out a cigarette and commences her speech.*)

SCENE 10

Mum's Point of View.
DAD *is sleeping.*

MUM: Sometimes I get gorged in my throat I see him sleeping – lump sweaty, beer gutted – farty – no hope – thick brained and me the other half of nothing fed with electric media swill – consumer me – *Hawaii Five-O – Z Cars – Coronation Street – Beat the Clock – University Challenge – Sunday Night at the London Palladium – On the Buses – Play of the Month – Play of the Week – Watch With Mother* – tea, fags – light and bitter – ha! ha! and ho! ho! Bingo – Eyes down – clickety click – *What the Papers Say* – Reg Varney – *The Golden Shot* – Live Letters – Tits – Green Shield Stamps (*Pause.*) Hallo dear how are you? Turn over shut up and let me sleep – fart belch the music of the spheres. Got a clean shirt? Who's running at Epsom? 500 more troops being flown in tonight – the Pill is safe – abortions rise – I would like to practise today – Tippett's 'Sonata number 3'; six hours of it, I must be ready for my BBC recital on Wednesday – then I may

26

pair it with Mozart's 'Concerto in C' – Terry Riley, mind
you, needs dextrous finger work – I'll leave that for now and
pick up my percolator at the Green Shield shop – Wall's
pork sausages for supper and Fray Bentos peas –
McDougall's flour for a smooth pastry – do I smell? Does
my mouth taste like an ashtray? Will my lover meet me after
I play Brünnhilde in 'The Ring' at the stage door to Covent
Garden and buy me filet mignon in Rules Café or the
Savoy? Will we drink champagne and discuss our next
production of Verdi's *Otello*? He's longing to play Otello –
but wants Bernstein to direct – I'd be happy with Visconti
really – Maria is coming to tea – must get some Lyons jam
tarts – I met Hemingway in the Brasserie Lipp today, he said
my poetry soars to heaven. Come and have some wine with
Gertrude, there will be some very nice people there.

FATHER: (*Waking up*) Shut your gob. Can't ya let me bleeding
sleep?

(*Blackout.*)

SCENE II

Mike and Les.

MIKE: How's Doris – the imbiber of thy resin with her holy
North and South?

LES: All right.

MIKE: Seeing her tonight?

LES: No!

MIKE: Oh! What happened?

LES: Loaded off her box to other's greedy paws.

MIKE: Almighty slag.

LES: I told her to get to a nunnery, in other words piss off.

MIKE: I thought you were a bit touchy.

(*Pause.*)

LES: I was on the bus today – I jumped on the 38 goin' towards
Balls Pond Road, the one that goes to Leyton – I mounted
at Holborn – just been to the British Museum to look at the

Elgin Marbles which were double fair but too big to half-inch and I was standing, since there were no seats, in the recess where the clippie normally stands – you know when it's quiet she stands there chattin' and making thin jokes to the seats that face each other, having a quiet fart as the bus makes its last journey down Piccadilly up Shaftesbury Avenue you know past *Jesus Christ* – up Charing Cross passed that cinema showing *I was A Go Go Dancer in a Saigon Brothel* – spins around the Centre Point Synagogue and skates down Holborn – up Mount Pleasant Post Office where the spade post office workers are skiving in the betting shop, past the Angel where Joe Lyons used to be, where one's mum supped famous cups of rosy amidst merry parlance, now it's boarded up, down Essex Road, past Collins Music Hall, now a rotten wood yard, past Alfredo's café, you know where one gets great toasted liver sandwiches, streaks past the ABC, now a shitty bingo hall to the end of Essex Road, now a casbah full of shishkebab.

MIKE: A veritable tour of our golden city.

LES: Shall I continue?

MIKE: Pray do.

LES: Anyway I jumped on at Holborn and stood in that recess where the clippie stands, when I saw the most awful cracker. A right darlin' – I stood there clocking it, wanting her to get the message, dulcet filthed, she was blonde with medium-length hair, dyed straw but soft and straight and her legs phenomenal. She had this short skirt on – and it had tucked gently between her legs in case she flashed her magic snare to some snatch bandit like me – and faces jumped on and off never quite hiding my angel from me but those legs with well-carved calves poured into some very high thick-wedged shoes. She was a darlin' – I could have breakfasted out of her knickers so sweetly pure she was – I could have drunk the golden nectar from that fountain, I could have loved her.

MIKE: What?!

LES: Wrapped her legs round my throat, her bright arse trembling in my hands. Divine she was and wore dark glasses but not so dark I couldn't see that finest glint as she occasionally clocked me vardering her like an ogre with a hard-on, ready to leap across the bus and say darlin' climb aboard this, but she was almost too perfect. I stood all the way – unable to leave, like a sentinel at the post and my lover was there – and I thought, Mike, I thought of Doris and I thought of all the fat scrubbers I get with soggy tits – I thought of all those dirty scrubbers and how, just once in my life I'd like to walk down the street with that. Why don't we chat up classy snatch? Why is it that we pull slags? We pull what we think we are Mike – it tumbled then – it dropped – the dirty penny – that we get what we ARE. What we think we are, so when we have a right and merry laugh with some unsavoury bunk-up or gang bang behind the Essoldo we are doing it to ourselves. We are giving ourselves what we deserve. It came to me then – here it was, the most delectable snatch in the world REAL with those INCREDIBLE pins and CLEAN – and then she stirred just ever so little it was but she knew I was lapping it up. She was going but maybe my wires got through to her and she thought why not give that geezer – he's not a bad looking bloke – a flash and as she uncrossed her DIVINE THIGHS I swivelled my sockets up there and some creep moved right in front of her but I just caught the slightest glimpse of heaven – the clouds passed over the sun but it reappeared again – she stood up on the platform waiting to leap off at Farringdon Road with that thin skirt on – a thin black cotton skirt – God she must have known that the sun pours through that skirt – no slip, just her AMAZING FUCKING FORM. Up to the ARSE. Like she was naked, standing there waiting for the bus to stop at Mount Pleasant where she jumped off – and I wanted to jump off Mike – I wanted to get off the bus and run after her – but what could I say – she strode down the street – strong on these DELIRIOUS PEGS with those nasty post office workers leering her beautiful form with their dim and faded jellies and I couldn't get off the bus – I didn't have the guts – I didn't know what to say to her Mike! What verbals could my gob spout?! And then I saw her cross into Clerkenwell Road when she disappeared.

MIKE: 38 bus! You want to get yourself a motorbike.

SCENE 12

The two lads wander upstage to a special spot – MIKE turns LES into a motorbike and jumps on his back using LES's arms as handlebars. The two clearly create the sound of a motorbike revving up and changing gear during the scene. The strength of the engine and the movement as it careers round corners should be apparent.

Oh for Adventures.

MIKE: I am a Harley Davidson with ape-hangers or maybe I am a chopper made to measure to fit me – a built-in Triumph 5000 cc. A Yamaha or a Suzuki 1500 cc. Yeah, but who wouldn't mind a Vincent HRD 10,000 cc.

LES: With apes?

MIKE: No – not on your Vincent HRD it's too classy, not on that – that's sacrilege. At a 150 a ton and a half of sublime speed tearing gut flailing flesh pulled – your glasses stabbing in your eyes – ice ripping off your face – the vibrations pulsating through each square inch of skin between your thighs power lies – at 2000 cc my throttle-twist grip lightly, oh so delicately held – not too much rev! We skate! We fly! Between my thighs I grip her tight – she won't budge – won't skid – road clears for us – it opens up like a river – the cars farting families in VWs and Fords, with dogs and kids smearing up the rear windows and granny spouting they ought to be exterminated – standing still they seem – we streak past the ponces and hairdressers in Minis, Sprites, MGs, menswear salesmen in green Cortinas, or ancient Cadillacs driven by ageing movie stars cruising for rough trade and liking the leather-loin boys with long records of glorious GBH tattooed on the helmets of their cocks. I slow

down to 150 miles an hour and chat it up – her face is
hanging off her skull, she sees what grows between my knees
and creams her jeans. 'Stop James,' she says and we split –
down to Joe's café at the intersection where the M1 sludges
reluctantly off into Luton, I mean who wouldn't be – there
behind the café behind the pantechnicons and articulated
lorries I ram it into her ancient North and South. 'Take out
your teeth you old slag,' and I leave her with a happy grin on
her toothless retchy boat. James carries her off with a nod
suggesting here we go again – never mind it's all in a day's
work – start up my beauty once more nice and gently – now
I feel it coming to life – warming, buzzing down there she's
loving it – she's randy now. Now kick the starter in the
jacksie – smash the brute down – she rises – like it had teeth
– like it was hungry – like it KNEW where to go and she
sings to me everything's checked, everything's beautiful all
checked.

LES	MIKE
Headlamp?	Check
Tail-lamp?	Check
Pilot bell?	Check
Carburettor?	Check
Alter-jet needle?	Right
Position?	Right
Float chamber?	Right
Tickler?	Right
Sparking plugs?	Check
Clean out?	Right
Oil your lubricator?	Lovely
Ready to start?	Lovely
How's your oil?	Lovely
Stand astride	Yeah!
Turn on the taps	Yeah!
Open your throttle	Yeah!

Song

    I am a Harley Davidson
    I am a Harley Davidson
    I am a Vincent HRD
    I am a Vincent HRD
    I fly like a king
    I kill like a sting
    I smash down the road
    I crush those other fuckers
    Those Hell's Angels like toads

MIKE: ⎫
LES: ⎬ (*Sing* 'Underneath the Arches'.)

(The two boys separate and become a raging duet enacting their passion for the bike. At the end of the song which is screamed out they go into 'Underneath the Arches', sung delicately, which covers the next dining scene and the table is brought on in the condition it went off – DAD *repeating the first part of the speech again.)*

SCENE 13

Dad's Soliloquy for Happier Days.

DAD: Years ago things were good, you got value out of your money, a dollar was five bob, a summer's day was hot and sunny like a summer's day – you weren't short changed, you got your full twelve hours' worth, then we take the train from Liverpool Street to Leigh-on-Sea and walk to Southend, go to the Kursaal Amusements. It was fun then. On Sunday you'd get cockles and whelks from Tubby Isaacs on the corner of Goulston Street, eat them outside and walk down Wentworth Street to the station past the warehouses – 'Got the sandwiches mum?'

MUM: Yeah – all packed. Bottle of Tizer – your Mike only five then before he saw the inside of a detention centre or Borstal. That was his bad environment that was – all those dirty rough-necked Irish bog-diggers whose kids set him up to snatch handbags – never got it from me . . . Never mind. Then we jump on the train - mum and Ethel, her sister – she don't half gas but what a larf . . .

MIKE: Who's Ethel?

DAD: You know. Big fat Ethel, covered in warts. No disrespect but she looked like a tree trunk coming down the road.

LES: She suffered from tree trunk legs.

DAD: Elephantiasis is the correct medical name. I looked it up. Here, young Mike was a terror even then. Unscrewing the light bulbs and chucking them out of the window.

MIKE: I did that?

DAD: Of course you did, all the way down to Southend. (*Bop bop bopbop*)

MIKE: I never.

DAD: You did, five years old you were. You stood on my shoulders! I still have the bill in the sideboard from Eastern Region. They banned us in the end . . . we'd go up to the station and say five please . . . they'd say piss off out of it! . . . no more light bulbs! You remember, we became known as no more light bulbs! Weren't we, mum?

MUM: (*Distant manner*) What? . . .

DAD: Never mind. The East End was rough then, still half down, and the kids would catch the water skaters from those septic rancid tanks near the bomb sites. All the abes used to sit outside in Anthony Street 'cause they liked a natter and would you believe it – they had the nerve to open a theatre where you had to understand Yiddish – what a gall! Many a time I'd been over there for a quiet afternoon kip, paid my one and six and they'd say, 'You understand Yiddish?' I'd say what you mean 'Yiddish' and they'd say piss off out of it!

LES: In the middle of London.

MIKE: It's not like a language . . . it's like a code.

DAD: You're right son . . . it's a bloody secret code.

SYLV: Do you know any dad?

DAD: Of course I do . . . I do know a bit . . . I went to night school.

SYLV: Say something then.

DAD: Let's see . . . turn the cogs back a bit . . . umm . . . 'My life!' That's Yiddish, that's four thousand years old that phrase.

LES: Sounds English to me.

DAD: Of course it's not bloody English . . . it's four thousand years old . . . that stems from the heart of Yiddisher land . . . it's been fooling the bloody Arabs for years that phrase . . . walking down Jerusalem high street they're all going, 'My life, my life'. They haven't a bloody clue . . . they think it means something else . . . they think it means the tanks are coming. Of course it doesn't!

LES: What's it mean?

DAD: What's it mean?

LES: Yeah.

DAD: I'll tell you what it means . . . My life actually means . . . My life!

LES: What's bloody secret about that?

DAD: I'm glad you asked that. You think that because it's a foreign language it's a foreign code . . . but it's not . . . that's the whole point . . . you get it! (*Pushes* LES *over.*) You dumb shmuck. Anyway, we'd go on the train on that hot Sunday morning, music playing in Liverpool Street Station (still do that do they?) (*Sings 'We'll Meet Again' in falsetto.*) Vera Lynn. Magnificent woman. She's 96 y'know.

LES: No.

DAD: I went to school with her.

SYLV: You were at school with her?

DAD: I was at school in the same class . . . we were very close friends.

MUM: But you ain't ninety-six.

DAD: Of course I'm not ninety-six you stupid bonehead.

MUM: Well how could you be in the same class?

DAD: She was a slow learner . . . she didn't start her schooling till forty-three on account of disease . . . very backward . . . she used to sing all the time . . . what do you mean sending her up! She's done more for her country than you have. She's served in four bloody world wars she has. At the bloody

front serving . . . what do you know about it you bloody
raging suppurating faggot?

LES: (*Faggoty*) I don't know what you mean.

DAD: She was honoured by our great and glorious Queen. She
went down to Buck House last week in our great and
glorious Jubilee year . . . ninety-six years old . . . knelt before
the Queen . . . she's not just bleeding old boring Vera from
Bethnal Green any more . . .

MIKE: Oh, what's she now?

DAD: (*Authoritatively*) Sir Vera! (*Laughter*) You fell for that one
. . . well it's true. Anyway, Sunday morning Vera singing in
Liverpool Street Station, past Hackney and then head up for
the coast – what a larf we had then – candy floss, the train
out to the end of the pier singing 'Roll out the barrel, we'll
have a barrel of fun', listen to that!! Sung to the rhythm of
the train 'We'll have a barrel of fun' – wholesome stuff know
ya? – never knew what the pox was in those days – didn't
exist except on the blacks and no one got near them or on a
few scabby Chinese off the boats in the West India Dock
road. A pack of Woodbines was a shilling and a pint was
tenpence ha'penny.

MUM: (*from the distance*) Ninepence.

DAD: The oracle has spoken . . . what she say?

SYLV: Ninepence.

DAD: Ninepence! Ninepence! . . . She's right! She's right! I tell a
lie it was ninepence. Doris was all right in those days. She
weren't fallen apart with all that grease – makes you sick. I
wonder why women become such old cart horses after they
marry – after Mike came her tits dropped so low they could
be seen dangling at the end of her mini skirt which she never
should have worn – a mini at fifty! And all she's got in her
box is a space – you could climb in her for a quiet snooze
like the other night . . .

SCENE 14

Scene of the Two in Bed.
MUM: Fred. (*Pause.*)
DAD: WHAT? (*Pause.*)
MUM: Are you fucking me? (*Pause.*)
DAD: (*Dry*) No.
MUM: Yes you are – I can hear you!
    (*Blackout.*)

SCENE 15

Mum's Lament.
MUM: He's a dirty bastard at his age. If he comes home pissed
    out of his head he grabs me and calls me his doll – I'm used
    to being left alone now – get no sensation no more – years of
    neglect have taken away the edge – so when he starts on me
    it's like being assaulted, it's dirty. We always keep our
    underwear on – in bed – just his horribly belchy breath –
    once he belched in my mouth as he was giving me a reeky
    kiss – I slapped him so hard he let out an enormous fart –
    that made me so cross I slapped him again and he pissed the
    bed laughing – we haven't kissed since then. I could still do
    it I've no doubt, just the desire's faded – I almost did once –
    have an affair – a short one – I was in the Poplar Cinema –
    just past the Troxy off Commercial Road, it's now been
    condemned I think – watching Anna Neagle in that
    beautiful film *Spring in Park Lane*. Some geezer started to
    fiddle with my skirt and then touched my suspenders. I was
    about to speak my mouthpiece when I thought 'Shut up
    Doris behave like a bloke' – dirty like – so I did. His hand
    was very slowly lifting my skirt up – so slowly like he was
    afraid that at any second he'd feel an axe come down on it –
    go on boy I thought, and he was only a kid – fuck me, just a
    sweet kid of sixteen or seventeen – couldn't see me in the
    dark and I didn't like to look – shy like. So he took my hand

36

rather boldly I thought – and placed it on his chopper; cheeky! . . . and he had a beautiful silky hot one, all ready primed and juicy – I was getting ever so flushy and each time the usherette went past we'd freeze like two statues – I kept on pumping away – he'd be fumbling with my cami, my camiknickers that is, and then it shot out all over the back of the next seat, whoosh!

(DAD *in the front seat reacts as if the great whoosh of sperm had landed on his head –* DAD: 'Was sat!?' *– looks up as if something has landed on him from the balcony and goes offstage mumbling* DAD: Something seems to be leaking out of my head. MUM *then continues her speech.*)

The film had just ended – Anna Neagle was just making up with Michael Wilding, and he was wiping his spunk off the front seat, not Michael Wilding, this boy next to me. When the lights come on – Oh dear – I did turn queer when I saw our Mike – dirty bugger – takes after his dad – I copped him out when he got home.

SCENE 16

Les's Speech: A Night Out.

LES: I fancy going down the Lyceum tonight. I double fancy that. (*The Lyceum music starts and* LES *and* MIKE *dance with invisible partners.* DAD *and* MUM *come on and dance in their own style –* SYLV *enters* MIKE *asks her to dance – the Andrews Sisters is played on a tape. The dancing of* MIKE *and* LES *is stylish '55 Lyceum style. A bar is created (*MUM *becomes barmaid.) Much drinking goes on. A fight nearly starts. Everyone leaves – then the two boys re-enter at a run, hit the centre spot, the music stops and the scene continues as before.*) Being as it's Sunday we'll have Mr Ted Heath the famous band leader, not the acid bath murderer or notorious political impersonator cum weekend transvestite – and Dicky Valentine in a blue gabardine, button two, flap pockets, hip-length whistle and flute.

MIKE: I'll wear a roll-away collar, a Johnny Ray collar, that sails out of your neck and a skinny tie – a slim Jim.

LES: French cuffs on a trouser with a fifteen-inch bottom. What about the handsome Donegal tweed with DB lapels? Button one, patch pockets, dropped loops, cross pockets on the trousers, satin lined, eighteen-inch slip up the arse on the jacket, skirted waist.

MIKE: What, that one?

LES: Er – yeah – it's beautiful – fingertip length velvet collar, plenty of pad in the chest ('Come on Morry, I said, more padding'). Of course when we were geary we pulled –

MIKE: Not all slags neither.

LES: But you need wheels – no point in pulling without wheels – or you'd end up taking some scrubber down Edmonton and walking all the way back to Commercial Road at three in the morning with as often as not nothing to show for it except a J. Arthur reluctantly given at the point of a seven-inch honed and sharpened shiv menacing her jugular. When we got our wheels we pulled handsomely a much better quality of cunt. There was not much good quality cunt about then. And most of it were from Billingsgate.

(LES *exits leaving* MIKE *in his spot.*)

SCENE 17

Mike's Cunt Speech.

MIKE: I disagree with Les. We always found good cunt at the Lyceum. Friendly cunt, clean cunt, spare cunt, jeans and knicker stuffed full of nice juicy hairy cunt, handfuls of cunt, palmful grabbing the cunt by the stem, or the root – infantile memories of cunt – backrow slides – slithery oily cunt, the cunt that breathes – the cunt that's neatly wrapped in cotton, in silk, in nylon, that announces, that speaks or thrusts, that winks that's squeezed in a triangle of furtive cloth backed by an arse that's creamy springy billowy cushiony tight, clinging knicker, juice ridden knicker, hot knicker, wet knicker, swelling vulva knicker, witty cunt, teeth smiling the eyes biting cunt, cultured cunt, culture vulture cunt, finger biting cunt, cunt that pours, cunt that spreads itself over your soft lips, that attacks, cunt that imagines – cunt you dream about, cunt you create as a Melba, a meringue with smooth sides – remembered from school boys' smelly first cunt, first foreign cunt, amazing cunt. Cunt that protects itself and makes you want it even more cunt – cunt that smells of the air, of the earth, of bakeries, of old apples, of figs, of sour yeast, of fresh fish cunt. So – are we going Les? We might pick up a bit of crumpet.

SCENE 18

At the end of the last speech the two boys return to the chairs – MIKE *starts slowly to speak the song 'Daisy, Daisy Give Me Your Answer Do' acting it out to* SYLV *who reacts favourably eventually. They all join in until it becomes a fracas – at the peak of the noise when all are jumping up and down shouting –* MIKE *leaves the group – followed by* LES *– they share the next speech – remaining in the same two areas they opened the play with.*

SCENE 19

Resolution.
MIKE *and* LES. (*The lines can be split or spoken together, as suits the actors.*)
MIKE: I'm sick of my house
LES: I'm sick of my family
MIKE: In fact they make me sick.
LES: I don't mind
MIKE: One day like the brothers Kray
LES: Like Reg
MIKE: We'll be flying along happily
LES: A chopper in one hand

MIKE: A dagger in my flute
LES: We'll see the boys in Dean Street
MIKE: ''Allo son, I'll have a hundred suits'
LES: The East End's my manor
MIKE: I mean that's what we know
LES: Trolling down the Green
MIKE: Bethnal to you –
LES: Going down the Lye –
MIKE: The Lyceum Strand –
LES: Kicking Cypriot berks to death
MIKE: With Johnny and the gang –
LES: Where's Big Harry gone?
MIKE: And Curly King?
LES: Where's hard Arthur?
MIKE: Where's all the hard men?
LES: Where have they been?
MIKE: We'll open a porn shop
LES: A knocking shop too –
MIKE: We'll spring the Krays
LES: Handsome –
MIKE: The Richardsons too.
LES: We'll threaten and murder,
MIKE: Connive and rob
LES: The law's on our side –
MIKE: We'll pay the slobs
LES: We'll get our piece –
MIKE: We'll protect their bit of trade
LES: The hard porn and tit shows
MIKE: They'll give us our pay
BOTH: Every week
MIKE: We'll eat at Mario's
LES: Where the hairdressers go
MIKE: We'll get fat
LES: We'll kill
MIKE: And we'll knife
LES: I hate all you pseudo bastards
MIKE: I hate you with my life.

SYLV *'s Speech of Resolution.*

We will not end our days
In grey born blight – and stomp
Our hours away in fag end waste.
And kiss the minutes till they budge
While we toil in some stinking
factory – But what's the future lads
for us – where were the stars when we
were born that ordained that our birth
and death should be stamped out like
jelly babies in a jar to be sucked out
and chewed, then spat out at the end to
croak away before a flickering light
– and fill in forms at dole queues and
stand behind the sacks of skin that are called
men and women, translated into numbers
crushed in endless files – we will not end
our days like this – waiting, while ma and pa
make little noughts and crosses upon
coupons called hope-or-death – we will not
end our days like this.

MIKE: Bung us a snout. Les?

LES: OK Mike. I'll donate to thee a snout.

MIKE: ⎱
LES: ⎰ Now you know our names.

GLOSSARY OF SLANG

berk (Berkeley Hunt)	female pudenda
boat or boat race	face
bundle	fight
charver	sexual intercourse
china	friend
chopper	axe or penis
clobber	clothes
clock	pointedly look at
curly king	East End tearaway
double strong	keenly
flute	suit
give a kick	eye up
hickory dickory	time
J. Arthur (Rank)	wank
jellies	eyes
knuckle-sandwich	fist
Kray twins	East End murderers serving life
Lyceum	centre for hard tearaways in the late fifties. Formerly the theatre where Henry Irving played.
minces	eyes
mucker	friend
north and south	mouth
pegs	legs
pins	legs
pull	pick up
Richardsons	South London murderers serving life
snatch	female pudenda
snout	cigarette
sprach	speak
talent	good-looking bird
vardering	looking (early sixties gay vernacular)

WEST

or

WELCOME TO DALSTON JUNCTION

CHARACTERS

RALPH
MIKE
KEN
SYLV
LES
SID
PEARL
STEVE
MESSENGER

AUTHOR'S NOTE

West was first performed at the Donmar Warehouse, Covent
Garden, in May 1983. That was its world première, although I
believe a version was performed in Wagga Wagga, Australia,
three years before, in 1980. But they had tampered with the text
and even included a scene from *East*, thus disqualifying
themselves from being the first to present *West*. *East*, my play
about the East End from a young hero's point of view, was the
first of a series which, naturally, inspired *West*. The BBC actually
commissioned it and then found it not quite dull enough for
television – much to my delight, as I was then able to stage it at a
later date. Limehouse Productions and Ian Albery sponsored its
first showing in London, and Limehouse have filmed it for
television at the time of writing, so I hope that as *West* played
before its thousands, it will soon play before its millions.

    West is about courage: the courage to live according to your
spirit and not the guidelines laid down for you by others, to be
true to yourself, which may involve alienating others, but your
truth is worth pursuing since it defines who you are. It shapes,
forges and hones you into something that is not vague but clear-
cut and definite. Mike's truth is to live for simple principles and
to put his courage where his mouth is. He defeats the Hoxton
monster and will continue to fight monsters so that others can
rest safe in their beds. While the play is an allegory about
demons we must defeat, it is also about an area of time and space
called London and, specifically, Stamford Hill or Hackney, N16.
You wore tailored suits and strutted your gear at the Lyceum,
Strand, on Sunday nights. Movements were short, percussive
and cool – Oscar Rabin led the band, Lita Rosa sang and the
Kray twins would stand and survey their domain. I never saw
them dance. Stamford Hill stood at the crossroads of
Tottenham, Dalston and Hoxton and was subject to attacking
forays from many directions. Such skirmishes were few, but I
remember when, instead of sending a gang each time,

Tottenham would send, symbolically, one of their toughest fighters to come and spread terror and challenge our leader. There was one young man from Stamford Hill who somehow elected himself to take on each one, and he did in fact beat them all. He was a frightening cur who actually put his fist through doors for practice. His name was Harry Lee. Mike is not based on a hero but is an amalgam of feelings that I had at the time and my observations of the environment.

West was first performed on 2 May 1983 at the Donmar
Warehouse, London, presented by Omega Stage Ltd and
Limehouse Productions Ltd. The cast was as follows:

RALPH	Ralph Brown
MIKE	Rory Edwards
KEN	Ken Sharrock
SYLV, Mike's bird	Susan Kyd
LES	Bruce Payne
SID, Mike's dad	John Joyce
PEARL, Mike's mum	Stella Tanner
STEVE	Steve Dixon
MESSENGER	Garry Freer

The HOXTON MOB are played by the same actors as Mike's gang
with some subtle changes, i.e. cloth caps and chokers.

Director	Steven Berkoff
Designer	Nadine Baylis
Music	Mark Glentworth

A television production of *West* was broadcast by Channel 4
Television on 14 November 1984.

ACT ONE

Pub sequence. The stage is bare but for a line of chairs upstage whereby the cast act as a chorus for the events that are spoken, mimed and acted. A piano just offstage creates moods, adds tension and introduces themes. The piano starts up and the cast sing as the lights come up. They sing cockney songs out of order – 'My Old Man', 'I'm Forever Blowing Bubbles', 'Roll out the Barrel', 'You are my Sunshine'. LES joins in. Time is called. They exit from the pub, leaving the boys and SYLV. The GANG explodes on to the stage and freezes.

LES: Breathless, I was aghast when I saw / standing between the full moon and the blinking lamplight, this geezer / all armed, a certain aim he took / and felled the swarthy git from Hoxton with a deft and subtle chop / I never witnessed Mike I swear such venom and gross form in leather stacked / his coat stitched and embellished with fine lattice work of studs (to be more deadly when swung) no other weapon being handy like.

MIKE: Armed you say?

RALPH: From top to toe.

STEVE: From head to foot.

MIKE: Then you saw not his face?

KEN: He wore his titfer up.

MIKE: By Christ, would I had been there.

LES: He would have much amazed you.

MIKE: Very like, very like.

LES: His face / his rotten grizzly boat looked like a planet that'd been boiled in nuclear wars or struck by meteors / razed by hurricanes, criss-crossed by deep canals and rank defiles / those scars were mute but telling witnesses of battles fought with weapons / grim with deadly promise / and fought to bitter ends before the shout of 'Hold, hold enough!'

RALPH: No shout of 'hold' was uttered then / not when he earned those lines / the tailor that did redistribute his face

49

served his apprenticeship in Smithfield's bloody stalls / had
habit of a thrust and chop to fell a bull and by the likes of
this man's deadly cheeks / was put to death / no waiting time
allowed / they fought until the streets were strewn in blood
and bits of human flesh did gladden many hearts of sewer
rats that night / or so I heard.

MIKE: He must be a right ugly bastard!

KEN: The face doth resemble the asshole of an elephant.

MIKE: A face like that won't launch a thousand ships or pull the
scrubbers to their beds in Edmonton / Gants Hill / or
Waltham Cross / so let him have his scars / his medals that
he flaunts to all / to put the shits up any villain that doth take
a fancy to him / for a bout of bundle round the back. That
don't go down with me / you hear / you scum,
impressionable as the tides that lick on any shore and gather
up the muck and floating rubbers from some hectic night
that others have / you who feed upon the blood that others
shed / and wipe the bums of hard-faced villains / living by
their very farts that you gulp down / and think you are so
favoured to be near / that don't go down with me you
chorus that exaggerate some slimy punk / as big in your
esteem as you are small / when seen through normal eyes
and not those / bent with envy / and weighted down with
fear / would seem a normal sort of bloke / a fraction harder
than the most at most / but not a raving Cyclops crossed
with Hitler and Goliath thrown in as well / so pack up all this
natter / and confess the utter wholesome gen [*truth*] you
fancy not my chances with this Kong?

RON: Of course we doth, my dearest lovely Michael.
    (*They walk on the spot.*)

LES: We were only uttering the like of what we saw / destruction
of the King of Hoxton's hardy pack / you know that
gruesome mob / they're hard men Mike / as tough as
hobnail boots / from days and nights of doing bird and
eating porridge within the flinty walls of Pentonville.

KEN: And Brixton.

STEVE: Scholars of notorious hatchet men of Broadmoor / served

their apprenticeships at double time in Parkhurst, Isle of
Wight, 'neath the twins / who taught them ultra-subtle ways
with carving knives.

RALPH: They're brought up hard / since snot-nose kids they
never knew / the softer life / electric blankets when you're
snug at night from pulling scrubbers / from the Locarno
Streatham / or the Ly / that cold walk back to home and
hearth / a glass of Tizer in the fridge and mum's left chicken
soup for you to nosh.

STEVE: A bagel warming in the stove.

RALPH: Those dulcet ways doth soften us Hackney lads.

KEN: Sure we'd be good for bang with gang upon a bird / or the
occasional toe to toe with hard-faced Arthur or blond tyke /
from Tottenham / I've seen you fell the best / but those from
Hoxton / they're not human Mike.

LES: They feel no pain / they don't wear coats in winter even.

KEN: Not to spoil their whistles / crush their shoulder pads / they
don't even like pulling talent / lest they disembark their
energy they wish to save / for making love to violence.

MIKE: So that's why all those tarts and slags come running to us
panting / drawers at half-mast when they see a lad from
Hackney or from Stamford Hill.

LES: (*Walking downstage*) Of course / their blokes just given them
clobberings / and pints of crummy bitter / if they're lucky /
and a game of darts / a kicking if they get in front of Arsenal
v. Spurs on telly on a Saturday / their day of rest from
hauling bricks around the sites, to harden gnarled hands to
bunch into thick mitts or knuckle sandwiches / to finish off a
pleasant evening at the Royal, Tottenham / they're not for
you / I know you're hard my royal Mike – the King of
Stamford Hill / I've seen you put your dukes through
wooden shit-house doors for practice.

RALPH: But those hands were made for better things / like
dealing royal flush and trump beneath the deck.

ALL: Right!

RALPH: Unhooking bras one-handed / whilst the other like a
subtle snake seeks other pastures.

ALL: Right!

RALPH: Or making rude and gamey gestures from fast cars at thick-brained yobs from Romford / who in slow and worn-out bangers / can only yelp and scream vile insults lashed in hate / about the nature of our origin / and flash their rotten teeth / as we slide past in fast Cortinas.

KEN: Birds galore in black / squashed in and squeaking / flapping in their awesome glee at your horsepower man.

LES: So let's forget the bundle / let's scout out what muff walks lonesome streets tonight / and drag them back to forty watts of Eric Clapton or Queen.

MIKE: Swallow it, you mean! And wear a hideous yellow on my back / to strut before a wanton ambling nymph / that's what you see for me / Mike the King of N16 / I'll drown more villains than a mermaid could / deceive more slyly than old Shylock would / and set the murderous Hoxton King to school / can I do this and cannot get his crown / balls, were he Al Capone I'd pluck it down / now listen men of little faith / beneath my gabardine and / poplin shirts / beneath my Crombie satin-lined with slanting pockets / there beats a heart of steel and will of iron / I'll crack open his skull / with this / I do a thousand press-ups every day and forearm curls / a score of chin-ups on the bar / have made my arms a vice to crush a bear / bench-press 300 pounds / those triceps aren't just ornaments you feel / 500 squats a day with poundage on my back of two grown men / have made my thighs the girth of oaks / and five score pull-ups on an inclined bench have carved a marble sculpture on my gut / feel / go on punch and break your fist on me you snivelly worms / just 'cause my mum fed me with bagels / cream cheese and rich bortsch you think I am a powder puff or soggy stuff thus to be shaped to humping ladies' underwear round retailers or flogging stockings out of suitcases in Oxford Street or doing knowledge on a moped with a dream of owning one fat stinking taxi cab / and sit spine-warped with 30p upon the clock / where to sir? To some ponce who vomits in the back / or has a quick charver . . . no boy / that's not for me.

LES: Our mind's made up.

STEVE: Yeah / let him come / we'll show them what we're made
of.

MIKE: That's the way. I see you now / straining like greyhounds
in the slips at Harringay / let's away / arm yourselves my boys
/ the heat is on / those that do not fight with us this day will
think themselves accursed / they were not here / get chains
and mallets / choppers and fine steel / we'll give those evil
bastards something to feel / we'll wrap a warning round their
skulls / and they'll not bestride our streets no more / their
ugly mugs scaring the police horses / causing our pregnant
ladies to abort upon their sight and smell / no more banter /
let's go pell-mell to meet in heaven or hand in hand in hell.

ALL: Smash! Splatter! Punch! Kick! Nut!

(MIKE *starts the words with a physical action appropriate to
each word. The others take it up until it becomes a choreographic
and vocal symbol of an advancing army. This action reveals a
casualty – one of the lads from Mike's gang,* HARRY, *lies dying.*)

HARRY: Food for w-w-w-...

MIKE: Worms, Harry ... worms ...

RALPH: Quick, have it away / afore the law doth mark us for
accessory!

(HARRY *dies. They race off, running on the spot, then turn
upstage and run to their chairs, leaving Mike's mum and dad,*
PEARL *and* SID, *with newspaper each side of the table.*)

Mike's mum and dad, SID *and* PEARL, *in their room.*

SID: It says here – pass another cuppa Pearl / that last night
violent street gangs clashed / causing gevalt and misery / six
taken in with wounds / one fatal / caused by they say / rough
Gurkha knives and chains.

PEARL: It's not safe Sid to walk the streets at night / you'll want
some more toast with your eggs?

SID: No, that's fine.

PEARL: A piece more cheese?

SID: Those lousy gits are getting bolder every day it makes you
sick / the youth today / you got some Swiss?

PEARL: No, only Cheddar.

SID: That'll do / are all the fish cakes gone?

PEARL: You ate the last one yesterday.

SID: That's all you made!

PEARL: When I make more you leave them.

SID: So – they can't wait in the fridge and give a warm-up underneath the grill.

PEARL: Tomorrow I'll make some more.

SID: Then it's too late / my yen for fish cakes may be gone.

PEARL: That's why you leave them if I make a lot.

SID: 'Cause you don't tell there's some remaining / I always have to ask – you know I like them Pearl! A thousand curses on their guts those swine / the youth today / they don't know what to do but spraunce about.

PEARL: They're spoiled by overpay and telly.

SID: I should smile / filth that comes out streaming from the box and films!

LES: (*As chorus*) Shit, cunt-face, scabby bollocks.

SID: Ugh! You couldn't take like years ago your family out / to queue in one and nines and have a laugh / a sandwich in the bag to munch between the films.

PEARL: You'd always have a laugh.

SID: That's right / you're right / feel safe and cosy / where's little Mike?

PEARL: Bless him!

SID: He's tearing up and down the aisle / laugh! ice-cream from Wall's at twopence.

PEARL: Choc ices.

SID: Ice lollies.

PEARL: Vanilla cup.

SID: Chocolate whirl.

PEARL: Bag of peanuts.

SID: Never ate them / stuck in my dentures.

PEARL: I did.

SID: Yeah, you did / all the way through *Road to Bali*, munch, munch.

PEARL: *Road to Singapore.*

SID: *Road to Mandalay.*

PEARL: *Song of the Desert.*

SID: *Wizard of Oz.*

PEARL: *The Red Shoes.*

SID: Beautiful, beautiful, what a picture.

PEARL: *King Kong.*

> (CHORUS *mime end of* King Kong *sequence –* MIKE *on table as* *Kong and* CHORUS *as planes shooting at him.*)
>
> Get off the table, Mike, you'll upset your father.

SID: That was a shocker / a cuddle in the back.

PEARL: You never!

SID: Didn't I? Yes I did – and then we'd have a cuppa in Joe Lyons with a pastry / right / they'd make a great cuppa then.

PEARL: They were famous for it then.

SID: The pastries were delicious then.

PEARL: They made the best then.

SID: Rum baba / chocolate éclair.

PEARL: Custard tart.

SID: Lemon meringue.

PEARL: A gossip with our friends all content like don't see them any more.

SID: They don't visit.

PEARL: You don't ring them.

SID: They don't ring me / I should ring them!

PEARL: They should ring us.

SID: That's right – never ask about the kids / never say like years ago / come over Sid and have a cuppa, a game of solo and natter.

PEARL: You asked them once.

SID: I did / you're right / I won't keep begging them / I should beg them! / What have they done for me? I ask myself. Except to ask a favour.

PEARL: That's all.

SID: Hey Sid – lengthen a sleeve – Norman's grown out of them / take in a seat / you couldn't put a new lining in / could you?

PEARL: There's one in hospital who's still in coma fighting for his life.

SID: They get what they deserve / what they sow / they reap / they get as good as they give / I should worry for them? / An overstretched health service / and they get a bed at once / they should have let them bleed to death.

PEARL: He's still a son to some poor mother.

SID: Unwanted bastard of some brass no doubt / brought up by waiting by the pub.

LES: (*As chorus*) When we goin' home, Dad?

SID: Outside the door in all weathers / waiting for his dad and mum who's sinking down the pints inside / and now and then peek out to see the kids all right / buying them a bag of crisps to keep them happy / makes you sick / their little noses running / blue knees and shivering / while ma does . . .
(*Chorus sings 'Knees Up Mother Brown'.*)
. . . 'Knees Up Mother Brown' to some joanna that's the life they had / witness the clouts their mums have suffered at the hands of doltish drunken dad / and emulate the like as they turn into them in turn / coming home from school all starving with a bit of bread and dripping on the table and a note / do not disturb / while mum performs with 'uncle' up the stairs / breaking in and entry in their teens / and then a term or two of Borstal sets them up to be the citizens of our fair capital / when once we walked down Leicester's famous Square and had / the Corner House / a quartet playing / lunch at half a crown.

PEARL: Those were the days.

SID: The Salad Bowl.

PEARL: Mixed Grill.

SID: The Guinea and Piggy.

PEARL: All you could eat for a guinea / imagine.

SID: I kept going back for more / remember? he couldn't believe his eyes.

MIKE: (*As chorus*) You back again?

SID: Five times he saw me / fill it up I said / the plate was up to here / I wolfed it down though / went back again / all you could eat that's what it said / there's nothing they could do.

PEARL: They closed it down that's what they did.

SID: Not on account of me! 'Cause hard-faced layabouts would lay about at night / and put the wind up decent folks.

CHORUS: Hey Jimmy, gie's a drink!

SID: That's why they closed it mate / the West End's now a karzi. (*Chorus mimes vomiting.*)

SID: Now you dare not walk the streets at night / lest some unsavoury mugger / some huge shvartzer maybe / takes an eye to you.

CHORUS: What you lookin' at?

SID: Or drug-crazed hippie dying for a fix decides to stick a bayonet in your guts for half a dollar.

PEARL: I'm nervous going to bingo even and that's only down the road.

SID: Nobody phoned, eh?

PEARL: No, shall I ring Rosie / ask them round for tea on Sunday?

SID: We should ring them! When do they ring us?

PEARL: You're right Sid / you're quite right.

SID: Be independent / don't be proud to be a little independent.

PEARL: When you're right, you're right / maybe she rang and we were out.

SID: So did she try again? / You'll make fish cakes tomorrow.

PEARL: Yeah, I'll make a load / only who will eat them?

SID: I'll eat them / don't worry / I'll eat them!

Hospital. A bed. The face of HARRY, *dying, quite still. The table is the bed.*

LES: It was our fault that little Harry fell / his memory shall be honoured for all time / stabbed in the field by coward's hand.

RALPH: This will not go unanswered / he shall be avenged.

KEN: Eye for an eye / tooth for tooth.

LES: We had them on the run / they fled beneath our might / but one fell rat draws out a knife to leave his mark behind.

KEN: The canker of the nether word / they are a plague that we must crush / or else they'll grow / contaminate by touch.

RALPH: What's the answer / blood for blood? (*Music stops.*)

MIKE: You must strike at the top / cut off the head and then the

body's dead / confusion then will spread about / then we
mop up / to get into the hornets' nest and kill the king / not
battle in the streets / but plan concerted armed attack / he's
hard you say / invincible to some / but he's only a human
like us all / with feeling senses / if you kick him does he not
hurt / if you stab him will be not bleed?

LES: To go into the lions' den is begging for it / they'll smell us at
a mile / they'll see our homespun spotless faces / not scabby
/ lined with tracks like Clapham Junction / they'll sus us out
before we're even near and wipe us off the streets.

MIKE: A little camouflage is what we need / divest yourselves of
your smooth gear / and imitate the clobber of that mob /
cheese-cutters and football boots / a choker round our neck
in white / a black shirt here and there / and dirty up.

RON: That's great / I'll drink to that / let's make a ding-dong at
Dave's pad to celebrate this plan / you're all invited / bring
some booze the birds laid on / some slags he pulled from
Dalston double-hot in keenness / and mad to make
acquaintance of you Mike.

KEN: Yeah I double fancy that / right on mate / I'll change my
knickers / let's get the booze.

MIKE: Do not forget what we have said tonight / don't let this
booze-up blunt our dreaded purpose.

LES: Nay! / We will speak further on it / oh come on Mike / let's
mix our grief with some small joy / to celebrate destruction
of the beast / we'll make our plans tonight and fix the day!

MIKE: OK, at the Duke's Oak we meet / that's on the way.
(*Boys' pub talk:* 'Five pints, Bert.' 'Straight glasses, if you
please.')

*Mike's bird, SYLV, in her room. Boys and family act as simultaneous
background from their areas: pub at top; PEARL and SID in centre;
SYLV at a bottom.*

SYLV: It was November / the last dead leaves of autumn / were
falling off the perch / the day was cold as ice / flawless sky
mind you / like it was washed in Daz / the pigeons picking at
the hardened chunks of dogshit / it's silent, like a Sunday is

round here / and I went down the road to get the *Sunday Mirror* / and some fags / the OAPs were snivelling in their scarves they wrap around their sunken sucked-in cheeks / as they bought cat food for their sole companions / their chat was shrill with 'Hallo Dot and how's your chest' and 'Innit parky, half a gallon of paraffin' / and back they went swaddled in veins and rheumatism to their grim / stove on the landing / room / cold water and a pic of dad / when he was fighting for his king for three and six a week / a postcard on the mantelpiece from daughter seen just once a year / at Xmas maybe / or a death / it's funny that I sit in now and wait for him to ring / he said he would today.

MIKE: Go on, Les. Put something on the jukebox.

LES: What d'ya want – Rosemary Clooney?

PEARL: Must we watch telly all the time? Let's play cards.

SYLV: Mike usually decides to come over / that's so nice / we sit in watching some old flic on telly / or playing Perry Como or some Brahms particularly he likes the Fifth by Beethoven / it gets him all worked up he says though / I like dancing really to some Latin / we jump around a bit and shake a leg / we'll have a fag or two / or smoke a joint / maybe a benny just before our lunch / I'll warm a frozen curry from the store / maybe Fray Bentos / though Chinese from the takeaway is nice / some chop suey and some chips / that's good, I fancy that and he don't half love it as well / I'll get that in a minute and what else / I think that's all . . . oh come on Mike and bloody phone you bloomin' bore.

MIKE: Not too much, Ken.

LES: Five more pints, Bert.

SID: Oh my ulcer! Pulverize a couple of pills, Pearl!

SYLV: Suppose I get it all and he don't come / I'll keep it for tomorrow / I'll do that he ain't half nice – really he is / he has his funny ways / I mean who don't / and sometimes I could strangle him / but when he looks at me with those hurt eyes / I just want then to mother him / he's really handsome like a movie star / but rugged like not poofy but a cross between Paul Newman and Brando / with little hints of Redford and

a touch of Cary Grant or maybe Boris Karloff / he don't half
make me laugh sometimes / we'd laugh so much they'd
knock back on our walls / those from next door – that
woman who is always sick and lives with her mad son who
never works / oh come on Mike.

MIKE: So go on, ask me: do I care?

BOYS: Do you care?

PEARL: Dorothy said she might pop in tonight.

SID: I'm out!

SYLV: I can't remember did I take the pill today or not / oh piss I
lost my little card / oh never mind / but then suppose he
wants to then what do I do / oh never mind one day won't
hurt or will it / no I shouldn't think it would / or would it /
rules are rules and if you break them then you take the risk –
men! Much they care – but then they're not supposed to –
really / they never do.

STEVE: Seein' Sylv tonight?

MIKE: Nah. Givin' her the elbow.

LES: How about Ange?

PEARL: Turn it off, for Christ's sake.

SID: It's the weather forecast.

SYLV: I can't go through all that again / no God forbid / I just
can't go back to that vile place / and let them in to murder
part of me again / like opening your doors to killers in white
coats and saying / it's in there – you will be quick / it won't
hurt it – will it? / No! No! Not again / oh come on Mike I'm
getting bored hanging around – it's Sunday – come on ring
you sod.

RALPH: So I said, pal, do I look like a tin of dog food?

SID: Go to bed.

(SYLV *takes fag out – looks in mirror. Lifts her skirt – suspender
belt, garters.*)

SYLV: Couldn't resist it really – he likes that – its cheeky / I feel
funny in the street / funny and nice at once / to know what's
underneath / and no one else suspects / how could they / I'll
give him a surprise / that's if he wants surprising that is /
don't know lately if it's getting / well . . . / better or worse / can

never tell with him / or maybe he's getting something else to
play with / bastard bet he has / oh if he dares! Maybe that's it /
it's wearing out / it's not the armed assault like once it was /
then he'd come at me like I was the last bird in the world / he
said he loved me then / after the op he turned all funny for a
while / chop suey or a curry – maybe a plate o spags / oh ring
you git I can't stay in all day and wait and wait.

LES: Here's to a smooth and slick funeral!

PEARL: It's just a blank screen, Sid!

SYLV: I fancy going up West / I'll treat him to a film and we'll sit
in a nice wine bar / I'd like to meet some people / for a
change / just watch them even / sick of staying in / oh come
on, ring me, please ring! Please ring – please ring.

RALPH: Do you all know the way to Dave's? First right, first left.

PEARL: I'm going to bed.

The gang at a table – harsh white light.

MIKE: A score of broken bones and busted shnozzles was the
price we paid by being unprepared.

RALPH: By being unprepared we was caught out with knickers
well and truly down.

STEVE: They came back for revenge last night / for the almighty
pasting that they took as if poor Harry's precious life was not
enough to slake the creature's thirst.

LES: The brute and monstrous thing rose from its lair into the
thick sulphurous night / while we were snoring gorged
appetites like swinish pigs / well bloated and obscene from
'evening in' with favoured bints / their perfumed limbs
enwrapped us like some marble seraphims / the sweetttnness
of their breath, so honeydewed mellifluous with tinkling
flute-like voices / beguiled us with soft porn suggestions / in
the dales and valleys of our ears / and we unpeeled them like
it was a ripened plum or mango / satsuma or sweet pear. But
they were poisoned fruit / within they carried venom /
between their loins a praying mantis / sucking us to our
death in lust-filled swoons / for they had plans / the birds we
pulled last night were fronted to attack / were set up to

assuage us in our guard by rendering unarmed our finest
men / attacking us where we are vulnerable / our sensual
centres / famed to all the world / those cornucopias of
passion / our Achilles' heel / our Samson's hair / where flock
the sirens of the Western world / to feed and drink in our rich
pastures / welcoming them all / turning none from our door /
those starved within the barren regions / of Dalston, Enfield
and Wood Green / who flocked to Stamford Hill.

MIKE: Oh horro! Horror! Horror!

RALPH: We planned too late our deed / we should have struck
when he was bloated in his bed as he found us / instead of
deeds / we fell to carousing as if to celebrate the victory
before it's won.

MIKE: Oh you my sinews bear me stiffly up!

RALPH: We were a cinch / lucky for you that you were out / the
stroke of fate that did decide by tossing coins / you were the
chosen one to buy the shish kebab from takeaway / or else
you may have suffered that like fate / that marched so
painfully upon our undefended loins.

MIKE: My fate cries out and makes each petty artery in this body
as hardy as the hardest villain's nerve / I'll tear him all to
pieces!

ALL: You shall not go.

MIKE: Unhand me / by heaven I'll make a corpse of him that lets
me / I say away! I warned you / what did I say! You were
seduced by snatch / your watchman fast asleep / his potion
drugged no doubt / allowed yourselves to be disarmed and
floating in the ether of vile lust / so's not to hear the hobnail
boots they always wear with toes steelcapped in dread / you
mugs / what are you / with friends like you I don't need
enemies / you were outshrewded by the Hoxton fiends /
who's celebrating now, no doubt in City Arms / carousing
with his chinas of / how easy it was after all / and laughing
with loud chortles / while the blast of shame sits on our
brows like the ill mark of Cain / now who comes here?
(*A* MESSENGER *approaches.*)

MESSENGER: I come unarmed from Hoxton's mighty King / to

give a message to him that calls himself / the Prince of
Darkness / the King of Stamford Hill or just plain Shtip-it-
in Mike.

MIKE: I'm known by many names but those will do / say what
your business is and blow / you emissary from the
underworld where sunshine never comes and days are
choked in hell's polluted smoke / say what brings you here
to gloat upon your master's cowardice and treachery.

MESSENGER: Cut out the patter man and cock an ear to what my
honoured master hath to spout.

LES: You dare to speak like that you pint of gnat's piss.

MIKE: Let him go.

MESSENGER; And wisely said / that you may learn a thing or
three / I see you are the guvnor / so here's the spiel / to cut all
these wars which doth confuse the citizens of our strife-
warm manor / to halt the battles in the Royal Tottenham
which hath us banned from dancing with our chicks / and
making parley with our mates / to cease the clash of skull
and iron in our streets which doth excite old johnny law to
exercise his tool on us / and bring the black marias out like
wailing banshees / round our council flats / in other words a
one to one / just you and he – step round the back – by some
remote deserted track / the Hackney marshes / or designate
a place that you prefer / I'll pass the message on.

MIKE: The marshes suits me well / tell him I'll come.

MESSENGER: Upon the stroke of twelve / one week from now.

MIKE: I shall be there.

(MESSENGER *exits.*)

LES: I do not doubt some foul play.

MIKE: A one to one / it's what I've always dreamed of.

KEN: What if he should lure you into some forbidden trap and
there . . . phut!

MIKE: What should I fear / when I now sense a giant strolling in
my veins / now I could slay whole armies all alone / a one to
one / I wish there were a hundred just like he / a week from
now / till then sit still my soul / for Hackney marshes will
become the bloody sea.

(*They trot off in quasi-military fashion. Exuent. Fanfare.*)

SID *and* PEARL *in their room. They speak but not to each other.*

SID: Soho's not what it's cut out to be.

PEARL: I get bored watching telly every night.

SID: There was a time when it was fun to walk the streets in summer / birds out on the game / all legs / then to stand about / flaunt themselves for all to see / you knew what you were getting / not that I got / but for a laugh you'd ask how much / and go up to the next / it passed the time.

PEARL: Sometimes I'd like to pack my bags and leave him to it / just run out and go / I don't care where / just up and off / and never see his face again / it's too late now / I should have done it long ago.

SID: Where did it go wrong I ask myself / she never had to do a stroke of work / I brought home all my wages every week / not all mind you but they never went short.

PEARL: He's not taken me out in years / not once in years like / come on Pearl let's drive to Brighton for the day . . .
(*Tableau as* BOYS *and* SYLV *join in and re-create the scene.*) . . . it's sunny out / we'll pack a lunch and take the kids I used to like it years ago / the pier and stroll along the prom / sit on the beach and watch Michael throw pebbles in the sea / and then a game of housey housey it's called bingo now / we won a silver-plated teapot . . . (*Scene disappears.*) . . . where has it gone I wonder?

SID: The others all made profits from the war / I was an honest joe / I could have made a fortune / with a little simple graft / black market was the rage.

PEARL: But for the kids / I'd have slipped out long ago / but when you're tied it's difficult / how could I leave them / or support them in a furnished room / it's just for them I live – it's for the twinkle in my baby's eye that I can soldier on / not that he's an angel but he's all I got / and she's as good as gold.

SID: They're ingrates that's the truth / give us a quid or two dad / or a tenner / or a pony maybe / pay you back? No never /

sponge on my old bones till I drop dead / I'd like for once to
see him looking smart / a decent hair cut / a well-cut suit
instead of that costume he wears / the layabout.

PEARL: I look at him and think what have I got but habit and
some sleeping pills / to send us to oblivion at night or ease
the pain of our arthritic bones / to soften his loud snores and
give an hour or two of sweet forgetfulness / one day I'll take
the lot.

SID: Harry's boy did well / matriculated and all that / then college
/ then degree in this and that / and a clever lad / stopped in
most every night to fill his cop with knowledge / he's no
shmuck / and the skill to stand up in a court and be a man /
defending companies in the quagmire of business laws /
what a man is Harry's boy / his mum and dad he bought a
home in Chingford with a garden and drives a Ford estate /
what did my son achieve for us – gevalt and anguish fear for
every knocking on the door / in case some johnny law
should say we're looking for . . .

PEARL: Some wives have husbands who's a joy / so proud they
entertain / and lay a table for their friends on Sunday
night . . .

(*Party tableau.* 'Hello, lovely to see you', *etc.*)

. . . a drink of port / and tell some jokes / maybe a game of
pontoon / silver laid / and lumps of children everywhere /
daughters and sons / grandchildren too / to fuss over / their
grannies take them out / their fathers proud and braying the
achievements in the world of their most honoured kids /
they don't invite us any more . . .

LES: 'Bye, Aunty Pearl.

SYLV: Lovely meringues, Pearl.

MIKE: Ring you.

PEARL: . . . and I can't go alone / he says he's too tired to go out /
and what have they done for him he says / you've only got to
entertain them back / so we sit in and watch the telly.

SID: I showed him how to earn an honest buck / I only told him /
get out now and graft / did I do something wrong / to turn
him to a villain / lousy sponger / low-life that he is / who

comes home when he does with busted teeth and broken bones and God knows where he's been or what he's done / if he stayed in and copped a book or two or got a decent job when he was young instead of dancing out all night with stinking whores no doubt / the filth he mixes with is rife in bad contagion / if he had worked he's got some brain / he could have been a manager at least of Cecil Gee's / or maybe an accountant / Tucker that's a job! For that you need a noddle in your bonce / faa! A pervert for a son / to tell the truth no blood of mine but hers.

PEARL: He set him no example if he's bad.

SID: From her and all her spoiling he's no good.

PEARL: When did he get a father's love / I ask myself.

SID: She always favoured him / right from the moment he was born.

PEARL: He never took an interest in him the way a father should / to show him what it is that he should know.

SID: What time does *Hawaii Five-O* come on?

PEARL: Eight o'clock.

SID: Turn it on, will you love?

GROUP: I fancy going down the Royal / I double fancy that / the Mecca is my temple of fate / who shall I pull / who shall I meet, will she be wrapped up like a Xmas treat / the fireball is turning, the music starts / your eyes survey the crumpet / and you say, do you wanna dance, do you wanna dance?

BOYS: Do ya wanna dance?

(MIKE *takes* SYLV *on to the floor, just the two of them. The* BOYS *are upstage, acting as a chorus line with invisible partners.*)

MIKE: Do you wanna dance / we slid on to the floor like two seals in a pool / wearing an ashen look about her face / smelling like a perfume counter at Boots / she had that look about her / like I couldn't care if you dropped dead look / her eyes scanning other talent / searching out the form / of course we do not get too close / just enough to give a hint of things to come / a lasso of lust waves encircles her.

SYLV: He ... he looks like any other / with easy grin / street-

66

corner patter / so we dance a bit and then he asks me.

MIKE: Do you fancy a drink?

SYLV: With him / as if he bought me / for a dance / whereas I stand or sit with or without mates / watching lines of faceless trousers stomping up and down.

MIKE: She looks nice.

SYLV: He looks OK / nice eyes / love crumbled grey / and smoking already for me / he says he don't half fancy taking me home / back to my gaff / an arm squeezed.

MIKE: Fancy her / not much I don't half.

SYLV: Yeah another gin and it / lipstick smudged / I'll do my hair / excuse me.

ALL: Thanks luv / that was nice / enjoyed that / fancy a drink / where d'ya live? – oh!

MIKE: I got to the karzi / full of geezers doing their barnets and who has who.

STEVE: I'll take the ugly one.

LES: Yeah all right!

KEN: What a cracker.

RALPH: I didn't get nothin'!

MIKE: And all that / I take the future of England in my hand and ponder her body which seems to me as if a shoal of silvery fish were gathered in a net / and wiggling and slithery and her silken skin encasing her incredible form.

LES: Mind the strides, pal.

MIKE: Whilst I read what Kilroy has been up to / so after much chat and I don't know / the night was wearing thin and I became afeared that unless she yielded to my heart-felt quest / to take her home that is / these chicks / these panoplies of exquisite and sensual delights / would be booked up by other snatch-bandits staking out their prey for the night and if at twelve o'clock I walk home on my tod sloan I would be well and truly choked.

SYLV: Not tonight, let it not be tonight.

MIKE: All right just to the door / unless . . .

SYLV: No, I said not tonight.

MIKE: Why wait / what makes it better if you wait / it's cold out

here / let's go inside / her make-up's cracked beneath the
light / our breath steams and snorts.

SYLV: He should wait / else I'm just another receptacle to stomp
out his butt / he pushes himself against me like I was for him
a sanctuary that he was struggling to get into.

MIKE: Like I was pursued by wolves / and she took my breath
away.

SYLV: And he asked me out next day / and from then on all I
wanted was to be a sacrifice / like an offering / I can't help it /
how often can you feel that / and that's how I felt / and he
felt good to me all the time / and often / not like the others
but someone wanting someone like me / and now why won't
the bastard ring?

The lads jump in attacking stance.

MIKE: Like stepping round the back was what was expected of
you / like a clobbering now and then / was mixed up with
pulling birds round there for stand-up charvers / like that very
spot where now you gaily spray your spunk / was where two
nights ago you splattered blood / 'gainst that very wall / you
pulled in passageways / in doorways / in any nook and cranny
so you'd only exercise your passion in the dark and private /
with a bird / or bloke for violence or love / or be in love with
violence / so when two tearaways decide to bundle / to inflict
some GBH upon each other's form / they might be making
love / and seeking out the soft parts to inflict upon them some
unsightly woe / and finish off the night in blissful satisfaction /
of adrenalin well pumped and flushy bleeding faces / all lit up
with joy / and many hand thumps on the back.

STEVE: You did all right, mate.

LES: Yes? / you din half give him one / boot in like –

RALPH: Kicked the shit out of –

KEN: I like the bit when –

STEVE: Well and truly.

LES: Handsome / ta da!

STEVE: See ya!

LES: Look after –

KEN: See you, plater.

RALPH: All the brest.

KEN: So he decided that it had to be and so prepared himself for
the onslaught / toe to toe and nose to nose / the weapons
chosen / and us chinas to be there in case the others thrust
their grubby maulers in.

Gym. MIKE *training with weights / during this last speech / pushing
weights in conjunction with music / muscles bulging / veins swelling /
sweat pouring off in shower / the mates continuing their forboding text.*

RALPH: I've seen the brutish thing he has to slay fancy his
chances / I don't know / I hate to tell my mucker / my best
mate / that I might carry in my heart / a little doubt / so I'll
keep shtoom / and render him my total confidence in this
night's caper.

LES: The other bloke annihilated last week / was in a coma for
some days / between the sheets he bled / and put tubes in
both his ears / to see if he was leaking red from broken
tissues / or the brain / that's what they do / and shoved up
little things into his nose in case he haemorrhaged and
formed a clot and shaved his head and searched his skull in
case his mind was cracked / or broken / but he recovered to
tell the tale.

STEVE: And was it worth it after all / I'd be rather all tucked up
and wrapped around a softer creature / dragging kisses up
from the deep / than face a bunch of fives well clenched / I
do not fancy kissing that at all.

MIKE: But who can undo what has been done / or wipe the
writing off from on the wall / what has to be will be.

*Walking home after the gym, bag over shoulder. Music. Each one
follows the other and takes over the walk.*

RALPH: Walking home alone beneath the stars / up Amhurst
Road / to Manor House / and down to Finsbury Park /
where little ducks sit quietly at night / like toys in a lake of
glass / to lonely back streets after / nights of rock and roll at
the Rainbow / or James Bond giving her one at the Essoldo /

maybe a binge at some vomity local / going home in pairs /
to make it in the back of steamed-up Minis / I could not
help but wonder on this night of all the talent getting well
and truly laid / and all the grinding going on / and how many
and how much / and all the wails and screaming going on
right at this moment / could almost in the silent aching
streets / hear across the city all the sighs / rising and falling
like sirens / thousands, maybe tens of thousands creating a
vast and lubricious symphony / a concerto / and in the secret
places / alleyways and back rooms at parties / some in crispy
beds / and some round backs of lorries or in graveyards /
some getting their oats before their time / by dint of threat /
in lonely fields / dragged there by snatch-crazed fiends.

LES: Digging in and hacking away like crazy robbers / smash and
grab of flesh / and tides rising and falling together / while the
mad moon / a giant's eye spying it all out / the murdered
and the robbed / and geezers out for bondage in Earls Court
/ and in the night the steam is rising / from the heaps of
bodies twisted in shapes like vampires feasting on their prey
/ and the cars passing / occupants all warm and cosy / he's
driving / Zappa in stereo / hand on knee / maybe one will
stop for me / and some delicious and horrendous piece /
swathed in filth-packed flesh will utter / can I give you a lift
young man / drooling sibilantly from scarlet lush-filled lips /
opens the door / smelling like honeysuckle in the dark the
hint of things to come / the promise of Elysium / and we'll
shoot off into the night searching for treasure.

KEN: But nothing / only the jeers of dawn carousers heading for
their unmade beds in Walthamstow and Leyton / reeking
stale beer and fish and chips / Fray Bentos pies from all-
night stands in Spitalfields / then home belching their
unholy gut rot into their scummy slags that hang around
hair lacquered like Brillo pads / and waking in the light of
day / one white arm / with digital / cheap one upon his wrist
comes snaking out the pit where scrubber lies a-snoring.

STEVE: And searching in his trousers for a pack of fags / starts the
day in cough-wake / dragging ropes of phlegm / from vaults

well stocked within / blue smoke rising / while the sunshine peeks reluctantly in / exposing a big juicy yellow pimple on her back / comes then spewing through the radio some idiot / so the day starts in a bath of rancid bacon and eggs.

MIKE: I'll get into my little bed / thus strengthened by steel for the battle ahead / I'll drink a pint / say my prayers / and wait for mum to wake me in the morning / French toast and tea / I double fancy that.

ACT TWO

Song of the Hoxton Mob. They march around the stage with East End macho-animalistic precision, jutting heads and threatening stares, to a drum beat.

CURLY:

I'm known as the avenger / when
they see me they do quell / for
they see before their runny
eyes a short pathway to ultra-
violence / with a swift descent to hell.

They scare before they get here /
they tremble at my name / to look
upon my face is quite enough to
send them packing off before
they've time to clench their
sweaty fists to deal out pain.

I'm known as the avenger / and they
seek to claim my crown / but the
hardest villains are the ones that
soonest / come tumbling down.

So come on boy / I'm waiting
I hear you're on your way /
I'm hungry for the blood of
victims / I need another jerk
like you / a mama's boy to slay.

MIKE *jumps into a pool of light and becomes a Cockney Lenny Bruce for five minutes.*

MIKE: Every day in the morning – while the sun rose like a
biscuit behind the glue factory / quivering in the smoke / I'd

get up at seven to go to work mum packs some sandwiches /
which would get soggy by the time it was opened / I would
crush myself in the tube and others behind me would crush
and we'd all get crushed together / which was all right if you
happened to have your leg wedged between the thighs of
some radiant fair-skinned blushing and divine darling but
not if some stinking gentleman from an exotic country of
the East was breathing the shit he calls food all over your
face / and as the doors slid open this composite mass of
sludgy flesh would wobble like a wall of jelly / and some
schemer would put a foot in the door and attempt to weld
himself into the compost heap quivering together / on the
Piccadilly Line poo! who farted? was it you? I'd read the
latest filth scrawled up when the doors open no one would
move to let anyone in / we were staunch allies in our square
foot of space / the doors shut and the pack got squirmier / I
was thinking about that bundle all the while and making
horrible little flickers in my mind about the outcome / eyes
staring into their daily tits that they'll never feel only ogle /
hands would wander about in the pit of hell / old ladies
gasping their last breath / glaring at some young sod in a seat
/ and umbrella stuck up your ass / fags stubbed out in your
face / and the ads advised you on the merits of speedwriting
/ revealing some grotty slag smiling deliriously like an insane
gorilla / while chewing on an improvised cock drawn by a
future Picasso / and I stare all the time at the ads like it was a
meditation / while performing frottage against a piece of
taffeta / lovely / working as typist in Oxford Street / oh no,
don't get out yet / I'm not there yet / you may not be dear
but I am! / oh sod it / Oxford Circus / and the train heaves us
like a bad case of diarrhoea / then I'm channelled up the
elevator still holding my dangle / and briefcase with the
squashed-up sandwiches / churned up like the debris of
human rejects / bits of machinery on the conveyer belt going
back for repairing / or destroying / and I hoped I'd see that
bird again / she was lovely with great gooey eyes / maybe I'll
wait for her tomorrow / wend my way to my office in Bond

Street where I was a managing director of a firm of
wholesale jewellers / flogging pearls out of a suitcase in
Oxford Street for Xmas (genuine three-strung diamanté
pearls / a quid / with beautiful engine-turned, bevelled
edges) / come on don't just stand there / gentleman over
there / lady over there / watch out there's a johnny / nip into
Woolie's or the ABC for a quick cup of bird vomit /
travelling salesmen swilling down some unidentified goo /
grins stitched to their unfortunate faces / collapsed spine /
frayed cuffs and souls / and breath to fell a dragon / I saw a
geezer shove his fork into a pie at one of these filling stations
/ of garbage manufacturers / but it was empty except for a
mouse that was curled up inside with a happy look on his
face / sleeping / and he didn't want to disturb the mouse like
he thought it could have been a pet / since a lot of these
chain cafés have a lot of mice around / so he took it back /
this mouse has eaten my pie miss / he said / this waitress
who was slithering around in the dead grease / with bunches
of varicose like gnarled roots on her pins / says: what and it's
still alive! / I'm glad something likes our pies / here never
mind the humour I want another pie / he was sweating now
since he used this day's voucher up / she says I'll send it
back to the makers and if they find it faulty they'll refund
your money / but this didn't solve the problem / and he
screamed that they didn't need to send it back / the evidence
is there in the mouse / so after all the rhubarb and shouting /
he's kicking up a big pen and ink / the manager comes
sludging over / a fag hanging out of his head / and one off his
ear / and one up his ass no doubt / so this greasy manager
comes wiping his fingers on his apron / since he'd been
making ham sandwiches / had distinguished himself in
service by cutting the thinnest ham in the world / and was
straightaway employed by Forte's / so here he was and said
if you make a fuss like this in a good British café / three
million men fought the Second World War on food like this
/ so the salesman bowing to his superior size says all right /
and the manager seeing that the salesman had calmed down

said / was there something he could do for him / and the
salesman brightened up a bit says / perhaps you could warm
the mouse up please / certainly sir, right away sir, came the
immediate response / but the mouse sussing something is
up with all the movement going on cocks an ear and runs
down the waitress's leg / she screamed / farted loudly
enough to shake the windows and slides over on the greasy
floor / keeling over a table on the way down / whose aged
occupants were shocked into a sudden coma / well after that
I didn't fancy going back to that café any more / it's all true /
don't look at me like that / I'm worried about that fight /
anyway I gave up flogging bent gear in Oxford Street after
that / they say there's a big future in flogging magistrates
with bags over their heads / they pay well.

(*They all mime a tube in rush hour, the words of the* CHORUS
syncopating with the train:)

ALL: Breakfast, shit, work, lunch, bed.

*Back on the tube or walking the streets – slow motion – best on the tube
– only a few strap-hangers or passers-by become* MIKE*'s friends.*

LES: Hallo Mike / I wish you luck for tomorrow.

MIKE: Thanks.

RALPH: How do you think you'll do?

MIKE: Very well thank you / how's your mother?

RALPH: She's OK.

MIKE: Still washing your knickers?

RALPH: No fear / I send them to be read by a fortune-teller.

LES: Are you scared?

MIKE: Not a jot / not a jot.

LES: I bet you are.

MIKE: How much / wanna see my pants?

SYLV: Don't go Mike / they're goading you on.

MIKE: What are you doing on the Piccadilly Line?

SYLV: Giving head to accountants in the rush hour.

MIKE: That's not very nice / is it?

SYLV: I waited in all day for you Sunday.

MIKE: I had things on my mind.

SYLV: That's what they all say.

MIKE: Who's they?

SYLV: I wish I knew.

STEVE: Going down the Royal tonight?

MIKE: I can't / gotta preserve my strength.

STEVE: Pity, we had something really dishy lined up for you.

MIKE: Keep it warm for me under the grill / I'll be back.

STEVE: You hope.

MIKE: What do you mean?

STEVE: Oh words words words.

MIKE: They're trying to undermine my fierce endeavour.

KEN: Hello Mike / coming for a ride up West?

MIKE: Not tonight Ken / not tonight old son.

KEN: Who's going with you Mike?

MIKE: I'll go alone unless you want to hold my coat.

KEN: Do me a favour / I wouldn't go down there for all the salmon in Wentworth Street.

(*All except* MIKE *leave the train.* PEARL *and* SID *get on.*)

SID: You could have been an accountant or a manager of a string of menswear shops.

MIKE: I'd rather be bounded in a nutshell and count myself king of infinite space.

PEARL: Michael, my son, my joy and pride / jewel of my loins / apple of my eye / the be-all and end-all / the sun in the morning and the stars at night / where are you going my son?

MIKE: For a fight to the death / a battle of honour / destruction of a monster / to kill the plague / to slay the dragon / to defend the weak / to prove my worth / to destroy the mighty / to avenge the dead / to annihilate the oppressor / to be a mensh / to have a punch-up.

PEARL: Well wrap up warm / it's bitter out.

SID: Come on, Mum.

(*They leave the train.*)

MIKE: Stars hide your fires / let night not see my dark and deep desires / maybe I'll go dancing after all to keep my mind off it.

The CHORUS *is seated as in a dance hall.* MIKE *takes* SYLV *into the centre of the floor. Gradually the others dance around them, holding invisible partners.*

MIKE: Do you wanna dance / I took her on the floor / the crystal ball smashed the light into a million pieces / a shattered lake at sunrise / the music welled up / and the lead guitarist / plugged into ten thousand watts zonging in our ears / callused thumb whipping chords / down the floor we skate / I push her thigh with mine / and backwards she goes to the gentle signal / no horse moved better / and I move my left leg which for a second leaves me hanging on her thigh / then she moves hers / swish / then she's hanging on mine / like I am striding through the sea / our thighs clashing and slicing past each other like huge cathedral bells / whispering past flesh-encased nylon / feeling / all the time knees / pelvis / stomach / hands / fingertips / grip smell / moving interlocking fingers / ice floes melting / skin silk weft and warp / blood-red lips gleaming / pouting / stretching over her hard sharp and wicked-looking Hampsteads / words dripping out her red mouth gush like honey / I lap it up / odours rising from the planet of the flesh / gardens after light showers / hawthorn and wild mimosa / Woolie's best / crushed fag ends / lipstick / powder / gin and tonic / all swarming together on one heavenly nerve-numbing swill / meanwhile huge mountains of aching fleshy worlds are drifting past each other holding their moons / colliding and drifting apart again / the light stings / the journey is over / the guitarist splattered in acne as the rude knife of light stabs him crushes his final shattering chord / the ball of fire stops / and I say thank you very much.

SYLV: OK.

MIKE: Speak again, bright angel.

SYLV: I fink I'll have a gin and tonic.

LES: You're avoiding your destiny by diversions.

MIKE: Tomorrow and tomorrow . . .

SYLV: I waited for you all day Sunday.

MIKE: I had something on my mind.

SYLV: Come on home / I'll cook you a plate of spags.

MIKE: I'd rather eat the air promise-crammed.

SYLV: You must be starving.

MIKE: I'm preparing myself for the battle on Sat.

SYLV: Will you come over after?

MIKE: Yes long after / if I am here.

SYLV: Are you scared?

MIKE: Not a jot.

SYLV: Why are you so mean / you told me you loved me once.

MIKE: You were the more deceived.

SYLV: Heaven help him.

LES: Oh blessed Mike / why art thou not in constant training for
the event?

MIKE: How do you know what I do all day / who watches my
mental exercise / detects the secret plans I make / an
armoury of weapons / stored in the forceful regions of my
brain / I'll hypnotize the beast / and psych him out / drinks
all round.

LES: Here's to the end of the Hoxton King.

RALPH: Destruction of the stinking dragon.

STEVE: The ogre falls.

KEN: Hideous and most sweet revenge.

LES: No more trembling in the strasser.

RALPH: Pull the birds we like.

STEVE: Safe conduct to the supermarkets.

KEN: Unimpeded entry to the Essoldo.

LES: Sleep tight at nights.

RALPH: Noisy mouthpieces / no frighteners.

STEVE: No knifing from bumper cars at Battersea.

KEN: Our motorbikes safe from slashing tyres.

LES: No more dreaded smells.

RALPH: No more terrified cats.

STEVE: Shaking OAPs.

MIKE: The Hackney marshes.

ALL: The Hackney marshes.

PEARL: You could have been had you tried / a manager / a
solicitor / or even a representative of a firm of ladies'

underwear manufacturers / your uncle would help you / I'm sure you would have liked getting into ladies' underwear / look at your cousin Willy.

STEVE: Wife – three kids – responsibilities.

KEN: House in Colindale.

SID: Detached.

LES: Mark 2 Cortina – £15,000 a year.

(*They follow* MIKE *as he runs away from the train of responsibility that pursues him, and they circle stage and sit.* MIKE *whips round and makes a speech to the audience.*)

MIKE: Why should I yoke myself to nine to five / stand shoulder to shoulder with the dreary gang who sway together in the tube / or get acquainted with parking meters / be a good citizen of this vile state / so I can buy an ultra-smart hi-fi and squander fortunes on pop singles / what do you do at night between the sheets but dream of mortgages and oh dear the telly's on the blink / we're going to Majorca again this year / you who've never raped a virgin day / with adrenalin assault upon your senses / but aggravate your spine to warp / while grovelling for a buck / or two / smiling at your boss / and spend heart-wrenched hours at the boutique deciding what to wear / ragged up like Chelsea pooftahs / or chase some poor mutt on Sundays / mad keen to commit some GBH upon it / and birds like screaming hyenas with teeth and scarves flying / make your usual boring death-filled chat in smelly country pubs / with assholes like yourself / no that's not for me / I'd rather be toad and live in the corner of a dungeon for other's uses.

The HOXTON GANG *with their leader,* CURLY. *They appear to lean against a lamp post, each facing out, like four gargoyles, a hard light from overhead.*

CURLY: Night and silence / that's what it's all about.

BURT: You're right Curly / oh son of night – the atmosphere is double-strong / star-filled / the perfect evening for a fight.

PAT: It's what you need / a cobbled street / just wet a bit / to give a little image of a broken moon / a yellow lamplight / flickering a bit / still lit in gas.

REG: The echo of our studs on lonely streets / the smoke of
cigarettes / thickening in a blast of light / like fiery dragons /
in our lair we hover / smelling blood / our leathern wings
glistening in the dewy air.

CURLY: The odd moth hanging about / and eyeing up the scene /
banging his fretful wings / oh let me in it says / to the hungry
flame.

BURT: Then out he goes / like a light double-choked / to be so
scorched up.

PAT: Right burnt up he was about it.

ALL: Laughter – cackle – silence.

CURLY: In just such a manner doth our fretful moth of Stamford
Hill / bang against the light that we give out / he wants to be
let in / and then . . .

PAT: Phhht!

CURLY: We wait / we've time / I don't think he will be late / I
sense him now weighing up the scales of chance / thinking
thick regrets / and oh what a mug am I, swallow it, he thinks,
turn yellow / at least you'll keep your face / the one the birds
do like to chase / you'll lose the other / the one you'll never
again show to mates.

PAT: He's as chicken as a chicken coming to a fox / his pants hot
lined in shit / I hear / that fear has wrenched from out his guts.

BURT: He does it to be king of his bankrupt domain / to cancel
out the bum he is at home / so he can spout out to the world
that he's got clout / and make the teenyboppers moist their
flowers / and holler, oh Michael / so he can stand up West
and join the firm of grievous / rape / robbery and death /
solicitors to the realm.

PAT: He desperately wants his diploma / and that is you / to
launch him on the path of hate / that's lined in gelt and not a
caper down the Ly / a bundle for a laugh / but turn pro /
that's his game.

CURLY: I'll not disappoint him / I am guaranteed against
default / reckless in my desire to give value / fear no marks
upon my well-worn face / have nought to save / but
welcome all / I'll make love to him / my caresses will start

their long journey in hell / he'll not see it coming / only
feel / I'll embrace him like a hungry bear / my hands will
find his body's treats / and practise on his bones / we'll
dance and then I'll look into his eyes / wet with tears of
thankfulness / as I do renovate the house he lives in / he'll
whisper like a gasping lover / to the background of
splintering sounds / as he hears the music of his body's
walls snap and crack / his heart will beat a terrible drum /
and want to burst to spread some numbing death relieving
darkness / so come on scum.

The café of Mike's mates.
LES: Two teas, Joe.
JOE: Sugar?
LES: One, ta.
RALPH: Got any sandwiches?
JOE: Sold out.
RALPH: Do you suppose it's possible to organize one?
JOE: Not now.
RALPH: Why not?
JOE: Because it's late.
RALPH: Ah, go on, don't be a fat pig.
JOE: Closing.
LES: Sod you, you slimy middle-aged fart.
RALPH: I hope you starve / the time will come when nobody
    comes in this dung heap and your family is condemned to
    catch rats to eat / while your children crawl in lice and your
    wife's hair falls out / may your daughters be gang-raped by
    blacks / and your house burnt down with your kids
    screaming / while you sit here counting your gelt you
    scheming piece of dogshit.
    (*Record on juke-box: 'You are the sunshine of my life'.*)
JOE: All right I'll make you a sandwich / what do you want?
RALPH: Roast beef and coleslaw in toasted brown.
JOE: Just watch it / next time you'll go too far and say something
    you'll regret, OK?
STEVE: Half-hour to go / Mike cut his hair and greased it / he

can't grip that / so as to introduce his knee upon Mike's head.

KEN: That's shrewd.

STEVE: We should have been there / we should.

RALPH: Then why weren't we / case the others jump him if he's out in front?

STEVE: Dunno.

RALPH: You're his mate aren't you?

STEVE: Well, so are you.

RALPH: Yeah.

STEVE: He's mad to go / what does it prove / to swallow it's no shame / we know Mike's tough / ignore those bums / that's what I say.

KEN: He'll swallow nothing / so he'll taste nothing bitter in his mouth like us / he goes because he has to / and for us / you know that's true / he goes for you!

SID *comes downstage, alone.*

SID: Once in Soho, a while ago, round the back streets / walking one night to catch the tube I wandered round the alleyways / a saunter for no reason but to stretch my pins / up in the window was this bird / a right cracker she was / I stopped and caught her staring down / a red lampshade that tells all I don't know why / but I was tempted by all the mysteries that glow foretold / I pretended to be staring in the shop below / transistors and electrical equipment / but up above was the socket I needed for my plug / a card said 'Sally, two flights up' / I found myself upon the stairs / grim smells and rot / knocked on the door.

SYLV *at home pouring a drink, upstage.*

SYLV: I hate to drink alone / sometimes I must / it quells the energy I have which I'd rather spend on someone / some him / or him / he leaves me with it bottled up and spare / I drown it out / my youth is going up the spout / in love that's wasted / I hate to stay in alone / how many others are like me / alone in boxes / waiting for someone or the phone to ring /

what's the use to wait / and if he does / a thing of shreds and
patches.

SID *and* PEARL *downstage.*

SID: So well, I knocked upon the door / and this scrubber
opened it / looking like nothing on earth / while far below it
was a mystery / I thought / she smiled / and showed a gap or
three / the rest was black / and on her face a cake of slap /
one inch thick at least / I thought I can't do this / I had my
wages in my belt / not much since times were hard / and
mum needed the gelt / for rent and clobber for the kids / a
coat as well / but even so I couldn't now turn back / I hurtled
through a quick time for . . . don't ask / it cost a bomb.

PEARL: You promised, Sid, you said I could have a new coat.

SID: And found myself outside the electrical store / and nothing
to show except a rancid shag / and wages short / felt sick and
empty / I couldn't buy my wife her winter coat / I sacrificed
my wife for that / I'm sorry Pearl, I said, I earned a few bob
less / you'll have to wait a week or two / felt real vile / she
said.

PEARL: You promised Sid / you said that I would have a new
coat Sid, this winter / that's what you said.

SID: I know / don't go on / don't start nagging / I sweat out my
guts for you / I break my balls that you should not go short.

PEARL: Don't shout in front of the kids!

SID: I sit down by a bench all day / machining trousers for five
bob / and dust choking my lungs / and the noise of the
machines / you wouldn't believe it / and fifty in a room / ten
pair of pants a day / I slog to make / cut and trim / then
throw them to Greek to finish off / and put a fly in / and at
the end a Mick to press them / I got callused hands already
from the shears / a spine that's curved forever / and a cough
that can't be cured by all the medicines in the world / that's
known to man / to make a haven for my family / which is a
little heaven / so don't get on my tits.

PEARL: OK / I'll wait / sure I can wait / wanna cuppa?

SID: I wouldn't say no to nice cuppa, Pearl.

PEARL: I hope Mike's OK / I haven't seen him since yesterday.

SID: Does that surprise you / you look surprised as if that's new /
that he appears when you see him and not before / a plague
he's been to me (*To himself*) . . . it cost a bomb.

PEARL: What did?

SID: Nothing, what did I say?

PEARL: You said it cost a bomb.

SID: Oh I was miles away.

In the café, or MIKE *walking. The following can be said either by a
chorus of* LADS *or by* MIKE, *lecturing the* LADS' *still faces. For
continuity,* MIKE *should be alone.*

LES: At least the joy of being strong.

STEVE: Of owning your own body.

RALPH: Your capitals, your guts.

KEN: In your hands you hold the pleasure or the pain of the
Western world.

LES: Hands can be the instrument of life.

STEVE: Or death.

RALPH: What's it to be?

KEN: Either way you have to choose.

LES: You who watch and never had a choice.

STEVE: You look the only way.

RALPH: How many times did you want to lash out?

KEN: Give vent to what you felt?

LES: The bile that's choked within.

STEVE: Instead ate humble pie.

RALPH: How often did you want to impress the missus?

KEN: Be Charles Atlas and kill the dragon like St George?

LES: And how often did you tremble in your socks?

STEVE: Afraid in case you lost . . .

RALPH: Or broke a nose.

KEN: Ooh, painful.

LES: Damaged an eye even.

STEVE: There's lots to fear.

RALPH: And swallowed some offence.

KEN: A mouthful of slagging vile.

LES: And wished next day . . .

STEVE: When safe at home that you had taken chances.

RALPH: A memory to chat about on wintry nights to all the
kids . . .

KEN: Of how you were a hero.

LES: For a while.

STEVE: Never mind, you made a bomb in wholesale and made a
fortune in the market like a lucky Joe.

RALPH: Beneath it all you wanted at some time to be a hero with
your dukes.

KEN: To emulate John Wayne.

LES: Or other prince of celluloid.

STEVE: Because that's your courage that you stake.

RALPH: Your guts you gamble on the street.

KEN: Opposing some hard tearaway.

LES: And whip him.

STEVE: That's worth a lot.

RALPH: You know it in your heart.

KEN: How many carry an emblem of some shame . . .

LES: Some insult not yet purged away . . .

STEVE: That gnaws your very vitals?

RALPH: You forget, you say! Ignore that cad.

KEN: Don't get mixed up with riff-raff, darling, says your dolly
bird.

LES: You jump into a cab.

STEVE: Agree with her . . . they're not worth it.

RALPH: Ignore the mob.

KEN: Yet underneath it all you wish there were a Bruce Lee
tucked away.

LES: Or a Mike.

STEVE: Instead you pour a drink and gas about an incident at
school when for a minute you stood up to wrath.

RALPH: You play the incident again.

LES: And yet again.

LES: Re-run the entire scene.

STEVE: Imagine what you would have done . . .

RALPH: Had you the chance again.

KEN: Let him say it once more, you utter in your dreams.

LES: Too late.

STEVE: And if you had the chance again . . .

RALPH: Wouldn't it have been the same?

KEN: But knights are born not made.

LES: The others stand round and watch.

(*They march off as tight group and comfort* MIKE.)

MIKE: See ya tonight then.

RALPH: Bird's in the club.

STEVE: Don't feel well, Mike.

LES: Gotta fix me scooter.

KEN: Me mother's sick.

MIKE: Don't let me down, will ya?

ALL: Course, Mike, yeah, etc.

Sylv's pad.

SYLV: What are you doing here?

MIKE: Aren't you pleased to see me / I had to see you / wish me
    luck / I got a little flicker in my guts / I must confess.

SYLV: Of what?

MIKE: Doubt and sick all mixed.

SYLV: Then don't go.

MIKE: Have to.

SYLV: Why?

MIKE: Sylv, the Fates have wrapped me up / to be delivered this
    night / I've got to go / revenge is one / strong one for a pal /
    as for the rest / what else is there to do / sure there is always a
    day that has to come / that you would much rather avoid /
    postpone / and send a card / forgive me / but / I can't make it
    this week / you lie in bed and sweat / hope the daylight never
    comes / it's not tomorrow any more / it's now / the readiness
    is all / but after if I'm still around / I'll pop on over.

SYLV: I wanted much more than that / the occasional hallo love
    and how are you / you busy tonight shall I come round / to
    sit and wait is not my idea of paradise / in case you decide
    this is the night that you decide to come / and what do we do
    but pass the time until it's time to go and 'see ya! Be in
    touch!' / I'd like to be there for a man / who lives for the

moment / so I can live for the moment too / when we can
meet / and protect that which we grow together within me /
not here love – here's a ton / go get it fixed / a hundred quid
to kick it out / buy back the space I'd rather fill / a hundred
quid / to kill / that's easy for the man in love with death and
pride / you are more keen to see your Hoxton pal so you can
be a tearaway / the King of Stamford Hill / if you gave me as
much as you give him / I'd be so happy / if I obsessed you
half as much / you'll give each other all the thrills you are
afraid to spill on me / you are in love with him not me / so go
enjoy yourself / be free / far easier for a hand to make a fist
than hold it open for a caress / easier for you to smash
yourself into his body than to mine / to make yourself into a
ball of hate wound up / so you can hide yourself from what
you fear / be a hard man / 'cause hard covers the soft / the
soft that's underneath is what you fear / my woman's body
tells me / is soft to make things grow / its softness breaks
down your rocks / can destroy you like water wears down
stone / go to your lover Mike / go, and don't come back / go /
be alone / and who will put you together again when you're
a pile of broken bones?

MIKE: Thank you very much / I'll bear in mind all what you
said / I spit out all my angst / confess my guts / wished I had
bit my tongue first / before I let those soppy words crawl out
my gob / I had a shred or two of doubt I do confess / and
that is all no need to make a song and dance / accuse me of
some vileness in my act with you / it takes two to tango /
don't forget that / anyway I'm here aren't I / I come to you
don't I / there's no one else / at least . . . you get the best /
sometimes the worst / that's what it's all about / that's how it
goes / that's what they spout in church even / for better or
for . . . / I'm sorry you don't find me your ideal / you never
will / you birds have scored into your head / some geezer all
identikit / a mister right / but they never can and never will
fit the little pictures that you make / so without more ado /
I'll take my leave of you.

Street.

MIKE: Didn't wish me luck even! I dunno / I'm all alone, that's
how it goes / my mates have fled / left me for dead / and
most pernicious woman left me too / I need a friend / need
someone / something / just to tell it to / tell me I'm OK / I'm
good / nah I don't need / anyone / I need revenge / that's
something to get on with / that's a start / don't take away my
raison dirt track / don't take away my art / I'll be myself again
/ but now a numbing sickness is sliding down my gut / I'll
force it back / I clench my fist / it feels like jelly / like a baby's
paw / if only I had the strength of a kitten I could win / I see
myself reflected in a windowpane / a death's skull stares me
in the face / where is my resolution / where the spleen that
had me think I was the king of the master race / bearded
with the sweat of fear / a demon came and sucked my blood
/ they sense victims and hover like bats / the filthy beasts /
that's all right / who ever felt happy before a fight / you go in
sick but once you start and get the first sting in / your face
you then forget your problems / like an actor on the stage /
scared shitless in the wings but once he's on then he's the
king.

(CHORUS *rushes on – reflects* MIKE*'s walk upstage.*)

OTHERS: (*At random*) You can do it, Mike.

Didn't wish me luck even.

How do you think you'll do?

He's mad to go.

No blood of mine.

But hers ...

One minute, Mike.

LES: Hackney marshes.

(*The* CHORUS *leaves the stage.* MIKE *is alone. He acts the
battle.*)

MIKE: He hits me with a hook / I'm down / a bolt to fell an ox /
crumbles slow / then smashes me with a right / and now / I
sway / a drunk looking for a hold / a volley a hard straight
comes whipping out / smashing home / I go down slow like
the *Titanic* / but grab hold on the way / and drag him down

leaking red from all openings but still I hold him / close / he can't be hit / too close / and with my almighty arm I lock his neck into a vice / where do I get the strength / the brute's amazed thinking it was all done / but he finds his head being smashed into the wall / but like he's made of rock / he twists himself from out my grip like some mad demented bull and snorts screams and kicks but by this time I dodge the sledge hammers and hold him at bay / alive again as if the blows have woken me from some deep sleep / I'm myself again / we move and circle / it's quiet as the grave / all tense waiting / the beast kicks out and hard / I grab a leg / and down he falls / hard / but with almighty strength the brute is up again / sneers and foams / and rams his fingers round my throat / grips hard / the others round about / screaming / kill the bastard / tear out his guts / and rip his balls off / I pull off his wrist and then we twist / fall / rolling / each trying to find a hold / and lashing out from time to time / knee / elbow / head / boot / whatever finds itself unoccupied and free for service / we break away and stand streaming like two dragons breathing flame / fighting to the death / each waiting for the other to move / still / just the sound of breath / then in the beast goes and fast and throws himself on me like to annihilate me once and for all / I go flying back thrown by the mass of hate and crash both down in a welter of struggling seething flesh / twisting foaming heaving screaming / I'm stomped on / sounds unearthly are heard / I fear it must end / and bad / he's on my chest / his fist drawn back / one horrible almighty gnarl of bone and brought it crashing down on to my face / pow and then again pow and now again pow / I can hear the sickening crunch / but I protect what how I can / draw energy from the deep and thrust my hand up underneath his jaw / with the other I smash it home / the brute stumbles / pulled off balance / my face is crimson blind by blood / I wipe with one hand / I'm upon him now spraying his blood on both like we were swimming in it / this time grip his throat and hold it fast / tight / tighter / after long time we topple over / again / rise

slow like prehistoric monsters / the beast screaming / words /
spitting out / no meaning / splattered curses / he bows like to
pounce again / I then kick / it lands home dead square in the
face / then follow up both hands working like pumps / like
you never saw.

CHORUS: Pow-pow–pow–pow–pow / pow–pow–pow–pow–pow!

MIKE: But you wouldn't believe the strength of the brute /
inhuman like / grinning like a gargoyle / he stands there, says
come on do something / and charges again / I can't believe /
as if my own powers mean nothing / see hopelessness and
fear now flooding in as fast as strength is flowing out / we
grip each other for a hold / to throw one or the other down /
but I'm losing all belief / I'm down / as if it's better there /
just lie covering my face / I'm kicked pow / once twice pow /
feebly attempt to rise pow / kicked down / the fourth time in
his glee / too keen, he misses / slides over on the blood
slippery deck / heavy as lead / I climb up in agony / but do
not miss the chance / to connect the monster's head with a
bone-shattering well-aimed knee / it stops him dead / it
looks surprised / astonished / and for luck / throw all my
weight into a right which crashes open all in his skull / out go
the lights pow / the Hoxton King keeled over / toppled /
crashed down / in one terrible long rasping blood gurgled
moan / then it was over / he twitched / raised his head /
spewed between his bloody teeth the words / 'Nice one' /
then lay quite still / me yelling / the lads about looked sick
and pale / were shattered in their souls / and thought the
future black / I wiped the blood away / put on my coat / they
parted quickly from me when I left / I staggered into
casualty at London Hospital who fixed me up.

*Gang as group like cheerleaders. They trot around the stage to give
him a hero's welcome.*

MATES: Well done and welcome home / you done us proud /
terrific / so we heard.

KEN: Report was trumps.

RALPH: From far and wide.

LES: Your triumphs sung to the four corners of the manor.
STEVE: You look a mess.
ALL: But hold your head up / you're the ace.
MIKE: Oh yeah / my nose is broke / my lovely profile's gone.
RALPH: You'll get it back.
STEVE: You'll look better than ever once it heals.
KEN: Don't you fear.
LES: Sensational it were, I swear.
RALPH: My heart was out there for you . . .
STEVE: Stomping in my chest . . .
KEN: Like fifty insane drummers.
LES: When you got up and curled your right . . .
RALPH: I said a little prayer for its journey into space.
ALL: He didn't know what year it was / he didn't care!
MIKE: So where were you, deserted me ye men of little faith / all
    mouth and trousers when it comes down to the crunch / you
    could have shown a face at least to plonk your minces on the
    scene should tricky business raise its ugly face / instead you
    wait for news of my impending fate / it's over now / it's done
    / so what's it all about / I've had enough of this / I'm out.

MIKE *creeps into his house – enters Pearl's and Sid's room for the first
time.*
MIKE: Hallo.
SID: What the . . .? Look at your face.
PEARL: Mike, oh God, what happened to you?
MIKE: I had a fight . . . but I won . . . I did it.
SID: So, look at you, what do you want / a medal?
MIKE: No / I just wanted to tell you / it's the last one I'll have.
SID: So tell me something new.
PEARL: Leave him, Sid.
SID: He's proud / he comes in here to tell us he's proud.
MIKE: It was hard / yeah I'm proud / his gang did up little Harry.
SID: Don't give us this talk / this time of night / your gang warfare
    / a gangster I've got and he comes in yet like he's a hero.
MIKE: I just wanted to talk to you.
SID: So / you've talked.

MIKE: I needed to tell someone.

SID: So you've told me / what do you want us to do?

MIKE: Nothing, just nothing you miserable lump of complaint / that's all you've done all your life / what else are you good for / nothing / and you give nothing / I've listened to your miserable snivelling complaints for years / I've had enough of you / a swollen bag of useless opinions like all the old sods like you.

PEARL: Don't aggravate your father / his ulcer's killing him / go to bed / wash your face and go to bed / you don't look well, son.

MIKE: Ma / you've tied yourself to a lump of concrete / and it's sinking into the swamp.

PEARL: And who's complaining?

MIKE: I am!

PEARL: Don't worry about me / go to bed.

MIKE: OK.

(MIKE *exits.*)

SID: Tell him in the morning to go / he's got to go / I for one can't take any more / so tell him / Pearl he's our son / but he's got to get out of this house / I can't take any more of it.

PEARL: I'll tell him.

SID: Make sure you do.

PEARL: I will / I said I will.

SID: He's got to go somewhere and do something / but I don't want him around any more / I'm sorry.

PEARL: In the morning I'll tell him to go.

SID: Don't soften up and change your mind.

PEARL: I'll tell him it's best for all of us if he went.

SID: You'll tell him that.

PEARL: Yeah.

SID: 'Cause this can't go on like this.

PEARL: I know that.

SID: Then we can have a bit of peace in our old age.

PEARL: Yeah.

SID: You know what I mean.

PEARL: Of course / I'll tell him in the morning / I'll tell him he

must find somewhere else to live and not come back this
time.

SID: I did my best.

PEARL: Yeah.

SID: Didn't I? . . . You sound as if I didn't well / didn't I or not /
did I show him those ways?

PEARL: No, I did.

SID: What you talking about?

PEARL: From me he saw that not to fight was to give in / he saw
that I never fought back / so he had to.

SID: You'll tell him in the morning to go!

Epilogue.

MIKE: I can't go on like this / look at me / my nose is out of joint /
I can't see straight / I've got no job to speak of but I won / I
won / I beat the beast / with my own two hands alone / I
reached out and defeated what they feared / I conquered my
own doubts when sick inside / that's great / so tell me where
to go and what to do / and what's the trick that makes for
happy days and nights / the fireside and mates around for
Xmas / the wife cooking a bird / a baby going gaga / the
colour telly on / the Daimler shining round the front / what
did you do to get it / do you thieve / stay on at school / or
work your loaf / inherit some cosy chunk of loot from papa /
go on tell me the trick / what's the clue I need to know some
answers / or I'll make my own / you who sit comfortably at
home / who wake up with a grin and toast and eggs / tell me
what you do and how you do it / never mind I'll find out / I'll
get the wind on you / I'll break out of this maze / and sniff
around your pen / I'll be the beast you fear / until I get an
answer / straight up I will / you had me do your dirt / and
stood around to gape / while I put down the fears that kept
you sleepless in your beds / there'll come another beast / for
every one you kill / there will grow another head.

Further epilogue.

PEARL *and* SID. GANG *as respectable people stand behind them.*

SID: Don't you worry / we did what we could / he's not so bad / a little wild / but soon he'll find his head / and if he don't / well then / others will help / there are the courts / police and magistrates to guide him on the way / prisons to help persuade / and keep society safe / so all in all he's no real threat to you and me / we keep our noses clean / pay the rent and rates / smile our social smile / and leave when they call time.

PEARL: But he's your son.

SID: No son of mine.

Blackout.
Faces of characters.

GREEK

CHARACTERS

EDDY
DAD
WIFE
MUM
FORTUNE-TELLER
MANAGER OF CAFE
DOREEN
SPHINX
WAITRESS I
WAITRESS 2

AUTHOR'S NOTE

Greek came to me via Sophocles, trickling its way down the millenia until it reached the unimaginable wastelands of Tufnell Park – a land more fantasized than real, being an amalgam of the deadening war zones that some areas of London had become. Tufnell Park was just a word to play with – like our low comedians play with the sound of East Cheam for example – so no real offence to the inhabitants.

In my eyes, Britain seemed to have become a gradually decaying island, preyed upon by the wandering hordes who saw no future for themselves in a society which had few ideals or messages to offer them. The violence that streamed through the streets, like an all-pervading effluence, the hideous Saturday night fever as the pubs belched out their dreary occupants, the killing and maiming at public sports, plus the casual slaughtering of political opponents in Northern Ireland, bespoke a society in which an emotional plague had taken root. It was a cold place in my recollection, lit up from time to time by the roar of the beast – the beast of frustration and anger, whose hunger is appeased by these revolving scraps, which momentarily dull its needs. We were the world's greatest video watchers, since we had lost the ability to speak to each other. We sat like zombies, strangled in our attempts to communicate, feeding off the flickering tube like patients wired to support systems.

Oedipus found a city in the grip of a plague and sought to rid the city of its evil centre represented by the Sphinx. Eddy seeks to reaffirm his beliefs and inculcate a new order of things with his vision and life-affirming energy. His passion for life is inspired by the love he feels for his woman, and his detestation of the degrading environment he inherited. If Eddy is a warrior who holds up the smoking sword as he goes in, attacking all that he finds polluted, at the same time he is at heart an ordinary young man with whom many I know will find identification. The play is also a love story.

In writing my 'modern' *Oedipus* it wasn't too difficult to find contemporary parallels, but when I came to the 'blinding' I paused, since in my version it wouldn't have made sense, given Eddy's non-fatalistic disposition, to have him embark on such an act of self-hatred – unless I slavishly aped the original. One day a friend gave me a book to read which provided an illumination to my problem in an almost identical situation. The book is called *Seven Arrows* by Hyemeyohst Storm. It contains a passage of such tenderness and simplicity that I was immediately given the key to my own ending:

'How is it, Hawk,' I asked him, 'that I should not make love to Sweet Water, my mother?'

'Do you love her?' he asked me.

I answered, 'Yes, more than anyone else . . . But . . . children of such a love are born wrong.'

'Have you ever seen one of these children?' asked Night Bear.

'No, I have not. And I have never known anyone who has.' . . .

'Then it is like everything else . . . It seems an easy thing to hear when a son kills someone, even his mother, but it is hard on people's ears when they hear of a son loving his mother.'

Greek was first performed at the Half Moon Theatre, London, on 11 February 1980. The cast was as follows:

EDDY and FORTUNE-TELLER	Barry Philips
DAD and MANAGER OF CAFE	Matthew Scurfield
WIFE, DOREEN, and WAITRESS 1	Linda Marlowe
MUM, SPHINX, and WAITRESS 2	Janet Amsden
Director	Steven Berkoff

Greek was transferred to the Arts Theatre Club, London in September 1980. The cast was as follows:

EDDY and FORTUNE-TELLER	Barry Philips
DAD and MANAGER OF CAFE	Matthew Scurfield
WIFE, DOREEN, and WAITRESS 1	Linda Marlowe
MUM, SPHINX, and WAITRESS 2	Deirdre Morris
Director	Steven Berkoff

A new production of *Greek* was presented at Wyndham's Theatre, London, on 29 June 1988. The cast was as follows:

EDDY and FORTUNE-TELLER	Bruce Payne
DAD and MANAGER OF CAFE	Steven Berkoff
WIFE, DOREEN, and WAITRESS 1	Gillian Eaton
MUM, SPHINX, and WAITRESS 2	Georgia Brown
Director	Steven Berkoff

Place: England
Time: present
Stage setting: kitchen table and four simple chairs. These will function in a number of ways. They can be everything one wants them to be from the platform for the SPHINX to the café. They also function as the train; the environment which suggests EDDY's humble origins becoming his expensive and elaborate home in Act Two. The table and chairs merely define spaces and act as an anchor or base for the actors to spring from. All other artifacts are mimed or suggested. The walls are three square upright white panels, very clinical and at the same time indicating Greek classicism. The faces are painted white and are clearly defined. Movement should be sharp and dynamic, exaggerated and sometimes bearing the quality of seaside cartoons. The family act as a chorus for all other characters and environments.

ACT ONE

SCENE I

EDDY: So, I was spawned in Tufnell Park that's no more than a
stone's throw from the Angel / a monkey's fart from
Tottenham or a bolt of phlegm from Stamford Hill / it's a
cesspit, right . . . a scum-hole dense with the drabs who
prop up corner pubs, the kind of pub where ye old arseholes assemble . . . the boring turds who save for Xmas with
clubs . . . my mum did that . . . save all year for her slaggy
Xmas party of boozy old relatives in Marks and Sparks'
cardigans who stand all year doing as little as they can while
they had one hand in the boss's till and the other scratching
their balls . . . they'd all come over and vomit up Guinness
and mum's unspeakable excuse for cuisine all over the
bathroom, adjust their dentures . . . rage against the blacks,
envying their cocks, loathe the yids, envying their gelt . . .
hate everything under thirty that walks and fall asleep in
front of the telly . . . so they'd gather in the pubs, usually a
smelly corner pub run by a rancid thick-as-pig-shit paddy
who sold nothing but booze and crisps in various chemical
flavours to their yokel patrons who played incessant games
of cruddy darts, drink yards of stale gnat's piss beer and
chatter like . . .

DAD: See Arsenal last week? . . .

DOREEN: I think England's team's all washed up . . .

MUM: What abaht the way he dribbled the . . .

DAD: Nah nah, he's lorst his bottle . . .

DOREEN: Do leave orf . . .

EDDY: The stink of the pub rises and the OAPs sit in the corner
staring out into the dreams they never had with a drip of snot
hanging off the ends of their noses and try to make a pint last
four hours . . . start crowding up now and the paddy starts
raving fucking 'time' and pulling the glass out of your hand
while he's bursting your eardrums screaming like a sergeant-

major, his wife attempts to shovel some paint on her evil hate-all face which looks as if it's been applied by a drunken epileptic on a roller coaster . . .

MUM (*as chorus*): 'Allo luv.

EDDY: She foams . . . staring out of a yellow face with little snot-brown eyes like two raisins in a plate of porridge. And if by chance you lean over the bar too far some bastard monster cunt Alsatian leaps at you, its dripping fangs simply dying to rip your fucking throat out . . . so I gave up going to the corner pub with its late night chorus of lurchy . . .

FAMILY (*as chorus*): G'night.

EDDY: . . . and . . .

FAMILY: (*as chorus*): See ya, Tel.

EDDY: We got wine bars now, handsome. That's much better – sit down, a half bottle of château or Bollinger, some pâte and salad by a chick who looks as if she's been fresh frozen . . . you take your favourite woman there, my woman very nice mate, looks like she's been just minted and sharp as new mown grass, knickers as white as Xmas, eyes like the bluest diamonds . . . a pair of fiery red rubies for lips, the light hits them and shatters your eyes, she smiles and your heart leaps into your throat and you carry a demon between your thighs and up to your chin . . . the whole time . . . I wear shades to protect myself against the brightness of her teeth . . . no tobacco stains on them boy . . . breath like an ocean breeze on Brighton Pier . . . now could you take her to that pub? Could you ever! Nah! It's really for the old fascists singing war songs on the pavement and . . .

FAMILY: Knees up Mother Brown . . .
Knees up Mother Brown . . .

EDDY: So I go to my wine bar with the bird who's carved out of onyx and marble and laced in the smells of the promise of sex the way you wouldn't believe . . . I swim in her like I was plunging into the Jordan for a baptism. So anyway one day my dad calls me in the kitchen.

DAD: Come in son . . .

EDDY: He says,

DAD: . . . I wanna chat to ya, or we could go down the corner to
the pub, I'll buy you a drink.

EDDY: 'No! Not that pub,' I yelp in real and unfeigned terror.
'I'll throw some tea into a pot instead' . . . mum's out . . .
the *Daily Mirror* crossword half finished . . . well it is a bit
grotty but homely in a sickly sort of way if you're not used to
anything better, it's not like the interior of a Zen temple but
cosy. A few crumbs on the carpet, some evil photos of my
sister on the mantelpiece and a picture of granny looking
like Mussolini in drag which they all looked like in those far
off days of pre-history, the poodle's shit again behind the
cocktail cabinet . . . the old bacon rinds sit stinking in the
pan and the room renches of lard. I made dad a cuppa.
Mum's at bingo and sis is meditating in the bedroom on the
squeezing out of some juicy blackheads . . . her old knickers
lie sunny side up . . . she always left them on the floor for
mum to scoop up while I wouldn't have touched them
except with those pincers that pick up radium behind thick
walls. So we sit down and he confesses this story to me . . .
pulls out a fag and sits there with his flies half undone, and
the ash of his fag ready to drop all over his shirt. I try not to
look at him or his flies. I try to occupy my thoughts with my
latest Stan Kenton. I look out of the window and see the
grey clouds of Tottenham stray across the window pane . . .
a tiny sliver of sun is struggling to peep through, sees what it
has to shine on and thinks 'fuck it – is it worth it' and beats a
retreat. So dad says . . .

DAD: Look here son . . .

EDDY: I says 'yes dad' clocking his work-raped face, his tasteless
shit-heap Burton ready-made trousers and his deadly drip-
dry shirt that acquires BO faster than shit attract flies . . . I
clock all this fusion of rubbish and say 'yes, dad? what do
you want to chat abaht', never hearing much else out of his
gob than . . .

DAD: Send the darkies back to the jungle . . .

EDDY: . . . and . . .

DAD: ''Itler got the trains running on time' . . .

EDDY: You got a lot of Nazi lovers among the British down and
out. Lazy bastards wondered why at the end of a life of
shiving and strikes Moisha down the road copped a few bob
or why the Cypriots had a big store full of goodies not that
pathetic shit-heap down our street that flogs only Mother's
Pride mousetrap cheese and a few miserable tins of
pilchards and Heinz baked beans and a dreary cunt inside
saying, 'no, we don't get no demand for that' when asked
for something only slightly more exotic than Kelloggs. So
dad did not come out with any of that fascist bullshit which
relieved me since the Front were full of dads like this and
that cunt in the grocery ship . . . 'yeah dad' I said 'what's on
your bonce' . . . his face squeezed up like it's hard to say,
like those old ads for Idris lemon squash showed a screwed-
up lemon and comes out with . . .

SCENE 2

DAD: When you were a nipper / we went to a gypsy, a fortune
teller / bit of a giggle / an Easter fair / don't laugh / a caper,
what else / spent a tosheroon on a bit of a thrill, don't talk to
me about thrills / so in we went / the gypsy asks 'have I a
son?' 'I have' I says, I mean who don't have a son? His face
meanwhile staring into the ball / his eyes all popping / I'm
not taking it for gen, straight up, a lark / Easter and all / I've
got a lovely bunch and all that / his face gets all contorted and
twisted and he says / he sees a violent death for this son's
father / do what! but I'm his dad / come orf it / don't get all
dramatic / we get on like houses blazing / 'and I see' he says,
'something worse than death / and that's a bunk-up with his
mum' / 'I'll give you a backhand' I utter / 'you're having me
on / you been smoking them African Woodbines' / 'No' he
shrieks, 'I see it, and what I see I see / so don't pay me, just
scarper / leave my tent / keep your gelt' / outside we ran,
your mum was white as Persil / I as yellow as a Chinaman
with jaundice / course we took no notice / forgot about it

like, but not quite / waited till you got to be a bloke and then
one day I said 'Dinah / you remember that darkie in the fair
who came out with all that filth about Eddy', one morning
in bed just lying there, redigesting bits of past and sucking
still the flavour of some juicy memories /

MUM: Not many . . .

DAD: Our Dinah slurps . . .

MUM: Not many, I nearly dropped Doreen with whom I was six
months' pregnant then / funny times.

DAD: 'Well' I say, 'that fair is back in town, the same firm fifteen
years later / let's bowl down and see that geezer, tell that
Hornsey gypsy what a lot of old bollocks / how he upset my
missus with his pack of dirty lies / so off we went / doubted
somehow that he'd still be there, since he was pushing sixty
then / you never know, we waited our turn / it was the same
name 'Have your future read / Fantoni's magic crystal
gazer' / shall we go in? . . .

MUM: Do you think we should? . . .

DAD: Why not, it's now or never / we went pale a bit but in we
marched / same old schmutter on the table, the beads we
walked through and the bit of old glass and no, it weren't
him, so I said 'Where's the old geezer that we once saw
whose handle now you seem to have?'

EDDY (*as the* 'GYPSY'): My late old man . . .

DAD: He said . . .

EDDY (*as the* 'GYPSY'): Five years ago he uttered his last / and fell
off the perch / but taught me the trade / imbued his vision in
me / I got his powers now / so don't you fret / if he did good
by you / donate a quid and I'll do my best . . .

DAD: So Ed, your mum and I sat down just like before, the years
they shrank away / just like a hole fell out of the earth and
time and space had faded away / we seemed then to have
hurtled back those fifteen years / in that small tent / the
music tinkling through from the carousel outside and that
funny smell / the shouts growing faint, just the whiff of stale
grass under our feet / and like the tent seemed small / like a
trap and suddenly hot and nothing outside just quiet but his

face / his face getting all twisted up just like his dad / his mouth all white and tight like an earthquake was going on inside his nut and his lips were straining against it coming out. Dinah sussed but natch we waited / 'don't tell me' I said, 'you see a son of mine' / his eyes looked up, affirmed / no word, just that look and his tight mouth / like holding back something worse than vomit / 'and you see something worse', I says, 'like a nasty accident perhaps' / He nodded, parted his lips enough to mouth the word 'death' which he hadn't the guts to sound. He then stared hard at Dinah / but we had enough and wanted not to hear the other half but fled / I turned and snatched the quid back from the table / I don't know why / but like before when I got my money back / it seemed to say by taking back the gelt that it couldn't happen / his eyes looked like pity / like those sweet pics you get in Woolie's of those kids with a tear just ripe to drop / I know it's just a funfair Ed / a laugh, a bit of a giggle / I didn't blame the kid / what do you make of it son / you don't fancy your old mum do you son! You don't want to kill me do you boy?

DOREEN: Leave off you two.

EDDY: Doreen! His face hung there like a soggy worn-out testicle / mouth open and eyes like carrier bags / fancy my mum! I could sooner go down on Hitler, than do anything my old man so gravely feared / no dad / but all this aggro and of wives' tale gone and put you in a tiz / I'll leave home / split and scarper / the Central Line goes far these days and that's to foreign climes / I'll piss off tomorrow / I needed to escape this cruddy flat and this excuse seemed good as any / tata ma and pa. They waved to me outside the flats . . . my mum looked sad / her spotty apron wrapped round her like the flag of womanhood / I never saw her out of it / always standing in the kitchen like some darkie slave behind dad and me and sis . . .

DAD: Bung us the toast.

EDDY: Where's the jam?

DOREEN: Pig!

MUM: More tea love?

DAD: Bung us the toast.

EDDY: Where's the jam?

DOREEN: Pig!

MUM: More 'taters love?

DOREEN: I'm on a diet.

MUM: More cake love?

EDDY: No mum, I've had six slices already.

MUM: Go on have some more.

EDDY: I don't want no more, you rancid old boot.

DAD: Hey?

EDDY: I'd spray affectionately.

MUM: Oh he don't like my cake.

EDDY: She'd simper . . . 'all right bung us another slice and I'll
    wedge it down wiv a mug of tea to slop it up a bit.'

DAD: Bung us the toast.

EDDY: Where's the jam?

DOREEN: Pig!

MUM: More tea love?

EDDY: She gazes at us with moist eyes on all of us slurping like fat
    pigs in a trough / we'd leave a wreck filled table, ma's
    washing up, how well she knew that washtop / dad's picking
    out losers in the worn out armchair / sis is fitting in her cap
    for the night's activity cussing and swearing in the next
    room as she struggles with it . . .

DOREEN: Fuck it!

EDDY: And mum sits in front of the box watching some dozy
    cretin making cunts out of the cunts who go on to win a few
    bob / mum's giggling in her glee / her legs like a patchwork
    quilt from hogging the electric fire, while I was in my little
    room plotting and dreaming of ruling the world / take a
    Charles Atlas course / wondering if the Queen gets it often /
    or planning a dose of robbery with violets or glorious bodily
    charm / so in my little room I plotted, smoked / played Stan
    Kenton and wanked wiv mum's cooking oil. Now no more
    will I escape to my little domain . . . hearing the sounds of
    hughie phlegm in the next room through the snot-encrusted

walls. So all in a flash these thoughts slinked like maggots through my bonce as I waved my goodbyes to the fast-diminishing figures of my mum and dad wed together in the distance like mould on cheese . . . my dad was the mould / never mad about him . . . as I reached the end of the road I could only see the apron and lost the figure / the apron stayed in my mind the longest. When my old lady went to the happy hunting ground I would frame that apron.

MUM: Take good care of yourself.

DAD: Don't forget to write.

DOREEN: Got your photo.

MUM: Be a good boy.

DAD: Send us some money.

DOREEN: Miss yer.

MUM: Love yer Ed.

DAD: Take care on the roads.

DOREEN: Au revoir.

MUM: 'Bye, boy . . .

SCENE 3

DAD: The toast is burnt.

MUM: Saw Vi the other day.

DAD: Neighbours don't complain no more.

MUM: Matilda's had six kittens.

DAD: Where's my smokes?

MUM: 'Ere, 'ave you seen the cooking oil?

DAD: I miss our little Ed.

MUM: How will he fare, strikes up and down the country.

DAD: The City sits in a heap of shit.

MUM: Of uncollected garbage everywhere.

DAD: The heatwaves turn it all to slime and filthy germs hang thickly in the air / the rats are on the march.

MUM: Transport sits idly at the docks where workers slink around and for a hefty bribe may let you have your avocado or Dutch cabbage . . . petrol's obsolete as thousands of rusting cars lie swelling up our streets to vital services like ambulances which take a month to get from place to place.

DAD: The country's in a state of plague / while parties of all shades battle for power to sort the shit from the shinola / the Marxists and the Workers' party call for violence to put an end to violence and likewise the wankers suggest hard solutions like thick chains and metal toecaps / poisoned darts half-inched from local taverns / anyone who wants to kill, maim and destroy / arson, murder and hack are being recruited for the new revolutionary party / the fag libs are holding violent demos to be able to give head in the public park when the garbage strike is over and not to be persecuted for screwing on the top deck of buses.

MUM: Forte's catering is resisting the staff's demand to be paid wages and is recruiting workers from the jungles of South America.

DAD: Yet also strongly resisting the need to clear out the rats for which they are duly famous.

MUM: Most of the stores are closed but Fortnum's and Harrods soldier on shrilly packed with screaming advocates of limited nuclear drop on Hyde Park and so rid the country they say of a twisted bunch of rancid and perverted filth.

DAD: The nights in Hyde Park are lit by fires and the sound of tom toms from the Brixton Black Workers Revolutionary Gay Lib joins forces with White Is Ugly Forced Abortion / wanking is not a town in China but an alternative to the Filthy Men Female Party Group.

MUM: Meanwhile the rats head down Edgware Road up to Oxford Street preparing to turn right into Bond Street / get down Piccadilly and raid Fortnum's, pick up their mates at Forte's and join forces to make all resistance impossible seeing how all resistance is locked in internecine strife.

DAD: The rats march across Piccadilly avoiding Soho where the food is dangerous even for rats, heading down to the Strand, collect the Savoy contingent, overfat rats, not sleek for battle but just good germ carriers with rotten teeth, head across Waterloo Bridge and the National Theatre . . . try to

wake the theatre rats who have been long in coma from a
deadly attack of nightly brainwash.

MUM: Those that can be woken will begin the number two
division and streak up Drury Lane to Holborn and on to
King's Cross . . .

DAD: Avoiding the carcasses of rotting football Scots swollen and
putrefying on the streets / those who failed to make the train
and died while waiting for the next one / their flesh is deadly
/ the rats come marching in.

MUM: Maggot is our only hope, love.

DAD: If we only had more maggots to eat through the stinking
woodpile. But how is poor Ed going to manage in all
this? . . .

SCENE 4

EDDY: The shit has hit the fan as if from a great height / I walked
and walked / the sirens like wailing banshees from black
marias tear along the garbage-filled London street, chock
full of close-shaved men in blue and clubs in black / stacked
full of teeth hate-clenched / wiv fists all hungry for their
daily exercise . . . the Scotties line the kerb face down in
vomit which swishes down the rat-infested gutters . . .
dumb jocks down for their dozy game of football / some
excuse to flee their fat and shit-heap Marys in the tenements
/ they wear funny little hats with bobbles on and rotten
teeth, they belch into the carbon air their rotgut fumes and
sing a lurchy tune or two about owning some pox-ridden
scab-heap called Glasgow when they don't own a pot to piss
in. Then one blue-eyed bobby lays a skull or five (well
aimed, son) wide open.

FAMILY: SMASH . . . SPLATTER . . . CLOBBER . . .

EDDY: Take that you tartan git . . .

FAMILY: CRASH . . . SHATTER . . .

EDDY: Lovely . . . 'ere you, wot the fuck you doing . . . shut
up . . .

FAMILY: KERACKKKK!!!!

EDDY: The whores descend and drain their filthy wallets,
with their con of fuck and as the jock steps inside for
fantasies of London pussy. KERACK! A villain hard-
faced doth distribute a bit of sense with bars or iron / so
on they go, the foul ignoble mob / they watch the
match the wrong way round so pissed as newts and
then they stagger into Euston Station driven by a blind
sense of instinct or smell to join their follow tartans on
their journey back. 'Ay, 'ad a loovely taime'. Meanwhile
and spewing up the Mall down which I walked to
escape the deadly gas from ten-day haggis freshly
heaved upon our silver London streets. When what do I
espy but fuck and shit Macdougal and his paddies from
Belfast and raring to blow up anything that moves.
Thick-eared, with hands like bunches of bananas / their
voices from afar were like a pack of baying hounds.

FAMILY: Haste, hate, throw the bomb.
Hate, hate, throw the bomb.
(*continue low chant*)

EDDY: They were an army dressed in blue serge suits and
without exception pale blue eyes and liquid gelignite
stuffed in their macs and little bombs in innocent
sandwich bags . . . armpits concealing stinking sweaty
guns ready to blow some mother's son's head off and
spray the dusty Strand with thick rich ruby / knock off
some chick who God forbid could be some sweet of mine /
or take the legs off some poor cunt who happened to be
hanging about / and then they get all stinking in their pubs
and roar with leprechaunish glee . . .

MUM (*as Irish Woman*): I've only got six Guinnesses . . .

EDDY: And fight to say who was the one to toss the bomb . . .

DOREEN (*as Irish Woman*): Whose round is it now? . . .

EDDY: How many tommies did you spray apart?

MUM (*as Irish Woman*): My fucking husband's in the pub
again . . .

EDDY: How many boys were drowning in their blood / who

that very night had kissed the loving girls farewell . . .

DOREEN (*as Irish Woman*): Jesus, Mary and Joseph . . .

EDDY: How many mothers' daughters copped a face of shrapnel / lost an eye . . .

DOREEN (*as Irish Woman*): Fuck my fucking husband, fuck it! / . . .

EDDY: How many mothers douse the graves of kids of eighteen / wives and widows chatting to a piece of earth while you, you crock of gonorrhoea in serge, wolf back another gallon, leer home to your Bridget alone and waiting with six kids and unwashed climb aboard dragging across her fleshy wastes your skimpy shred of dirty prick / poke it about a bit and come your drip of watery spunk ten seconds later / she's lying there like a bloated cow / never known what coming is / only read about those soft explosions in the groin / heard rumours like / the only explosions Paddy here can make are the ones that make you scream in fucking agony and pain awash in blood not ecstasy and spunk. What a fucking obscenity that is . . .

DOREEN (*as Irish Woman*): FUCK FUCK FUCK AND SHIT / MY FUCKING HUSBAND'S LYING ACROSS THE ROAD / HIS LEGS ON ONE SIDE AND HIS TORSO ON THE OTHER. OH GOD HELP ME . . .

EDDY: OH, MAGGOT SCRATCHER HANG THE CUNTS / HANG THEM SLOW AND LET ME TAKE A SKEWER AND JAB THEIR EYES OUT / LOVELY / GREEK STYLE . . .

Hanging's no answer to the plague madam / you'd be hanging every day / I'm human like us all / we're all the same, linked / if you kick one his scream will hit my ears and hurt my mind to think of some poor cunt in shtuck / the way a kitten crying in the night will make you crawl out of your soft pit, say what the fuck's up little moggie / free Guinness, that's the answer and sex instruction initiated by luscious English birds well trained in fuck and suck, then instead of marching down the street with weapons of war and little

people on the side waving flags / they'll march down with
cocks at full alert and straining proud and strong / and
promptly get arrested. Still you can't help it / you're drowned
in aggro since a kid and dad has fed between your flappy
lugs not love but hate / has fed the history of ye olde past to
give you causes / something to do at night / has woven a
tapestry of woe inflicted on him from the distant foggy patch
called past. So what else can you do / your tired soggy brain
awash with Guinness laced with hate . . . I jumped into the
bushes and watched the curly mob in a storm of dust go past
. . . the place was on alert . . . the sturdy chiselled chins,
fresh shaved, of our fine and brave John English ready to
defend the Queen and all her minions who represent all that
is fine in this drab of grey / this septic isle . . .

EDDY (*Sings*): Rule Britannia, Britannia rule the waves, [etc.]
Two rhythms battling for ascendancy.

FAMILY: Hate, hate, throw the bomb . . .

EDDY: Eventually got on a train / found one whose carriage
wasn't entirely smashed and wrecked and rode in peace to
London's airport Skidrow, alone and reflective in my
thoughts except for some Paki in the carriage getting a right
kicking for some no doubt vile offence like inadvertently
catching the eye of some right gallant son of Tottenham, the
kicking lent a rhythmic ritual to my thoughts which were
beginning to get formed to take some mighty fine decisions
that would shoot me on my path to riches and success,
sweet-smelling pussy and golden arms and lashing tongues. I
fell into a kind of reverie . . . I fell asleep and dreamed . . . I
saw a dozen pussies on a bed nestled between some soft and
squeezy thighs, like little gentle kittens suckling on a
mother's teat / their sweet and ivory columns hanging loosely
fell apart revealing flowers in a garden that you water and
like a randy bee I buzzed from one to t'other / their petals
gently opened wide / sent forth their perfumes in the air / and
as I left they'd close again / and then the next and each one
subtly different / each like precious luscious plants / each like
a grasping toothless mouth, hungry like open beaks of little

birds while I, like mother, into their open throats would drop
my worm which hungrily and devouringly they'd grasp.
Then I awoke / and rudely saw the world just as it is and
started on my adventures, thrust all young and sweet into the
seething heaving heap of world in which I was just a little
dot. I arrived at Heathrow, gateway to the world.

FAMILY (*as chorus of airport sounds and noises*): All this confused
me / who needs to go / do I, do you, do he / I decided to stay
and see my own sweet land / amend the woes of my own fair
state / why split and scarper like ships leaving a sinking rat / I
saw myself as king of the western world / but since I needed
some refreshment for my trials ahead, I ventured into this
little café / everywhere I looked . . . I witnessed this
evidence . . . of the British plague.

SCENE 5

FAMILY *as waiters and kitchen/café menu sounds and phrases – in
rhythm:*

VOICE 1: Soggy chips.
VOICE 2: Beans on toast. } (*Repeated as they trundle round café*).
VOICE 3: Greasy eggs.

EDDY: One coffee please and croissant and butter.

WAITRESS: Right. Cream?

EDDY: Please. Where is the butter so I might spread it lavishly
and feel its oily smoothness cover the edges of the croissant?

WAITRESS: Ain't got none. There's a plague on.

EDDY: Then why serve me the croissant knowing you have no
butter?

WAITRESS: I'll get you something else.

EDDY: I'll have a cheesecake, what's it like?

WAITRESS: Our cheesecakes are all made from the nectar of the
gods mixed with the dextrous fingers of a hundred virgins
who have been whipped with bull rushes grown by the
banks of the Ganges.

EDDY: OK. I'll have one.

(*She brings it*)

   . . . I've finished the coffee now and won't have any liquid to wash the cake down with

WAITRESS: Do you want another coffee?

EDDY: Not want but must not want but have to / you took so long to bring the cake that I finished the coffee so bring another . . .

WAITRESS: OK.

EDDY: But bring it before I finish the cheesecake or I'll have nothing to eat with my second cup which I only really want as a masher for the cheesecake.

WAITRESS: OK. (*To another waitress*) . . . so he came all over your dress . . .

WAITRESS 2: Yeah.

WAITRESS: Dirty bastard.

WAITRESS 2: It was all thick and stringy it took ages to get off / he was sucking me like a madman when my mum walked in.

WAITRESS: No! What did she say?

WAITRESS 2: Don't forget to do behind her ears / she always forgets that.

WAITRESS: I wish my mum was understanding like that / I haven't sucked a juicy cock for ages, have you?

WAITRESS 2: No, not really, not a big horny stiff thick hot pink one.

WAITRESS: What's the biggest you've ever had?

WAITRESS 2: Ten inches.

WAITRESS: No!

WAITRESS 2: Yeah, it was all gnarled like an oak with a great big knob on the end.

WAITRESS: Yeah?

WAITRESS 2: And when it came, it shot out so much I could have wallpapered the dining room.

EDDY: Where's my fucking coffee? I've nearly finished the cheesecake and then my whole purpose in life at this particular moment in time will be lost / I'll be drinking hot coffee with nothing to wash it down with.

WAITRESS: Here you are, sorry I forgot you!

EDDY: About fucking time!

WAITRESS: Oh shut your mouth, you complaining heap of rat's shit.

EDDY: I'll come in your eyeballs you putrefying place of army gang bang.

WAITRESS: You couldn't raise a gallop if I plastered my pussy all over your face, you impotent pooftah bum boy and turd bandit.

MANAGER: (*Her husband*) What's the matter, that you raise your voice you punk and scum / fuck off!

EDDY: No one talks to me like that.

MANAGER: I just did.

EDDY: I'll erase you from the face of the earth.

MANAGER: I'll cook you in a pie and serve you up for dessert.

EFFY: I'll tear you all to pieces, rip out your arms and legs and feed them to the pigs.

MANAGER: I'll kick you to death and trample all over you / stab you with carving knives and skin you alive.

(*They mime fight.*)

EDDY: Hit hurt crunch pain stab jab

MANAGER: Smash hate rip tear asunder render

EDDY: Numb jagged glass gouge out

MANAGER: Chair breakhead split fist splatter splosh crash

EDDY: Explode scream fury strength overpower overcome

MANAGER: Cunt shit filth remorse weakling blood soaked

EDDY: Haemorrhage, rupture and swell. Split and cracklock jawsprung and neck break

MANAGER: Cave-in rib splinter oh the agony the shrewd icepick

EDDY: Testicles torn out eyes gouged and pulled strings snapped socket nail scrapped

MANAGER: Bite swallow suck pull

EDDY: More smash and more power

MANAGER: Weaker and weaker

EDDY: Stronger and stronger

MANAGER: Weak

EDDY: Power

MANAGER: Dying

EDDY: Victor

MANAGER: That's it

EDDY: Tada.

WAITRESS: You killed him / I never realized words can kill.

EDDY: So can looks.

WAITRESS: You killed him / he was my husband.

EDDY: I didn't intend to I swear I didn't / he died of shock.

WAITRESS: He was a good man, solid except in his cock but he
was good to me, and now I am alone / who will I have to
care for now. Who to wait for at night while he cleans up our
café or while he's at the sauna getting relief / who to cook for
or brush the dandruff from his coat and the grease from his
hat or the tramlines from his knickers / who to comfort in
the long night / as he worries about me / who will put the
kids to bed with a gentle cuff as he frolics after coming home
all pissed from the pub and smashes me jokingly on the
mouth / whose vomit will I clean up from the pillow as he
heaves up all over my face on Friday nights after his binge.
Whose black uniform will I press in readiness for his
marches down Brixton with the other so noble men of
England / whose photos will I dust in the living room of his
heroes, Hitler, Goebbels, Enoch, Paisley and Maggot not
forgetting our dear royals. Is it worth it any more? / I
married a good Englishman / where will I find another like
that? See what you did / and all over a stupid cheesecake.

EDDY: Wars, my dear, have been fought over less than that.

WAITRESS: I'll never find another like him.

EDDY: Yes you will.

WAITRESS: Where?

EDDY: Look no further mam than this / your spirits won me / cast
thy gaze to me / my face / and let thine eyes crawl slowly
down / that's not a kosher salami I'm carrying / I'm just
pleased to see you / sure I can do like him / polish my

knuckleduster / clean my pants / I'll give you a kicking with
the best if that's what you really want / you'll have my set of
proud photos to dust / I'd rather treat you fair and square
and touch your hair at night and kiss your sleeping nose / I'll
not defile your pillow, but spread violets beneath your feet /
I'll squeeze your toes at night if they grow cold and when we
through rose gardens walk I'll blow the aphids from your
hair / I'll come straight home from work at night not idle for
a pint and all my spunk I'll keep for thee to lash you with at
night as soft and warm as summer showers / I'll leak no
precious drop in the Camden sauna for a fiver ('don't be
long dear, others waiting') but strew the silver load in thee to
dart up precious streams / I'll heave my sceptre into thee /
your thighs I'll prise apart and sink like hot stone into butter /
into an ocean of ecstasy for that's what you are to me / an
ecstasy of flesh and blood and fluted pathways softest oils
and smells never before uncapped / I'll turn you upside down
and inside out / I'll strip you bare and crawl under your skin /
I'm mad for you / you luscious brat and madman, girl and
woman turned into one / I'll take you love for what you are!

WAITRESS: You've eased my pain you sweet and lovely boy / I
thought I'd miss him desperately but now I can when
looking at you hardly remember what he looks like. You
look so familiar to me though we have never met / so strange
perhaps the true feeling love brings to your heart. The
familiar twang.

EDDY: I feel the same for you.

WAITRESS: You remind me of someone or something.

EDDY: What, ducky?

WAITRESS: Oh, nothing.

EDDY: Confess my dear the quandary that doth crease your brow
and makes the nagging thought stay in your head, the way
an Irish fart hangs in the air long after its creator wends his
weary way to Kilburn High Street.

WAITRESS: 'Tis nothing sweet but this / I had a kid, just two he
were, sweet and blue-eyed just like you / a darling, then one
day disaster struck / and don't it just / an August trip to

Southend for the day / all hot and sticky with floss and
smiling teeth / hankies and braces / start off at Tower Pier
excitement, sandwiches and loads of fizzy Tizer.

EDDY: (*Aside*) Strange, I love Tizer.

WAITRESS: Then two or three miles out we hit a mine that slunk
so steadily up the Thames, like some almighty turd that
won't go down no matter how often you flush the chain, so
this had stayed afloat, it showed its scarred and raddled
cheek from its long buffets round the choppy seas and just
by luck as if the fates had ordained us to meet it blew us at
the moon / at least it made a hole so large that suddenly the
Thames resembled Brighton on a broiling day with heads a-
bobbing everywhere, my Frank swam back and I clung to a
bit of raft but little Tony, for this was his fair name, ne'er
did surface up . . . I hope his end was quick.

EDDY: No chance that some local fisherman may have snatched
him from the boiling seethe.

WAITRESS: No word, no sign, not even his little corpse did show
/ I stuck around all night, then as the dawn arose I saw his
little oil-soaked teddy bear, as if heaved up from deep inside
the river's guts. It lay amidst the condoms on the junk-filled
strand. I took it home and washed it.

EDDY: That's a sad tale / and I feel grieved for you my dear that
woe should strike at one who was so young and fair / and let
the others more deserving of fate's lash to get away with
murder.

WAITRESS: Fate never seems to give out where it's meant but
seems to pick you out as from a hat / like bingo and if your
number's on it boy you've had it.

EDDY: That little bear you mentioned, sweet . . . may I see the
precious relic?

WAITRESS: You really want to?

EDDY: Yeah, let's have a butcher's.

(*She goes and brings the bear in.*)

'Tis strange but often times I dreamed of such a thing a little
Refus just like this / I never had one, yet seemed to miss the
little furry cuddly thing as if my body knew the feel whereas

my mind could not / since then I've always liked small furry
things. Come, love, you've had your share of woe and so
have I and if fate heaps the shit it also heaps the gold and
finding you is like a vein I never dreamed of, so fate's been
kind this time / I think we're fated, love don't you?

WAITRESS: I do, my precious, for once I bless the stars that this
time made me such a man / you've got the same eyes as my
Tony – green and jadey like the sea.

EDDY: Your eyes are like the sunlight in the sea that speckles on
the rocks so deep below / all blue and gold.

WAITRESS: Your face is like all Greek / and carved from ancient
marble.

EDDY: Your body feels all soft like puppies, strong as panthers.

WAITRESS: Let's go to bed my sweet.

EDDY: OK.

DAD: Do you think that it could happen.
that the curse could come about
that Ed could kill his own dad,
pop into his mother's pants, I had to kick him out.

MUM: That's something we will never know dear
until the day, when suddenly you'll
see quite a different Ed than the one that's known to me.

DAD: You're right, dead right . . . oh Dinah
what did we do that such a curse
should be blasted on the heads of me and you.

MUM: Who knows my dear what evil lies in store
that we are unaware of, did we cause some
grief somewhere, inflict some unhealed sore. . . .

DAD: I've done nothing all my life
I've been an honest Joe
shit on that fortune teller
and his vile and evil joke.

MUM: It's funny that twice we heard it Ted
it's funny that a second time
another face years later should
sound the same old horrid warning line.

DAD: Perhaps we should have told him Dinah

perhaps we ought to tell
our son should know the secret
or we may end up in . . .
MUM: Hell you mean, you make me laugh
it's over now, it's past,
it can't be now undone with words
fate makes us play the roles we're cast.

ACT TWO

SCENE I

EDDY: Ten years have come and gone, scattered their leaves on us / drenched us in blazing sun and rain / toughened my sinews to combat the world. I improved the lot of our fair café by my intense efforts, aided of course by my sweet mate / got rid of sloth and stale achievement/ which once was thought as normal / I made the city golden era time / the dopes just died away when faced with real octane high-power juice / the con men that have tricked you all the while with substitute and fishy watery soup / went out of business and people starved for nourishment brain-food and guts just flocked to us / the fat-faced bastards you saw sitting on expense accounts and piles / too long defied the needs of our gnawing biting hunger / real food and drink / real substance for the soul / not those decayed and spineless wonders who filled the land / strutting and farting pithy anecdotes at boring dinner parties on profits made by con and cheap / they thought they were the cream and not the sour yuk they really were / we showed them the way / they died in trying to keep up with us / they faded in a heap.

WIFE: Ten years have flown away as Apollo's Chariot hath with fiery stride lit up our summers, thawed our frosts and kissed our cheeks / ten winters hath the hoary bearded god of ice encased our earth in pinch hard grip of chill / to be kicked out in turn by spring's swift feet of Ceres, Pluto, Dionysus / and April brooks do glisten giggling over rocks and reeds so pleased to be set free / ten years this splendid symphony of life hath played its varied song / hath saddened and elated / hath drawn the sap of life into the fiery poppy and frangipani and gripped them in its autumn sleep again / whilst we my man that is and me, for three thousand three hundred and sixty-five times did celebrate our own ritual in nights of swooning.

EDDY: While I each day and year have scored another niche into
this world of ours / have moved about and jostled / cut a
throat or two metaphoric of course and shown how what
this world doth crave is power, class and form with a dab of
genius now and then. We cured the plague by giving
inspiration to our plates / came rich by giving more and
taking less / the old-style portion control practised by fat
thieves went out with us / we put the meat back into the
sausage mate / now once more the world will taste good / no
more the sawdust and preservative colouring and cat shit
that you could better use to fill your walls than line your
stomachs / so foul that nations overseas would ban them
from their fair stalls and shops lest their strong youth should
fall into the listless British trance so often seen in Oxford
Street or on the Piccadilly Line at 8 a.m. / a nation half
asleep and drugged with foul and bestial things poured out
of packets / massed up by operators who conspired with
commies thick in plot to weaken our defences / feed the
nation shit and mother's crud and watch them crumble
down in heaps upon the pavement / then the cunning reds
just blow them over skittle-like / but now in out great chain
we energize the people, give soul food and blistering blast of
protein smack / sandwiches the size of fists chock full of
juicy smile-filled chunks / the nation blinks and staggers
back to work on this / not fast / it takes a while to use those
muscles starved so long / limp with only holding *Daily
Mirror* race results / and eyes so dim from weekly charting of
the pools / we'll get them back to work, no fear though they
may die of shock upon the way / we'll drag them out of
pubs, their fingers still gripping on the bar they know so
well, like babies reluctant to part with mother's tit / it's us
that has to do it / rid the world of half-assed bastards
clinging to their dark domain and keeping talent out by
filling the entrances with their swollen carcasses and sagging
mediocrity / let's blow them all sky high, or let us see them
simply waste away as the millions come to us.
(*Chorus sing 'Jerusalem'.*)

The SPHINX.

WIFE: The plague is not quite over yet. There's still a plague
around this city darling that will not go away, caused by
some say some evil deed that has not purged itself, but
continues to rot away inside the wholesome body of our
state / people are dropping like flies / armed killers snipe
from the shattered eyes of buildings and death stalks in the
foul and pestilent breath of friends whose eyes are drunk
with envy and greed at your success / people shake your
hand with limp grips as if afraid to catch it. The illness of
inertia, and should I shan't I, the country's awash in
chemicals that soup the brain to dullness to dull the dullness
of grinding hips long bored with ancient habit and lovers are
afraid to stroke each other's groins lest new laws against
spreading the plague outlaw them. Masturbating shops line
every High Street and the pneumatic drill of strong right
wrists ensures a girl a fat living, the country's awash in
spunk not threshing and sweetening the wombs of lovers
but crushed in Kleenex and dead in cubicles with red lights.
Meanwhile men in white masks are penetrating the holy
crucible where life may have slipped in, and armed with
scalpels and suction pumps tear out the living fruit and
sluice it down the river of sewage, the future Einsteins,
Michelangelos and future Eddys. The blood and plasma of
creation is swept and flushed away with gasps of 'don't'
inside the tender packages not yet fulfilled.

EDDY: That's the plague at work all right, there's something
rotten in the city that will not die / a sphinx I read stands
outside the city walls tormenting all that pass they say and
killing those who cannot answer her strange riddle / no
doubt she helps to spread the canker and the rot and yet no
one can destroy her.

WIFE: I heard that too, and yet she can at will dissolve herself to
air.

EDDY: I'll go and sort her out.

WIFE: Be careful darling / you are all I have.

EDDY: Don't fret, if I've come this far, survived the worst that fate can throw I'll come through this as well don't wait up I may be late but if I'm not back by dawn, I'll meet you in heaven, if not we'll met in hell.

SCENE 2

SPHINX *outside the walls.*

SPHINX: Who are you, little man / pip squeak scum / drip off the prick / mistake in the middle of the night / you've come to answer my riddle / the riddle of the sphinx / fuck off you maggot before I tear your head off / rip your eyes out of your head and roast your tongue / you nothing, you man / you insult of nature go now before I lose my cool.

EDDY: I'm not afraid of you . . . you old slag / you don't scare Eddy 'cause Eddy don't scare easy / I've beaten better than you in Singapore brothels / you can only frighten weak men not me / why do you exist to kill men you heap of filth / you detestable disease / because you can't love / loveless you can only terrify man no one could love you / who could even kiss that mouth of yours when your very breath stinks like a Hong Kong whorehouse when the fleet's in.

SPHINX: You make me laugh you fool man / you should know about brothels, they exist for you to prop up your last fading shreds / men need killing off before they kill off the world / louse, you pollute the earth / every footstep you take rots what's underneath / you turn the seas to dead lakes and the crops are dying from the plague that is man / you are the plague / where are you looking when you should be looking at the ghastly vision in the mirror / the plague is inside you. You make your weapons to give you the strength that you lack / you enslave whip beat and oppress use your guns, chains, bombs, jets, napalm, you are so alone and pathetic, love from you means enslavement, giving means taking, love is fucking, helping is exploiting, you need your mothers you mother fucker, to love is to enslave a woman to turn her into a bearing cow to produce cannon fodder to go on killing / can you ever stop your plague / you're pathetic, unfinished, not like me, never like us, a woman, a sphinx. Women are all sphinx. I have taken the power for all, I am the power / I could eat you alive and blow you out in bubbles / I devour stuff like you . . . oh send me strong men you scrawny nothing / look what they send me / mock up heroes / plastic movie watchers / idolizer of a thousand westerns / punk hero / flaccid man / macho pig / rapist filth and shit / oh nature's mistake in the ghastly dawn of time / when women were women, androgynous and whole and could reproduce themselves but somewhere and some time a reptile left our bodies, it crawled away and became man, but it stole our little bag of seed and even since the little reptile has been trying to crawl back, but we don't want it anymore, all we need is your foul little seed, you gnat . . . something that takes you thirty seconds of your life and us nine months we create build nourish care for, grow bigger and fat and after we suckle and provide. While you dig in the earth for treasure, play your stupid male games / go you biped of dirt / just a prick followed by a heap of filth, I feel sorry for you / I really feel for you / I've eaten enough men this week / so go / fuck off / stink scum dirt shit / go, before I tear you to pieces / go and plot and scheme, hurt, exploit and rape, oppress and wound, make a few more evil laws you shrivel of flesh, you poor unreliable penis. You have not even our capacity for passion . . . I could come ten times to your one / wanna try big boy? You are from my rib mister / me from you? what a joke / woman was Adam / she was the earth, woman is the tide / woman is in the movement of the universe / our bodies obey the phases of the moon . . . our breasts swell and heave and our rich blood surges forth to tell us we are part of the movement of nature / what signs do you have? / How do you know that you are even alive? / Do you bleed / do you feel the kicking in your womb / does a mouth draw milk from your soft breast / can you tell the future / can you do anything? What signs do you have / a date with death / the hour you must attack / unable to

create you must destroy / I am the earth / I am the
movement of the universe / I am liquid, fire and all
elements / my voice rises octaves high and communicates
with the spirits of the dead / my skin is soft and velvet and
desirable to those with rough faces and bodies hard and
muscled to labour, to toil across the face of the earth for us
/ the goodness of life / woman / we / sex / sphinx, the grand
and majestic cunt, the great mouth of life / the dream of
men in their aching lonely nights / the eternal joy that men
die for and envy and emulate / what they sicken for and
crave for and go insane for / so go, you are small,
insignificant, piss off you worm or I'll break your teeth and
pull out your fingers / go fuck yourself or stick a bomb up
your fucking asshole you heap of murdering bastard shit
filth . . . go, you make me vomit.

EDDY: Without me you are nothing / without me you wouldn't
exist without me you are an empty screaming hole.

SPHINX: You what! You think I need you. I need milk but do I
go to bed with a cow. I'll farm and fertilize you and keep you
in pens where you will do no harm / now go boy, I am
getting aroused, be grateful that for some reason I feel for
your pathetic attempts at heroism.

EDDY: I want to answer your riddle.

SPHINX: Then you must know that those that can't answer it die,
and then if you can't I will kill you, I will tear your cock off
with my teeth before I eat you up.

EDDY: With pleasure / if I answer it / what do I gain?

SPHINX: You can kill me.

EDDY: Then I will cut off your head for women talk too much.

SPHINX: I agree. You're a brave little fart. So here goes: what
walks on four legs in the morning, two legs in the afternoon
and three legs in the evening?

EDDY: Man! In the morning of his life he is on all fours, in the
afternoon when he is young he is on two legs and in the
evenings when he is erect for his woman he sprouts the third
leg.

SPHINX: You bastard, you've used trickery to find out the riddle.

EDDY: No, just reason. All right, sorry to have to do this, I was growing quite fond of you.

SPHINX: I don't care any more / to tell the truth I was getting bored with scaring everyone to death and being a sphinx / OK cut it off and get it over with.

(*He cuts off her head.*)

SCENE 3

EDDY: She would put you off women for life / but not me / I love a woman / I love her / I just love and love and love her / and even that one / I could have loved her / I love everything that they possess / I love all their parts / I love every part that moves / I love their hair and their neck / I love the way they walk across the kitchen to put the kettle on / in that lazy familiar way / I love them when they open their eyes in the morning / I love their baby-soft skin / I love their voices / I love their smaller hands than mine / I love lying on them and them on me / I love their soft breasts / I love their eyelashes and their noses / their teeth and their shoulders / and their giggles / and their desperate passions and their liquids and their breath against yours in the night / and their snores / and their legs across yours and their feet in the morning and I love their bellies and thighs and they way each part fits into mine / and love the way my part fits into them / and love her sockets and joints and ball bearings / and love her hip bone and her love-soaked parts that want me / I love her seasons and love her sleeping and love her walking and speaking and whispering and loving and singing and love her back and her bum nestled into you and you become an armchair / and love her for taking me in / and giving me a home for my searing agonies / my lusts / my love / my dreams / my sweetness / my honey / my peace of mind / and love pouring all my love into her with open eyes and love our fatigue and love her knees and shoulder blades and pimples and love her waiting for me and love her soothing me as I tell her about my day's battles

in the world – and love and love and love her and her and!
(WIFE *enters*.)

WIFE: Well done my sweet, now all will be well / my hero . . . yes
you are / my brave and shining knight / my lion, yes! And
I'm your mate / my brave and gentle lion / and now to
celebrate let's have your dear old pa and ma to dine and
reconcile the fairy tales and woes of past and be all gooey
nice together in family bliss.

EDDY: I have to laugh when I think of my soppy mum and dad /
locked up in council bliss / and £40 a week driving a 38 from
Putney down to Waltham Cross and getting clobbered each
Saturday night.

WIFE: Invite them over Ed, to share just once our colour TV,
hi-fi, home movies showing us in fair Ibiza and Thebes, of
you diving in the bright blue cobalt sea, your smiling new-
capped teeth all sparkling in the brilliant sun, invite them to
partake of our deep leather sofas / succulent wines / show
our video that records those programmes that you wish to
view when after working late at night in selfless graft you sit
with dog and slipper by your feet . . . let them enjoy the
comfort of central-heated bathroom . . . no more the cold
ass on a plastic seat but wool-covered and pipes all steaming
hot, of stairs thick-gloved in pile so soft that each tread is
like a luscious meadow. Would they not like a
Slumberdown or even our soft waterbed which thrusts our
pelvises so sweetly swished together, needlepoint shower
show your mum the joys of kitchen instant disposal waste,
no washing up, just time to enjoy our super apple pie.

EDDY: I'll send the chauffeur down to pick them up / that's if my
dad has rid himself of that old hoary myth that like a louse
ate inside his nut, to tell him of patricide and horrid incest /
or subtitled could be called the story of a mother fucker / a
tale of kiddiwinks to send them mad to bed and cringe at
shadows in the night, and in their later years to bung good
gelt to shrinks in Harley Street.

WIFE: When you told me that story Ed / I could not believe that
grown ups still could set such store by greasy gypsies in a

booth / and to kick you out all young and pink into the
seething world while you were wet behind the lugs / maybe
'twas a ruse to get you out the nest.

EDDY: Who knows my dear the wily minds of cruddy mums and
dads whose heads chock full of TV swill, the pools and read
your own horoscope / who believe in anything they read that
comes so fluent forth from out the gushy asses of the turds
in Fleeting Street / so what, it put me on the springboard
young and lively and I learned how to jackknife into the
surging tide with all the best.

WIFE: You're tuf that's what my love / you're a survivor in the
swilling mass of teeth and knives and desperate eyes all
anxious to carve out their pound of flesh / you did it and
you're still a beaut / still lovely brown and svelte / success
has not paunched you or stuck a fast ass on your hips or
burnt an ulcer in your gut / or made your mouth a stinking
ashtray where fat cigars hang like a turd that cannot be
expelled / but hangs on till the end / your sweet and honey
breath / your tongue's not coated with the slime of ten-
course meals taken with other con artists who flash their
gaudy rings and thick as pigshit wives who sit at home and
wank or play some bridge with other dozy bags whose only
exercise is stretching out an arm to screech out 'taxi' outside
Harrods / you're sweet and your body's like a river, flowing,
flowing, flowing into me / it moves like a flowing river . . .
your streaming muscles carry me along your river, along
your soft and hard and flowing river / when I'm in your arms
I'm carried along this endless stream and then I reach the
sea, I'm swept up by your sea, I'm carried by a wave, I'm
threshed up in your wave and then set down again only to be
re-gathered up as your volcanic wave gathers me as a piece
of ocean, as your sweet lustful pangs gather up its morsel
I'm swept up, I'm gathered up, I'm sucked up and spun
along a raging storming river . . . I love your body, I love
your fingers and round and round and tearing and gripping
and finding and searching and twisting and gathering me for
your sweet lustful pangs . . . and then and then and then

. . . your body is like a tree . . . like branches twisting and
breaking . . . like a wave like a wind, like an animal like a
lion . . . ferocious and sweet lustful pangs grow bigger
darling . . . as they grow bigger to make your sweet spunk
flow . . . they grow bigger and the lion's breath is hot and
the grip on me is growing tight and more ferocious and then
and then I know . . . that you tremble, you shake, you
quiver, you thrash . . . oh the river flows, oh . . . it flows, oh
it floods through me . . . as you tremble your quiver is shot
into me . . . oh I am flowing with the river in the wet and
warm and succulent flow . . . you turn me into a flow and
flood me . . . and the shivering and the quivering and the
shaking and the trembling, softly softly . . . softly goes as the
storm passes slowly . . . goes . . . slowly . . . rumbling into
the distance . . . slowly goes the breath less hot, but soft and
silky and sweat on your back and silky on your thighs and
warm between our thighs . . . oh / life my love / oh love my
precious / oh sweet my honey / oh heaven my angel / oh
darling my husband.

EDDY: But soft my darling wife / what noise is that / it must be
my cruddy mum and dad / who interrupt your lovely flow of
gob rich thick and pearly verbs that send my blood a-racing
to my groin so I might manufacture love-wet tides.

SCENE 4

MUM *and* DAD *enter.*

DAD: Look how he's got on / you really got on well son / I'm
proud of ya. He's got class and qualities drawn from me.

MUM: From me more, his mum whom he did love not this wet
fart that calls himself his dad.

DAD: Don't talk like that in front of Eddy's wife you sloppy-
titted, slack-assed lump, you raving scrawny fried-up witch.

MUM: Don't talk to me about my body / age has withered my soft
beauty but you will need cremating since your poisoned
flesh would cause pollution in the earth and make

widespread crop failures / you're death on two varicosed legs and a hernia belt.

DAD: I've got no words for you Dot . . . since you were gang-banged by that bunch of drunken darkies . . . a dozen it were, if I counted right, whose swollen truncheons flashed their golden sprints of foam into the sulphurous and heavy night, since that bad time you've not been right in ye old bonce . . . I know that night was dark for you in double horror and I fear that it may be the cause of your unseemly evil tongue that like a poisoned snake doth linger under filthy damp and rotting stone.

EDDY: Hallo dad, hallo mum – good to see ya again . . .

MUM: Oh Ed, it looks really lovely, and this is your lovely wife / oh! how lovely, oh, she's nice.

WIFE: Why thank you, I think you're very charming yourself.

MUM: Oh thank you. You are nice, have a nice day, you're welcome.

WIFE: Please feel free, make yourself at home, how very nice to meet you. Have you had a good journey? How is everyone at home? Isn't the weather cold now? It will soon be winter. You're looking so young. You really look well. You've lost weight. Are you going away this summer? Do you use Fablon in your kitchen?

MUM: You've a lovely home, it's really lovely, just lovely. Some people are lucky, some people have all the fun. Some mothers do have 'em. Mind you, I mean, it goes to show, well it does. Idle hands make wicked thoughts. He's all right, really, underneath . . . when you get to know him, he's lovely, have you been away this year? Water off a duck's back, dear.

EDDY: So what's the news my folks / my flesh and blood / chip off the old / apple of your / say what goes on in my old neighbourhood / where once rank violence stalked the dirty streets and filthy yobbos hung round the corners of old pubs like flies on dead carrion / say can you still walk down the streets at night? Or do you macaroni in your pants at every shadow that stalks out lest it be some Macdougal out

to line his coat with other's hard-earned gelt . . . around
this manor there's peace my folks. Move out that council
flat where urchins' piss does spray the lift which takes you
to your eyrie on the twenty-fifth floor and move in with us,
or do you still fear that old curse / that bunch of gypsy
bollocks, that you so avidly did gulp / though secretly me
thinks you used that as a ruse, to clear me out the womb
and save yourself some L.s.d. / you always said I'd eat you
out of house and home / round here only the poodles drop
their well-turned turds in little piles so neat. And au pair
girls go pushing little Jeremys into the green and flowery
parks / no ice-cream vans come screaming round this
manor / all's quiet / just the swish on the emerald lawns
close cropped like the shaven heads of astronauts / and in
the quiet of the evening silly chit chat from the strangled
vocal cords of well-heeled neighbours rises from the
gardens as they wolf down in the summer nights a half a
dozen gin and tonics. Nicely tired from a hard day's graft of
thieving in the city. So come and stay. You're welcome and
bring the cat as well, we've always got room for moggie.

DAD: Nah son but thanks and double ta. You're very kind to us
. . . how thoughtful / bless you, you're welcome, have a nice
day, but we're used to wot we got, can you teach an old dog
new tricks, a bit long in the tooth you're as old as you feel,
and I feel like a worn out old fart . . . we know the familiar
faces / our rotten neighbours / the geezer who collects the
payments on the fridge and on the telly every week / meals
on wheels that daily calls now that we're getting older, all
familiar trappings that have trapped us / now that our useful
working life has been sucked dry by the state we get a little
pension and some security for which I sign / now that my
boss god bless him sits back fat and greasy / not that I mind,
he got it by hard graft and cunning / good luck to him / he
gave me fifty quid when I retired, handsome and a watch
with fifteen jewels / right proud I was / so what I got asbestos
in my lung / so what I got coal dust in my blood / so what I
got lead poisoning in my brain / so what I got shot nerves

from the machines / so what I lost two fingers in the press /
so what I'm going deaf from the steel mills / so what I lost a
lung for our old king in Dunkirk / I'd do it again / yes I
would I tell ya / so what I got fuck all for it from our fair state
/ so what they're gliding past in their Rolls-Royces / and
their fat little kids come tumbling out on piggy little legs / so
what they thieve and murder and get away with it / so what
our lovely royals pay no tax / they're figureheads mate / so
what I starve waiting for your cheque which sometimes you
forget to send if you are busy entertaining, when you forget
your old ma and pa . . . son!

MUM: Don't listen Ed, he's gone a bit in the nut since they retired
him / all he does is grouse and quail. When you complain
remember others worse off than you / I think of mothers
whose sweet fruit of their most holy wombs / those warm and
precious sacks of giggling joy, who have been snatched by
sex-mad fiends. They stalk around the town . . . there are so
many around / you cannot pick up the daily snot-picker these
days without seeing between the tits and race results the
photos of the burns and scalds and broken limbs . . . the
staring eyes of kids / how one is burnt by fag ends / others
punched black and blue / screams in the night / neighbours
too scared or fastened to *Hawaii Five-O* to receive the
bloated cries that stab through the walls like an open hand
saying help me / others, babies with broken lips, their little
ribs all smashed by dads who have caught the British plague
that cements their heads and puts vitriol inside their hearts /
some kids chained to their beds for hours at a time and
others crawling in shit and piss . . . and whack and zunk goes
mum and splatter back hand crack goes dad . . . one kid's
nipples almost burnt off . . . what about the dad who picked
up his small innocent and smashed his head against the wall,
until his brains seeped out . . . what dreams did that kid have
as his grey thoughts ran down the wallpaper . . . and then the
judge says . . . 'off you go, you are basically a good character'
. . . and then he's off to celebrate in the nasty pub with his
old lady . . . and up and down the length and breadth the

straps are out and babies, bairns and kids are straightened
out, lashed out, whipped and made to obey, the nation's full
of perverts if you ask me / the plague still flourishes mate.

EDDY: The plague mum / the plague is still about? You never did
nuffin like that to me / you only gave me muffins and jam /
swaddles of lovely love and spoiling and playing and story-
telling. And swishing my pillow and a ride on dad's back
and chase around the garden, and a three-wheel bike. You
only gave me ten slices of toast every morning and Marmite
after school . . . I looked all Bisto like, and like those kids
whose shoes have a long way to go I was put on a path called
bliss with jammy mouth and sticky doughnut fingers / a dad
who put me on the crossbar of his bike and never once
introduced the back of his hand to my bonce not once
opened his eyes wide and hate-filled and sought to venge
some filthy taste for colouring my flesh in Chartreuse green
or bruisy blue. No! We'd race across the municipal lido.
How long can you stay under. *Dandy* and the *Beano* each
week and even the *Film Fun* as well.

DAD: You were loved son / we wanted to give you love / we luved
ya kid. You know . . . like open hands gripping your
shoulders and a squeeze at the end . . . palm on your head
and ruffling your hair, a clenched fist and a slow tap on the
chin . . . like chin-up when you didn't pass your eleven-plus
'cause you were a dummy . . . I didn't want you to hate us.

EDDY: Hate? I never used that word my folks, only pocket money
each week five bob and Sat morn flicks. Do you mean to say
you loved me because you were afraid I'd hate you? 'Cause
the gypsy's curse rang in your ears? Let's smother him with
spoiling and cuddling so he won't want to hurt his old dad,
you make me laugh . . . you would have loved me the same
without the rotten curse / I'm your flesh and blood, it's
natural.

DAD *and* MUM: But you're not our son, son.

EDDY: SHIT GIVE UP THE GEN / SPILL YOUR GUTS /
OPEN YOUR NORTH AND SOUTH AND LET
ROLL THE TURDS BEFORE I PONEY MY Y-

FRONTS. IN OTHER VERBS OPEN YOUR CAKE-
HOLE AND UTTER. LET ME EARWIG YOUR
HOBSONS. NOT YOUR SON. OH BOLLOCKS
AND CRACKLOCK.

WIFE: Don't say that he ain't your real produce of your blood-
swept thighs, not shoved out of your guts in warm sticky
afterbirth, not the sparkle in his dad's eye in the glinting
night when his pa heaved apart his woman's limbs and
unloaded a binful of hot spunk, not eyed her like a
lodestone or a star, or a jewel in the corner of his eye not
breathed hard or pulse raced to produce this lovely hunk of
super delicious wondrous beefy darling spunky guy / not
seen you walking from behind and wanted to grasp your
arse and deliver the mail up your wet and wondrous
letterbox?

MUM: Nah! 'Fraid not!

WIFE: Oh fuck.

EDDY: So what if I'm adopted / who gives a monkey's tit.

DAD: Like this it was. Cries and groans, shouts and shrieks. I was
fishing by Wapping, just down from the *Prospect of Whitby*
. . . a peaceful Sunday (you were fished out, what a find,
what I prayed for, a son) threw my line, the big steamers
going out to Southend. The old Tower Bridge opening up
to allow the steamers' funnels through like some big lazy
East End tart from Cable Street opening her thighs . . . on
the deck in the sun the people of Bow, Whitechapel and
Islington in their cheese-cutters and chokers, all doing a bit
of a dance on the deck, the steamers flickering, the
Guinness pouring . . . us waving from the shore as the old
steamer cuts through the scummy old Thames and sends
the swell over to us and makes our little boats kneel and bob
as she passes by. When all of a sudden boy / the sun's up
high, Hitler's just topped hisself. It's hot. Churchill's in
command, there's peace at last. Twenty million dead /
including my two boys, the radio plays we'll meet again and
mares eat oats and does eat oats and little lambs eat ivy,
remember. Well all of a sudden in that August afternoon no

bananas in the shops and coupons for four ounces of sweets each week, pictures of Auschwitz just come out / thousands of bodies like spaghetti all entwined / all done in the name of Adolf / all of a sudden in the hot blue day . . . they're all swimming look at them, look at all that blood and oil, bad mix, the sky turned black. What a terrific hell of a bang, and soot is dropping all over us plus bits of people, all the fish dropped dead, from shock, hey let's shalp them out. Look let's get some help, they're all in the water. Some jerry ball of hate stacked full of painful promise and carrying the names of the future dead blew the Southend tripper to the moon and down they fell in a deadly mash of Guinness and Gold-Flake . . . come on mate . . . 'I'll give you a hand'. We pulled them in all night, the others just bloated up like funfair freaks. Come on mum, don't fret, 'ere have a cuppa, where's your little Johnnie? . . . now, now he'll be all right, can he swim? No . . . oh. We'll find him . . . won't we lads . . . we'll find the little bleeder . . . shine your torch over here Bert, yeah, there's an old lady, give us your hand love, I'll pull you in . . . oh no, just a stump, she left it in the water . . . what bastard could do this . . . more blankets . . . bring more tea . . . there's just not enough of us . . . there's not enough people to help, who does this to people! What sick perverted bastard started all this shit . . . if he was in front of me, I would take a butcher's fucking knife and carve him slowly bit by fucking dirty piece and feed it to the river rats and any cunt that supports him, I'd fucking throw them in acid baths . . . when all had gone and the dawn arose we saw what seemed a little doll clinging to a piece of wood but on closer butchering revealed a little bugger of about two he were, struggling like the fuck and gripping in his paw a greasy old big bear, which no doubt helped to keep him up. We threw the bear back in the slick, and lifted the toddler out all dripping wet and covered in oil looking like a darkie so, no one about we took him home and washed him / he was a beaut / and mum was double chuffed to see a little round soft ball of warm goo goo / 'don't want to give him

up' quoth Dinah, 'must we' she said. 'Nah', I said 'his mum
will think he'd dead anyway' / so let her go on thinking it /
but think our Dinah rightly slurps of how its real mum will
fret and pine and waste away and mourn for her sweet lovely
soft flesh of her own / 'all right' I says 'we'll keep him for one
day only and then give him back.' A day turned into two /
then after a week we thought the shock now would be too
great and that the true mum would be adjusted to her sad
loss.

WIFE: Oh shit and piss and fuck. I just pissed in my pants. (*She
faints.*)

EDDY: My dearest wife and now my mum, it seems, this lady was
the very one whose baby you snatched / she told me the
selfsame and bitter tale of how she lost her Tony and if you
found him then I am he, he whom you found that belonged
to her was me. The he you stole and gave to her did once
belong to she . . . nice to see ya, have a nice day, so I am the
squelchy mass of flesh that issued from out the loins of my
dear wife / oh rats of shit / you opened a right box there
didn't you, you picked up a stone that was best left with all
those runny black and horrid things intact and not nibbling
in my brain. So the man I verballed to death was my real
pop / the man to whom my words like hard-edged shrapnel
razed his brain / was the source of me, oh stink / warlock and
eyes break shatter, cracker and splatter . . .! / Who laughs?
Me who wants to clean up the city / stop the plague destroy
the sphinx / me was the source of all the stink / the man of
principle is a mother fucker / oh no more will I taste the
sweetness of my dear wife's pillow . . . no more . . . no
more . . . no more . . . so I left my cosy and love-filled niche
now so full of horror / foul incest and babies on the way
which if they come will no doubt turn into six-fingered
horrors with two heads / poor Eddy. Oh this madness
twisting my brain / I walked through the plague rot streets
and witnessed the old and the broken / the funny faces
staring out of the dead vinyl flats / the flickering shadows of
the TV tube / I sat in cafés and thought of my desirable

lovely succulent and honey-filled wife and as I sat and
stared at the rheumy faces and the dead souls with their real
wives who were plastered forever in casts of drab
compromise, my own wife seemed like a princess / I
fastened her face on the horizon like the rising moon and
stared forever into space / and when the café closed I sat and
stared forever and forever, ran through in my mind every
combination of her face and smile and eyes and twists and
curves of her lips, I sat and projected her picture on the
moon and pored through every page of our life together like
a great holy bible of magic events I examined every feature
of her landscape and ate up every part of her and loved every
part whose sum total made up this creature, my wife. And
then the moon turned as red as blood / the clouds raced
across her face and became her hair and then her eyes and
the wind pulled her hair over her face / like it did when we
walked together through the fields and the forests, when the
trees shivered and the sun kissed us and the universe
wrapped us round in a cloak of stars and rain and crushed
grass and ice-creams and teas and clenched fingers / hold on
to me / hold on to me and I will hold on to you and I'll never
let you go, hold on to me, does it matter that you are my
mother, I'll love you even if I am your son / do we cause
each other pain, do we kill each other, do we maim and kill,
do we inflict vicious wounds on each other? We only love so
it doesn't matter mother, mother it doesn't matter. Why
should I tear my eyes out Greek style, why should you hang
yourself / have you seen a child from a mother and son / no.
Have I? No. Then how do we know that it's bad / should I
be so mortified? Who me. With my nails and fingers plunge
in and scoop out those warm and tender balls of jelly
quivering dipped in blood. Oedipus how could you have
done it, never to see your wife's golden face again, never
again to cast your eyes on her and hers on your eyes. What a
foul thing I have done, I am the rotten plague, tear them out
Eddy, rip them out, scoop them out like ice-cream, just
push the thumb behind the orb and push, pull them out and

stretch them to the end of the strings and then snap!
Darkness falls. Bollocks to all that. I'd rather run all the way
back and pull back the sheets, witness my golden-bodied
wife and climb into her sanctuary, climb all the way in right
up to my head and hide away there and be safe and
comforted. Yeh I wanna climb back inside my mum.
What's wrong with that? It's better than shoving a stick of
dynamite up someone's ass and getting a medal for it. So I
run back. I run and run and pulse hard and feet pound, it's
love I feel it's love, what matter what form it takes, it's love I
feel for your breast, for your nipple twice sucked / for your
belly twice known / for your hands twice caressed / for your
breath twice smelt, for your thighs, for your cunt twice
known, once head first once cock first, loving cunt holy
mother wife / loving source of your being / exit from
paradise / entrance to heaven.

(*Blackout.*)

SINK THE BELGRANO!

CHARACTERS

MAGGOT SCRATCHER
PIMP
NIT
CHORUS
COMMAND
TELL
WOODY
TOMMY
PRESIDENT OF ARGENTINA
FEET
SIR FISH FACE
REASON
SAILORS
FARMERS

For Clara

THE SET

The stage was divided into three areas. Upstage, on a rostrum running left and right, was the political area with desk, and behind it a large screen for projecting images. Downstage, on the main playing area, was drawn the outline of a huge submarine. The actors playing chorus and submarines would do their 'work-outs' and acting from this area. Stage left was a pub area which represented the 'voice of England'. Here the sailors would recline as the people back home and relate to the news as it came in. There was just a round table in the pub area and a dartboard facing off stage. Music accompanied the action, marked entrances and exits, and created a very strong atmosphere under the deft handling of Mark Glentworth. The actors played all the roles from Falkland farmers to Members of Parliament and, of course, the main roles as young, physically fit submariners. Props were kept to a minimum and were largely a change of hat or a red and white football scarf. The sailors wore track suits throughout which was a simple neutral uniform. The chorus were dressed in plain suits. I have not indicated the kind of slides I used since this would be a personal choice, but I have indicated where it might be necessary to project the text on to the screen.

S.B.

THE STILL SMALL VOICE OF TRUTH

On Tuesday 4 May, 1982, the House of Commons heard a statement from the then Secretary of State for Defence, John Nott. People, press and Parliament were given to understand that the forty-four-year-old USS *Phoenix*, survivor of Pearl Harbor, for such the *Belgrano* was, had to be sunk by our nuclear submarine, because she was converging on the Task Force. Albeit there had until that moment been no British casualties in action, I and others did not criticize. Daily from 2 April, we had publicly opposed the sending of the Task Force, and urged its return, but we recognized that terrible things happen, once conflict starts. No *Belgrano*, No *Sheffield*, No *Ardent*, No *Antelope*, No *Atlantic Conveyor*, No *Coventry*, No Bluff Cove, No Goose Green. But Mrs Thatcher would have been deprived of the military victory, which was what, for her, the Falklands War was all about.

I began to ask questions about the *Belgrano* in July 1982, when HMS *Conqueror* returned to the West Coast of Scotland. The Captain, Commander Christopher Wreford-Brown, DSO, made it clear that he had sunk the *Belgrano*, not on the impulse of defending the Task Force, but 'on orders from Northwood'. This was very different from the impression given to Parliament, press, and people. Small inconsistencies tend to be part of larger inconsistencies – small lies part of larger lies. For example, it was dragged out of Ministers that *Belgrano* had been detected not on 2 May at 8 p.m., but on 30 April at 4 p.m. A series of parliamentary questions and debates, the Old Bailey trial of Clive Ponting, the Minority Report of the Foreign Affairs Select Committee published in July 1985, add up to a picture of a Prime Minister, aware of the Peruvian Peace Proposals, ordering the sinking of the *Belgrano*, at Chequers, on 2 May, not for reasons of military necessity but for reasons of political advantage.

Tam Dalyell MP, July, 1986

WHY I WROTE IT

It had to be written. What a story! All those statements and contradictions in the House of Commons. All those 'statesmen' lying their little heads off in the Commons, and then when the facts emerged having to contradict themselves. What a pack of fakes, and what a disgusting bunch of rogues. It is apparent to everyone that the sinking of the *Belgrano* was a very dubious affair and led to severe attacks on the British Fleet and subsequent huge loss of life. How many people realize that before that calculated piece of sabotage not one British soldier had died! After unloosing that torpedo, under orders not from the submarine *Conqueror* but from England, on a ship way outside the demilitarized zone all havoc broke loose. It was a calculated gamble to end the war at a stroke and failed miserably. My play deals with the situation as I found it and was inspired by the book by Arthur Gavshon and Desmond Rice. I met Desmond on New Year's Eve in 1984 and, mutually expressing our disgust at the incident of the *Belgrano* sinking, led him to introduce his book to me. It made a fascinating and sordid read. I could never understand people who could order the taking of life so easily and weep later at the havoc they caused. I imagine such people to be 'armoured' in the full Reichian sense, dead to all real human response except to that which concerns them personally. The lack of imagination to foresee events is typical of right-wing thinking. The pollution of the environment and The Government's lame excuses for not dealing with it; the deadly poisoning of our seas with nuclear wastes; acid rain; bursting prisons – all seem to have one common heritage, and that to me is an abnormal disregard for human life and values, plus an overwhelming and religious belief in the sanctity of the marketplace. The *Belgrano* sinking was a typical product of that muddled and opportunist thinking. The irony is that brave Britons and Argentinians lost their lives needlessly. The play received mixed reviews and some virulent ones from the right-wing press. It was curious that their reviews, which were almost hysterical cant, resembled so closely the threats and poisoned mail I received from Fascist thugs. Special thanks to Desmond Rice and a special thanks to the Half Moon Theatre, and Chris Bond, who took the chance and gave his unstinting support.

Sink the Belgrano! was first performed at the Half Moon Theatre on 2 September 1986. The cast was as follows:

MAGGOT SCRATCHER	Maggie Steed
PIMP	Barry Stanton
NIT	Bill Stewart
CHORUS	Rory Edwards
COMMAND	Terence McGinty

Other parts were played by Tom Dean Burn, George Dillon, Eugene Lipinski and Edward Tudor Pole.

Director	Steven Berkoff
Designer	Ellen Cairns
Music	Mark Glentworth

This production of *Sink the Belgrano!* subsequently transferred to the Mermaid Theatre, when MAGGOT SCRATCHER was played by Louise Gold.

CHORUS: Oh you most brave and valiant Englishmen
Who never shall, no never bear the yoke
Of shame of curdled pride beneath the boot
Of some o'erweening greasy foreign bloke.
We smashed the damned Spanish might . . .
We put the Hun upon the British rack,
The Boers we kicked to kingdom come
And now the Argies sneaked behind our back.
Oh blasted glory for a few frail days
Oh cowards hiding under the sheep
Like Ulysses they sneaked while Britain dazed
Worn out with strikes and social strife
Numb with queues of unemployed that add
Their groaning weight to the nation's back . . .
But once aroused, oh ho! Old Albion snorts
The Bulldog, start-eyed, drools for Argy blood
Outraged its precious garden overrun
By foreign, greasy, dark unholy scum
Oh howl fair noble Grand Bretagne
Your people's voices crying out from afar
Like babies howling for the mother's breast
While dark satanic forces raid its nest
We put the greedy scavenger to flight
With fists of steel and hawk-like Harrier jets
Our submarines like silent hungry sharks
Went hunting for the juicy Argy game
But they were cautious, hiding, wouldn't show
Hoping for a *fait accompli* for their crime
And crawling behind the skirts of the UNO.

PIMP: Oh shit, your royal sweetest Maggot,
The lousy Argy swines unleashed their bile
On us, decided to invade our Falkland
Paradise, and dead of night they came like rats
Disturbed the peace and placed their rot,
Which means their scummy Argy flag upon our
Holy God-gave Promised Land!

MAGGOT: Those bloody junta bloody swine . . .!
How dare they, how simply do they bloody dare
When we've been so damned good to them
Never complained when their death squads
Got rid of opposition in mass graves . . .
Nor publicly showed our disgust at torture
For those that disobeyed (since naturally we
Wish to trade) and now those greasy Argy wogs
Show their thanks by stealing our sweet
Precious lands. Call out the Fleet, get planes
And tanks, I love to have a crisis on my hands.

PIMP: We'll get the UNO behind us first
Give evidence and facts to thwart their claim

MAGGOT: What bloody claim! When gangsters rob
What fuels their greed, you Pimp, is gain
Don't talk to me of robbers justifying
Deeds, the land is ours, that's plain to see.

PIMP: I know that and you know that but they
May say that we, that is those ghosts of past
Who made up our great history, did steal it,
Pardon the expression, first . . . In 1833 we staked
Our claim, backed by a warship, ma'am, or two
And threw the Argies off the land, and now
Although through time it's ours . . . Like some
Adopted babe we suckled, and watched it grow
Like our own flesh, the mother wants it back again.
So let's go to the world's great states
And get them behind us in our claim
The child we reared must then decide
The Islanders' wishes can not be denied
And naturally all of them will want to stay British.

MAGGOT: No! No! No! That's not the way, not that.
To sit around, regurgitate old tales
Who owned it then and now and chat
Until we grow old, like ancient cronies in a pub
Recounting how we owned this piece of sod
Discounting claims and waving old contracts

Possession is you know nine-tenths the law
And he who transgresses our hard-won right
Will get himself one hell of a bloody fight.

PIMP: We must of course recourse to written law
'Tis true that they have stolen our sweet lands
But then there will be time the world will judge
Without perhaps a punch-up strewn in blood
To save lives surely is the way
With honour we will live another day.

MAGGOT Oh bloody bollacks compromise you mean
And wait in turn for others to redeem our wealth
And sit in calm compliance while we hope
For others to present to us a deal,
While whispering give up old colonial ties
As they in turn make profits with their trade
Their greed to capture markets far and wide
Will sugar every bloody thing they say
And in the end we'll give the bloody lot away!
By the way, Pimp . . . Where is the Falklands??

Falkland Farmers

FARMER 1: Oh toil, oh strife, oh bleeding blooding graft
Is this the life for us I daily spout?
For sixty quid a week they bleed our veins
And us poor farmers slave for next to nought
We live in this pisspot, this dreary rock
Where no one has invested, not a jot . . .
The profits never go to thee or me,
Where then? The bloody bleedin' FIC.

FARMER 2: What's that?

FARMER 1: The bloody Falklands Island Company!

FARMER 2: What's that . . . ?

FARMER 1: Those who pontz from distant lands
Who own more than forty per cent
Of this, this wind-spat spit of rock,
And take the wool, our precious locks,

They own our house, they keep us poor
And we buy our grub at the company store.
FARMER 2: So bloody bleedin' bloomin' hell
While we sit on this blasted heath
They chat about our future rights
And say our wishes must be paramount
Bollacks and lockjaw, scum and dregs!
They've done sweet FA all these years
No roads are built, no hospitals . . .
When we are ill or hurt we fly
To Argy land where Argy hands
Repair our broken bodies or we'd die
So all that's cock and bollacks when they say
We fight for you dear folks in case one day
The Argies make you drive the right-hand way.
FARMER 1: It makes good PR back in gutter press
Who suck up lies more quickly than
Do buzzing flies the garbage in a bin.
They leave behind their maggot worms
That crawl across their daily sheets,
You think the Government has a heart
In thinking of the welfare of us men?
When really their souls couldn't give a fart.
Oh bullshite soggy Scratcher spews
Her eyes are on some distant parts
Antarctica or oil, that makes a start . . .
PIMP: How dare you pigs complain, you dogs
You curs that *want* always and gripe
Then know we care for you like we
Might care for chickens in our pens
You've never had it quite so good
Regular employment, lots of space
And all you do is trim some wool
And drink yourselves into an early grave
Of course we can't worry for you.
Eighteen hundred poor souls that sweat
And piss their lives away in hell

More than that number's killed themselves
Died by their own hand from dire grief
Of unemployment while millions weep.
The nation's fit and young queue up
In grey drab cities where empty days
Will lead to pointless nights, 'Time please'
And at the end your dole queue pay.

MAGGOT: So you think how lucky you are here
You might be back in England's drear
And pleasant land where miners strike
And other left-wing pests unite
Like filthy dogs disturb our rest . . .
Now shuffle off and do some work
While we take on the nation's pain
You're useless, any excuse to shirk,
You're lucky to have me, so don't complain . . .

NIT: (Rushing on) Oh, your precious whitened hairs
Though now so stained with Sassoon's dyes
Would stand on end if now you knew
How Argentina plotted and spied.

MAGGOT: Stop spitting in my tea, you nit,
Inform me where and when this came
Catastrophe, who can we blame!!
The Labour Party, they failed, you tit.
Wake up, you git, we need a war . . .
Establish once again our might and strength
Shake our old mane, out fly the moths
Oh God, I start to feel myself again
Now where is this damn Falkland Isle?

NIT: 'Tis just a tiny spot of land
That sits so neat in threshing seas
Not far but far enough 'tis nearer
To the Argentines than us I fear.
Some eight thousand sea miles from Cornwall's toe
And stands four hundred miles from Argy shores
Which thus have tempted them to claim
The Malvinas are theirs once again.

MAGGOT: Again! Again! They never were, you mug.
　　　They're British, damn you, sink that in your bontz.
　　　Again! Just 'cause they leapt across the straits
　　　While we were napping, dealing with the world
　　　They sought to steal our gateway to the south
　　　That precious stepping stone that we may need
　　　Since raging conflict 'twixt the super states
　　　May give a base to our dear USA.
　　　Suppose the Commie swine made use of it
　　　Oiling the Argy hand with swingeing bribe
　　　Eh? What then? Tell me that, you silly prat.
NIT: A dame of iron, for that is what you are,
　　　They never will question your metal now.
　　　Bring forth men soldiers only for thy
　　　Undaunted metal should compose nothing but wars.

CHORUS: And so the valiant British soldiered on
　　　Girded their loins with Vulcan steel
　　　The forge breathed fire night and day
　　　Preparing ships stacked full of cannon shells
　　　Like giant whales of death they steamed ahead
　　　The Harriers like mosquito's wings
　　　Did leap up in the sky were thirty-two
　　　Next stomach loaded full like gorged beasts
　　　Dread bombers, sixteen Victors tore the air
　　　Armed to the teeth with missiled brains
　　　To smell the Argy fear and chase
　　　Locked on to their frightened fleeing game
　　　Next, Scimitar and Scorpion tanks
　　　As deadly as their name suggests,
　　　Mine-sweepers . . . Laser-guided bombs
　　　Four hundred thousand tons of fuel
　　　One hundred thousand tons of freight
　　　To concentrate our Scratcher's boys
　　　Into one deadly fist of hate.
　　　We made a bridge across the seas
　　　Which measured some eight thousand miles

And poured twenty-eight thousand noble men
To gain back our sweet Falkland Isles . . .

Inside the submarine *Conqueror*

TOMMY: All right we've heard the news, let's get stuck in,
    And sail our deadly turd-shaped tube
    That will unleash pure havoc when
    Upon the surface of the deep we spy
    Some vessel filled with Argentines
    And shit some pain as it glides by
    With hunter-killer submarines
    Deep down we'll dive into the ocean's guts
    And wait . . . just still and silent till
    At last we see that great fat ship
    And then at last we'll have our . . .
CREW: (Sing) 'Sweet violets . . .'
SAILOR 1: Here, hang about and just a mo'
    Before we get all bleedin' hot
    Now sod all this, don't swallow shit
    Don't gulp down all you hear, you fool
    You ape, you asshole that is used
    By others who make up the rules
    'You're just a soldier now, go kill'
    'Go, Fido, fetch'. Don't think mate, no,
    Don't use no skill . . .
    Just obey orders that's your job
    Become a murderer's right hand . . .
    Don't dare to question what we do
    For what we are protecting and for who!
SAILOR 2: Protecting life and limb and British soil
    Sod you, who do you think made war?
    Who stepped up the British corn?
    Who, mate, bloody started this all?
    For self-determination of the Falkland folk
    To make an omelette you gotta break some yolks.
SAILOR 1: What's self-determination, mate?

Do you know what the fuck it means?
You just shove big words down your throat
Like when mum gave you medicine . . .
Now open up and down it goes, good boy.
Whenever hard truth won't go down
We grease the way with subtle quotes,
Self-determination, paramount, law and order,
All that crap. Old Adolf smashed Slovakia
To protect his German hordes
Sudetenland must have, he said,
Self-determination for those Nazi bores.

SAILOR 3: Then fuck off off this boat, you cunt
Don't fucking winge, you got no guts
A soldier's life's obey the Queen
The thinking's done by Whitehall nuts
We know there's right and wrong on both
But basically we trust our state
You must believe in England's green
And pleasant or fucking emigrate.

SAILOR 1: I'll fight . . . I'll hold a gun . . . I'll kill
I'll support the Union Jack, so help me I will
But I'll not stuff a sock in it
I'll not become a sponge for all
Just use your brains and think at last
Before it's blown away because
You kept your brainbox up your ass.

COMMAND: Now, now, lads, let's cool it down, eh?
The bloody war's not our responsibility
Now is it? Bloody hell . . . just think
If we had to unscramble every wrong,
Undo the twisted knot of history each time
We sink a foreign ship with our sweet bombs
We'd spend our time in Davy Jones'
Deep down still gassing, who did wrong?
Or else blown up upon the choppy green
Discussing politics as we cling
To shattered mastheads in the freezing sea.

No, boys, you volunteered, you came aboard
Because you like the adverts on TV
You want to be a hero, fire a gun . . .
Wear fancy helmets in your jets
As you ascend into the sky like Zeus
Like a god, omnipotent, a silver bird.
With nuclear claws you tear and kill
Or else beneath the deep as deadly sharks
Your finger on the button, death all round
You deal your piercing strike and wait
Until the bomb slips silently, no sound
Is made until it swiftly penetrates
Like a hot knife into butter . . .
It sinks into the bowels of the ship
Into steel plate it cuts and rips
And from the wounds issue its life
Machines and oil, smoke and blood
And then the sea replaces all that space
And claims the ship like carrion back again
That's why you're here, yes, that's your job!

SAILOR I: I see, we're just a bunch of yobs.

COMMAND: That's right, you've got it, boy,
    Don't look for principles in politics
    It's just a game they play, you're Whitehall's toys
    You're here to kill or die, not reason bloody why
    Did we go in 'gainst bloody Ian Smith
    When he seized power in '65? . . . No Task Force
    Then rushed in and said we're here to defend
    Rhodesia's black men
    And do not think for old Hong Kong
    We'll go in there and fight, no fear,
    China's a bit too big for us, my dear.

SAILOR I: So it's all a question of size or race?

COMMAND: You've got it, sonny, in this case
    You're the Task Force boys . . . we rule the waves
    'Cause if you don't, you'd better pray.

Cabinet

MAGGOT: Where's my Foreign Secretary Pimp
   And get me my good faithful Nit
   Those two defenders of Tory strength.
PIMP and NIT: Here, your worship most honoured Maggot.
MAGGOT: Well, what's the news today, my boys?
   Come on, Pimp, don't slobber and winge,
   If the news is bad just spit it out
   I've not all day to see you cringe
   I must get Denis's supper soon,
   And if you don't unheave your load
   I'll not get the best sides of bacon home
   So don't annoy me with your stutter
   Just open your cake-hole and sodding utter.
PIMP: It's good and bad, oh holy Scratcher.
MAGGOT: (Aside) *I loathe these fair and foul male turds*
   Still, I'll throw them out but screw them first.
PIMP: They want to make with us peace terms.
MAGGOT: They bloody what? Why peace terms now?
   After they shit on our front door.
PIMP: It seems (well not exactly our front door
   More like the garden gate or tradesman's
   Entrance so to speak) . . .
   It seems that having made their little *coup*
   Or *fait accompli* . . . It's up to you.
   They're willing now to sue for peace, i.e.
   A recognition of their claims . . .
   Historic rights when Spain left Argentina
   How Malvinas are to them their symbol
   Of the time when they kicked Spain
   Right up the ass and now they want
   To introduce the boot to us . . .
NIT: We seized the place in 1833 and now
   It's been so long it really does belong
   To us . . . it's practice . . . It's ours . . .
   For a century or more our folk

156

Have toiled the soil and reared their young.
MAGGOT: Oh shut up, Nit, you'll make me weep
And anyhow who asked you to speak
Just shut your trap, you're M.o.D.
That means defence if you can't read.
I have a well-paid politician here
Called Pimp who interprets history
Or bends it here and there if there
Be need . . . What say you, Pimp, the world's with us?
Have you checked old cowboy yet,
Old Geriatric Joe, is he for us?
PIMP: Without a doubt, he's for us like you
Can't believe . . . sends all his love
And will give all the info that we need.
Like how much weaponry they've got and where
How many planes, what ships, what subs,
He'll loan his radar, high frequency
To intercept and translate any code
That they may send, just point your
Guns and trust him, he'll do the rest.
MAGGOT Oh Jolly Joe . . . Old Cowboy Poke
Oh what a friend indeed when times
Are tough and then a friend we need
To help us smooth the way . . .
How sweet . . . He said all that? Aah Joe
I must invite the old sod back . . .
His wife's though such an evil bore
Why is it great blokes marry such whores?
BOTH: Hmmmn . . . hmmnnnn . . . hmmmmn ?!
MAGGOT: Oh never mind . . . just fuck all that,
Oh shit . . . a pound of bacon with no fat
I'll be back, just chat away . . .
I've got to get the groceries . . .
And please don't quarrel when I've gone
Or plot behind my back!! You scum.
BOTH: My lady . . . would we do that?
PIMP: Oh fuck, oh shit, oh piss, oh balls.

NIT: What's the problem, old boy . . . Do let me hear.
PIMP: We just bloody sold to Argentina
    Some missiles and some naval weaponry
    Two hundred million quids' worth flogged
    Which may be used against our Fleet
    Oh hot bollacks and spotted dick
    Our own weapons may like to find
    Their way back to their master's house
    Weapons of death carry no names
    The more's the problem, who can we blame?

SAILOR 1: Dear Tina, we've passed the Canary Isle
    One periscope-depth run each thirty hours
    Just to keep us on our toes
    This is beginning to feel like fun.

NIT: Oh Pimp, you pontz, you prat, you cur . . .
    You, the Foreign Secretary, that what you are?
    Did you not suspect that one day
    The bloody Argies would get itchy feet
    And aim their guns at the British Fleet!
PIMP: Who was to know? Well not for sure
    We sell death weapons to those who
    Pay. Who cares who they kill, it's their war,
    We only manufacture death, no more.
    We don't tell who to shoot and kill
    We flog the bloody stuff, that's all . . .
    But usually it's not our doorstep
    We have deigned to shit upon.
    South Africa's too far away . . .
    We made a bomb in Lebanon . . .
    Excuse me! . . . I mean a killing . . .
    Oh no! I mean we made a fortune
    Selling death all round the world
    Is it my fault that now by chance
    A bloody boomerang's been hurled?

SAILOR 2: Dear Janet, we've been going five days
    I miss you but it won't be long
    I'll take some pics, the blokes are nice
    For supper we had ice-cream and rice.

MAGGOT: (re-entering) Well done . . . I got the last half-
    pound . . .
    He likes it lean and meaty . . . don't we all?
    Bastards were just about to close,
    I said now what's all this, you work part-time?
    The Brits are such a lazy bunch of sods
    No wonder there's three million unemployed.
    The buggers simply now refuse to work
    And then the Labour scum will point at me
    It's not our bloody sodden fault
    It's dole money the state doles out,
    They get for free by queueing up
    Just once a week, not so much less
    Than they would get in full-time graft.
NIT: Then ma'am, why not get wages up?
    And so temptation's not so great
    The difference being far too much
    Between the dole and a week well paid!
MAGGOT: No!! . . . Get *dole* down, and then you'll see
    A scramble for the factories . . .
    No skiving now, the whistle blows . . .
    All present and correct . . . they know
    There's now no safety net, that's what they need
    That's monetarism, Nit . . . are you agreed?
NIT: Yes m'lady, I dare say there's truth in that . . .
PIMP: Too bloody true, what . . . ! Lazy scum!
    Can't wait to strike at any turn
    Been spoilt, what!, by the Welfare State
    When what they desperately need is a swift
    Kick up the ass, mate.
MAGGOT: That's all very well, you know,
    But the barometer of fate

Has placed us in the opinion polls
Behind the scummy Socialist crud
Behind old stinking 'Feet' we limp
While you just drag your feet
Old 'Feet' just stumbles on and bleats
Like some old flasher on Hampstead Heath.

PIMP: About this invasion, my lady . . .
MAGGOT: Shut up a mo' . . . I'm thinking hard . . .
PIMP: Of course, of course, what action to take?
MAGGOT: No! Whether to fry it in butter or lard!
PIMP: Oh myself, I like my bacon grilled . . .
A few tomatoes sizzling there
Bung in a mushroom or two
And if you've time then just prepare
Two slices of fried bread, that's a treat
Or if you like two scrambled eggs
Quick whipped and fluffy like molten gold
Coffee steaming from fresh ground beans
. . . That's my definition of ecstasy . . .

MAGGOT: You're wasted as Foreign Secretary
Your talent there is hardly used
We need a decent bloody chef
The Commons kitchen's the place for you!
(Aside.) *Ah! I have it . . . I have it, Nit!*

NIT: Yes, my lady, what have you got?
Have you come up with some inspired plot?

MAGGOT: I'll make a Spanish omelette!
At first I'll crack some Argy eggs
Throw in some tasty British herbs
Well flavoured with strong British earth
Then, round and round the cauldron go
In the poisoned entrails throw
Hate and good old Tory guile
Plots to cover up our sins
Lies and slander to beguile
Then throw massive outrage in,
Synthetic will do just as well.

To make the mixture rise and swell
Then add more then one thousand dead
Tears of children's salty brine
Broken hearts and widows pining
Mothers mourning for their lost boys,
Collect those dewdrops to make the paste
Soldiers' howls as they lay burning,
Throw in the lot and keep it turning
Olé, your Spanish omelette!
PIMP: But who will eat this foul stew?
MAGGOT: The entire British press, you fool!

The Conqueror

SAILOR'S SONG
Rule Britannia, Britannia rules the waves
Britain never never never shall be slaves.
We've spent twelve thousand million quid
On our defence in twelve short months
And now you see money well spent
We'll give a demo of our strength
We've got the class and discipline
The training, thank you, at your expense,
Communications are next to none
Weapon-locating radar, chum
We're on our way from Scotland's shores
Until we reach the battle zone
We're going fast beneath the deep
On our way to the Argy Fleet
Attracting curious sharks and whales
Who cannot believe this giant fish
That slides armed with its deadly eggs
That will be laid when we will, mate
War's just another way to fornicate
We'll fuck their slaggy Argy ships
Action stations, we'll rehearse a hit.

SAILOR 3: Dear Sheila, just cleaning my gun
I tell you it's great . . . it's just fun
We're not going to kill anyone
We're just keeping the Argy on the run.

SAILOR 4: Dear Rita, we crossed the Equator today
It weren't half hot, the guys sunbathed
We'll be there in about a week
We're safe as houses and the roof don't leak.

SAILOR 5: Dear Doreen, I feel so proud my love
To be part of this great Fleet
A hundred and seven ships on the way
And each man will say . . . 'I was there that day.'

SAILOR 6: Dear Mum, I can tell you I'm scared
Don't know what we're facing down here
It's so quiet beneath the surface and still
But each night we can watch a film.

SAILOR 7: Dear Dad, it's getting colder as we close in
The South Atlantic's cold as ice
I can't imagine what it's like
If we had to bloody swim.

SAILOR 8: We're told there's now a TEZ,
Total Exclusion Zone I mean,
If we find enemy ships within
Then we can blow them to smithereens.

SAILOR 9: Dear Judy, I don't want to kill
In fact of war I've had enough
The zone we're told's two hundred miles
So they'll stay out, unless they're tired of life.

COMMAND: Two-hundred-mile Exclusion Zone
So if the buggers stay outside
All we can do is be like cops
And whack them if they stray across.
Still I'm not sentimental, this is war
The Argies began it, but I've no hate
But I wouldn't half like it if they want to play
I've got a lovely bunch of coconuts . . . called Mark 8.

Argentina v. Britain

PRESIDENT OF ARGENTINA: No, we don't wish to fight no more.
It's a question of principle, that's all
We have to settle this old score . . .
The Malvinas belong to us
It's on our continental shelf
It's part of our long history
You have no contracts sealed and signed
You came in 1833 and stole
What was rightfully our land
We never sold it to you
We never gave it to you
So please give it back thank you
We tried so many times to call
To ask you when and how and why
You put us off, we're foreign scum
You ignore the warning signs
'End colonialism in all its forms'
Resolution 2065 . . .
The United Nations wrote that line
Nineteen hundred and sixty five
For seventeen more long years we wait
And get nothing . . . nothing at all
You would not even negotiate
What did you do for your Malvinas
Nothing, but bleed it, suck it dry,
We supplied the Islands' needs . . .
You gave nothing, nothing at all,
Oh yes, perhaps a little greed . . .
PIMP: All right, old chap, now settle down
Don't get your knickers in a twist,
History is made by time
And in that case you must believe
The Falkland Islands really mine
Or rather ours, sorry slip of the tongue,
You cannot separate the strands of memory

Who's right, who's wrong . . .
'Prescription' is the word that I would choose
Defined in our good dictionary
As 'a claim founded upon much use'
We've had our good old British stock
For so many long winter years
Toil the earth and break the rocks,
And backs as well with sweat and tears,
It's just a little piece of England now
So be a good chap and piss off
Or else we'll blow you to kingdom come.
You know we're on the way, old boy
So why don't you just scuttle off
And show your boss that we mean biz,
OK? There's a lot of muscle on the way
He'll understand that there's no deal,
Just stay put in Argy land
I know it's tough, inflation's high
Five hundred per cent and going up
Wages are low, your debt is huge,
But . . . don't use the Falklands for your subterfuge.

CHORUS: Oh for a brace of Exocet missiles
That would ascend the brightest heaven of invention
The sky would be their stage
Super Etendard jets to fly
Six hundred and eighty miles per hour above the waves
The deadly Exocet once it is launched
Cannot be stopped until it strikes
Since radar with its seeing eyes
Can only read what's in the sky
Below ten feet its eyes are blind
Oh who would know the cunning fiends
Had fixed them to their flying wings
We did not dream nor could not know
The bastards had such weaponry
This flying spear of death is quick

You can't shoot down an Exocet
When hurled above the choppy seas
You don't see it till you are hit!

Cabinet

MAGGOT: Well done, Pimp, the bastards know
What follows as the night the day
If they won't move, those junta creeps,
That Britain won't just watch and pray
And see our Islands given away . . .
PIMP: I told the bugger, it's up to him
The message could not be more plain
I spelt it out, withdraw or else
The answer could be a lot of pain.
MAGGOT: You're sure we're quite prepared, my Nit,
No fuck-ups now, no tricky biz
The press has swallowed all that shit
And the country's right behind us too.
PIMP: Yes, my lady, we're nearly there
And your speech yesterday when you compared
Yourself to Churchill was a wiz.
Hitler's very useful in times like this.
MAGGOT: Never mind all that, just give us facts
We must be certain we will win
Not land our boys into the fat
Because you screwed up, you nit.
NIT: We're all prepared, the Yanks are there
We will know when it's time to hit
Old Cowpoke's loaned the electronic toys
We can even hear them take a shit.
MAGGOT: Spare me your squalid anal jokes
Your public schoolboy legacy, Nit!
NIT: Yes ma'am . . . sorreeeeee!
MAGGOT: What about those bloody Exocets
Those rotten greedy French have flogged
The French are not averse to deals that stank

They'll climb down sewers to make a franc.

NIT: It's all arranged, they'll spill the beans
And tell us the secret of those stinging bees
The intimate details, how fast how high
And how easy it will be to swat them from the sky
We have no need to worry, ma'am
We know all they can hurl at us
An inventory you might say
The French have been a good ally.

MAGGOT: How long, how long before our arm
Can swat you might say, with our might?

NIT: Three weeks is all we need, three weeks
And then we'll be right there on sight.

MAGGOT: OK, Pimp, here's the plan, unplug your ears
For three weeks then you show restraint
Talk peace, remonstrate the wrongs,
Make amends, negotiate, discuss
The pros and cons, offer a plan . . .
A waiting time before it's time to go,
'Time please' we go out gently from
The pub with easy and all friendly smiles
The landlord must lock up the doors
And so like us he will away
Into the night, we had our day
And quaffed down our pint
Just look after our good folk
Perhaps a golden handshake and Amen.

PIMP: Oh goody then there'll be no war!
Just threaten and then make a deal
A long lease back, divide the oil?
The Islanders can go to hell.

MAGGOT: No, Pimp, you rotten little turnip
You greasy stupid dotty sod . . .
That's what they'll *think* – why divvy up?
When we can have it all . . .
If we let UNO back in,
Sit down for weeks with Garlic Chops

Debate our terms with the gangster mob
We'll look like we've been shat upon.
We're not a third power yet you know
We've got some balls in the old bird yet
Though I doubt the pair of you
Have got much there to boast about
If we decided to talk to them . . .
To negotiate with those we hate?!
Then goodbye Tory Party from the land.
We're two percent behind the Reds,
That's all we need to show how weak
And spineless we are to old 'Feet'
They'll shit on us from a great height
Can you see Feet in Downing Street?
Because we couldn't make the pace?
Besides I don't intend to move,
I just redecorated the bloody place.

CHORUS: Around the land, in every pub,
    In every dining room and lounge
    The voice of England can be heard
    Discussing the Falklands with angry sounds
    As if the family jewels had been thieved.
    Outraged. The telly on, the pot of tea
    Refuelling parched throats for verbal war
    You'd never believe until last week
    They didn't know Falklands from Leigh-on-Sea.

The Commons

MAGGOT: We didn't know, no, not a thing.
    Bolt from the blue . . . I couldn't believe . . .
    There we were eating their meat,
    Enjoying West-End Musicals inspired by their chiefs,
    How does it go? It's really quite sweet
    'Don't cry for me, Argentina'
    We were shocked, shocked we were . . .
    You know it's quite a strain

We weren't prepared, no ships, no planes,
Not a dicky bird was said . . .
If only they had asked us nicely . . .
Said, 'Please Maggot, can we have our Island
Back', polite and quietly,
We would have considered, I would have said,
'Piss off, you greasy fascist pigs'
(Cheers.)
'Go screw your mother, you filthy wogs'
(Cheers.)
'You want to put your dirty toe
Upon our cropped-lawned island home.
You've got some hope, don't make me laugh
Or I'll shove the junta up your ass!'
(Cheers.)

FEET: The Labour Party now demands
That we avenge this bloody deed
For bloody bloomin' bleeding war
Should we declare right now, no less
Foul and brutal aggression must not succeed,
Labour's not a pack of Tory weeds,
We'd be there, yes damn right we would.
What happened to 'Intelligence', they all dead?
Fingers up your assholes, blind dumb and deaf?
They've been telling us for years
They're going to give the mighty boot
What have you been doing, love
Fiddling the books? Or plotting
With asslicker Nit, or Pimp the pontz, the crooks.
(Boos.)

SIR FISH FACE: I think we should ban Argentina
From entering the soccer World Cup.
(Cheers, 'Piss off', etc.)

NIT: I take great exception to Cheesy Feet
Accusing us of dragging our foot
When we were never even warned
Or if we were we didn't hear . . .

FO didn't tell us or the post went astray,
The lines were bad I believe that day,
Or else, oh yes we were away . . .
The file got buried or got mislaid
Oh, then we were on holiday . . .
Yes I remember that, the weather was fine . . .
You know how memos pile up high . . .
We did write a letter, I remember that . . .
But forgot to send it . . . The last chap was a prat.
But you know what we do with prats
Or silly buggers who make a balls,
We give the bastards the bloody sack
And they sleep it off in the House of Lords.
Anyway who are you to talk
In your worn-out elbows and smelly cords?!
You march against the nuclear bomb! (Shame, shame.')
I've seen you stride with long-haired poofs
All the way to Aldermaston! ('Disgusting!')

MAGGOT: Can you imagine old Feet in the shop
When we'd come back to check the stock
He'd have the whole damn country in shock!
(Bravo! Cheers!)

REASON: Surely, before we shed young blood
We must seek an ointment for the wound.
To heal must be then paramount
No more killing, not quite so soon
('Bollacks', 'Appeaser', 'Coward', etc.)
There must be time, no blood's been shed
Not one young English life's been lost
You seek a medicine for the sore
Not hack it with a bloody knife.
All human flesh belongs to God
You take one life, you take the world
Did Jesus say, 'Throw your stones first,
Those who are innocent of any sin.'
('Balls', 'Rubbish', 'Coward', 'Appeaser'.)
The world's become a tinder-box

You set a match and watch it flare
Death has become a TV screen
That we watch from our soft armchairs
('Sit down', 'Piss off', 'Left-wing pontz'.)
If you can call yourself Christians
If you believe in Christ our Lord
Then you will seek the bloodless way
Not solve it with a flaming sword.
('Commie', 'Bollacks', etc.)

The Conqueror

SAILOR 1: Dear Janet, love, we're there, it's cold
  We do six-hour shifts, I'm bored
  Scotland lost the match, we hear
  There's not much else I can report.
SAILOR 2: Dear Sheila, still cleaning my gun
  I'd love a decent cup of tea
  Or even read the daily *Sun,*
  You know, we still ain't killed anyone.
SAILOR 3: Dear Rita, there's not much about
  We saw a couple of old freights
  A sitting duck . . . but couldn't shoot
  The sods were outside the TEZ.
SAILOR 4: Dear Doreen, still feeling so proud
  But I can't wait to see their ships
  It's dark and silent as the grave
  I'm dying for us to make a hit.
SAILOR 5: Dear Mum, we don't know what's going on
  We hear no news except the crap
  They send us from HQ at home
  And politicians' daily chat.
SAILOR 6: Dear Judy, I don't want to kill
  I can't imagine what it's like
  The waves are like giant hills
  The sub feels like a block of ice.
COMMAND: Two-hundred-mile Exclusion Zone

A lot of bloody bollacks that
To steam around and watch the buggers
Stick their tongues out, safe and fat,
Hold on, we've had a signal here
'Go out and sink a bloody ship'
'Which one?' 'Who cares, just something near
You've got to make a bloody hit'
There's nothing in our target now!
'The other sub will make the kill'?
Give us a chance, we'll look around
We'll get some juicy Argy ship
Chock full of arms and fighting men.
'Westminster wants some action' . . . Shit
We've got our hands tied by the law.
Can we attack them from the rear
When they're outside the lines *you* draw?
That just ain't cricket, is it, dear?
Or they may say, and it will be true,
Britain doesn't rule the waves
She simply waives the bloody rules!
Wait, hold on . . . just hang about
I'm picking up a distant tune
Let's go to periscope depth and peek . . .
A silhoutte against the moon . . .

PIMP: (On phone) Hello, hello, Maggot, that you?
And how are things at home, my dear?
I'm chatting up old Cowboy Joe
And it could be that peace is very near.
MAGGOT: Hello, Pimp, speak up, you drip
And don't believe all that you hear
Those greasy wogs are cunning sods
With all their talk of peace plans now
That our Task Force is bloody there.
PIMP: Well, to spell it out, the sods agreed,
Immediate cease fire, number one . . .
And then withdraw all Argy troops . . .

That's what we want to flaming hear
A third party to govern it,
While we thrash out conflicting views
And then the Islanders to have a say
Before the final solution day . . .
Well, it's not bad, is it, what d'ya think?

MAGGOT: What do I think . . . ? It bloody stinks
Who cares about the rotten Islanders!
It's not what this is all about,
You stupid simpering silly pontz.
You think the wishes of those few
Will dictate how and what we do
We're not negotiating with them
It's us, Great bloody Britain, mate
It's our corn that they stepped upon
You think we're going to war for them?
Spending four million quid a day
For eighteen hundred Bills and Ben!

PIMP: I know, I know, but still they say
Their wishes will be . . . etc . . .
And they can make peace this very day
It's up to us, they've cleared the decks
What shall I say, ma'am . . .
Can I say . . . yes?

MAGGOT: No, no, no, no, no and no!
And that does not quite spell out yes.

PIMP: But, ma'am, they have agreed our points . . .
Old Cowboy's flogged himself to death
We've been up all night . . .
For nearly a week . . .
A hot line between Joe and them . . .
We've squeezed the best possible deal . . .
Squeeze any more the marrow is next . . .
Give them a morsel . . .
Don't put it to the test . . .
They'll withdraw . . . we've won
Talk terms . . . no blood behind a desk. . . .

172

MAGGOT: Tell Cowboy Joe, I need a fight
    He needs it too, expose the sore
    That may spread inside the flanks
    Of England if we have no war
    There's twenty-eight thousand Brits
    On whom the world's eyes hold in awe
    Are we going now to turn around,
    Say, 'Sorry, lads, false alarm'?
    Tell Cowboy, if we do, then farewell,
    England falls to Socialist claws
    Who will tear our land apart
    Then who will support his Cruise missiles
    Planted like teeth in our fair land
    To scare off the Russian Bear
    Or bite any invading hand?
PIMP: But then we're nearly almost there . . . !
    What can I say then when they ask
    What did your old Iron Lady think
    Of our strong plan we made for peace?
MAGGOT: Stop whining, you sickening spineless wimp,
    Oh God if only I had men around
    And not this pair of leaking drips
    That dribble daily in my mind.
    Tell Cowboy I support *his* wars
    Prop up *his* Nicaragua
    Ignore his murder squads he sends
    To clean up vile El Salvador
    So screw this pissy peace plan, Pimp!
PIMP: OK . . . I see the danger, ma'am . . .
    The troops return . . . the drooping flags
    No 'Knees up, Mother Brown' in pubs
    Or clinking glasses in Buck House
    No medals, no heroes lined up . . .
    Before the Nation's TV screens
    No celebration of the deed
    That spells out British victory
    No revenge for the filthy slur

No hands in mouths waiting for news
No photos in the *Daily Muck*
Of Tommies clambering up hills
With smiling faces, British flags,
Atop a craggy mount . . .
No Islanders with whoops and cries
And cream teas for the hungry lads
Wide-angle lens of history
Being made by Fleet Street hacks
Who follow us with hungry lens
Ready to frame for all the world
The conquered lying in the dust
And Maggot Scratcher raised up high
And then, vote Tory . . . written in the sky.

MAGGOT: A teardrop now steals from my eye
    Oh, Pimp, for once you now speak true
    At last, you see the truth at last
    At long last you must see our cause
    Thank God, the scales fell from your eye
    You see, we must defend the state,
    Not just some piece of rock with sheep
    Dropping their rotund turds so thick
    Or gentle Islanders shedding wool
    Or rocking chairs for weary feet.
    It's England, now at last you scan
    The breadth of history . . . The pulse
    Of England must be strong, we *must*
    Punish those who commit wrong . . .
    You know we've got them beat,
    We paid the deposit . . . Let's just complete.

PIMP: So what shall I tell Cowboy Joe?
    They're sewing up the peace plan now.

MAGGOT: Say you couldn't get through,
    You know the phones are always bad
    By then we'll scuttle their little 'plan'
    But make up a tale for the man.
    (**She hangs up.**)

PIMP: Now I shall have to lie *again*
　　　She always leaves me in the shit!
　　　Oh well, it's nothing really new
　　　Not when you're taught by the master bitch.
　　　(Into phone) Hello Joe, how are you and how's the wife?
　　　Listen, I can't get through right now
　　　Nobody home, and embassies are closed . . .
　　　Weekends, you know, nobody works . . .
　　　Yes, the plan seemed fine to me
　　　A hiccup perhaps just on one word?
　　　What word is that they want to change . . .?
　　　'Wishes' . . . to 'Aspirations' on the clause . . .
　　　Oh well, I'll have to call HQ
　　　To see if 'aspirations' now will do
　　　I know it's only just one word,
　　　I know that time is running out
　　　But we must analyse the sound . . .
　　　Weigh it carefully on the scales
　　　Make sure we have value for a pound
　　　I'll call you back without delay
　　　OK? . . . and, er . . . have a nice day.

CHORUS: Now you see and now you don't
　　　Imagine pounding on the rocks
　　　A score of Harriers now unleashed
　　　Shredding their targets like angry hawks
　　　Then sweeping into the sky
　　　Dissolving in a womb of cloud
　　　Only the deep and throaty sound
　　　Is heard as it again prepares
　　　And down down it dives
　　　Ploughing up earth rocks and trees
　　　And sending fear into our enemy
　　　Who cower, trembling hair on end
　　　Affrighted by this show of strength
　　　Watch them as their spines will bend
　　　Beneath the blast of British breath

Hot, fierce as raging angry lion
Protecting her young cubs from death.

Lunch at Chequers

MAGGOT: We've not much time, the sands are running out
    And at the end we'll be checkmate
    By compromise and deals, my friends,
    Unless we give the most almighty clout.
TELL: (Off, the war) Damn it all, we're hitting the buggers
    hard
    All day we rained down great dollops of pain
    We attacked again and yet again
    Port Stanley will never look quite the same
    Our chaps are doing all they can but
    If the buggers stay outside the line
    The boxing match is fought with gloves,
    Let's get them off and get some knuckles
    Cracking on the swine . . .
WOODY: Hear bloody hear . . . What! Bloody shame
    I call it . . . sod it, let's clout the buggers
    As you say, knock one off and they'll not
    Come out to play another day. . . .
MAGGOT: Trouble is they have accepted all our terms
    The very minimum we would accept,
    They have by now accepted, bar one word
    One bloody word will be the straw
    To break the camel's back. The word
    Will not go down, not if we choose
    Not to accept their peace-meal stew.
    But once they inform Joe that it's on
    We can't then change our minds and say
    It's off . . . Can we . . . How say you, Tell?
TELL: Bloody hell, that's what I bloody say
    Damned good lamb New Zealand eh!
    That's it . . . buy British or nearly . . . tasty . . . what!
MAGGOT: Have some mint sauce, Tell . . . Yes can we

Say it's off? I mean, can we say, sod off!
Too late, the balloon's gone up?
WOODY: Smash the buggers, in or out the bloody Zone
Reclaim what's ours, if we don't we'll be
A right example to the rest, besides
We could then test our toys, warn Russia too,
We'll make an example of all those that
Think the Lion is just a sleeping cat
I'm dying to see how Sea-cat missiles
Fare and Tiger-fish torpedoes blasting
Holes, at half a million quid a time,
Bit costly that, but think of all the orders
We will get once they see them in act
Tests and war games aren't the same
As seeing them work on living game.
TELL: Right, let's get to work, let's heat it up.
MAGGOT: Oh Tell, you speak the words I want to hear
Where can we clout the sods before they
Crawl behind the UN skirts in fear?
TELL: Sink a bloody Argy ship!
Hit them where it hurts the most
A packed full, well armed with young men,
A thousand maybe more, hit in one below
Condemn to darkness their young pride
Then watch them cave in when they feel our punch
You take one out, you take them all
They'll be on their knees, you'll see.
MAGGOT: Oh Tell, I'm thrilled with ecstasy
More lamb? Go on, it's piping hot
Some roast, 'fraid they're just overdone,
Now go on . . . sink one!? Bloody hell.
Then it's all over really? You think so, Tell?
TELL: Could be very well . . . They'll see
That we mean business . . . won't risk
Coming out and lose an arm, maybe a leg
We've got them well and truly pegged.

MAGGOT: They wouldn't attack *our* ships, would they, Tell?

TELL: Can't see how, we know their strength
    Got all the facts, thanks to old Joe
    Who fed us all the info that we need
    To know, give us the word, let's go.

MAGGOT: You don't need me, just do your work
    I'm right behind you, lads, you know.

WOODY: We've trailed a lovely Argy ship
    Stacked full as Tell has just described
    We've got them in our sights . . . could
    Blast them now to kingdom come.
    One battleship just steaming on
    With two destroyers by her side
    Like taking two alsatians for a walk,
    They'll bark a bit maybe
    But won't do much when they will see
    Their master's bleeding guts,
    But then they're just outside the TEZ.
    Please change the rules and then you'll see,
    Madam, a swift sharp British victory.

MAGGOT: Can we do that? So easily.
    Or won't it seem in the world's eyes
    That we have been a mite extreme?

WOODY: No, bloody hell, let's say we saw them
    Start to stray across the line . . .

TELL: They posed a threat to us, our boys,
    Were steaming straight just hours away
    We had to sink the bugger without delay!

WOODY: They're bristling with fire-power, ma'am,
    With two missile-packed escort destroyers
    Like armed guards ready to defend the boss
    Who himself carries fifteen six-inch guns.
    We had to sink it or face our loss
    God knows how many lives we'll save.

MAGGOT: You think we'll save lives?

WOODY: Of course, we'll stop the war
    They'll have no bottle left to fight!

TELL: Attack them now. Before they go,
    There may not be a chance again
    And then we'll bite our nails and sigh
    Oh why didn't we do it then, you'll moan.

MAGGOT: What do you mean, 'before they go'?

TELL: Well . . . info is, that they're heading back home
    They're on a track, you see, two-ninety degrees,
    Between ten and eleven knots, we'll lose them
    Though we've had them in our sights
    A day or more, we're waiting for the light.

MAGGOT: Sunlight?

TELL: No green, give us the green one, madam!

MAGGOT: I may say, now forgive me if I winge
    That to sink a bloody ship (sailing away
    You say) in cold blood gives me just a twinge
    I know it's right, I know . . . but when I think
    Of hundreds of young boys, they could be ours,
    Stopped dead and floating in the drink
    It does . . . just for a second . . . make me think . . .

TELL: Don't! . . . ma'am don't, be hard as steel
    The Iron Lady, come, not brass not tin
    Like leaking oil can in *Wizard of Oz*,
    But iron! Rigid, hard, inflexible . . .
    Your reputation earned the whole world wide
    The Iron Lady with a velvet glove??
    No! Iron fist to match a steely heart.

MAGGOT: (Inspired) Then sink the bloody sod, that's what I say
    We'll change the engagement rules . . . OK.

TELL: We'll drink to that.

WOODY: Can't wait to give the bloody orders
    They will be pleased, they're getting
    Bored sailing around the endless seas.

MAGGOT: What shall we say? Let's all decide
    To tell the same story, on the day.

TELL: Get Nit . . . to extricate his tongue
    With due respect from out your ass,
    And tell the press and parliament . . .

'A heavily armed surface attack group
Close to the Exclusion Zone, was closing
In on our Task Force . . . only hours away . . .
Ignore them at our peril,' that's what he'll say.

MAGGOT: But that's not strictly true, they're sailing away
You say, some forty miles south-west of the Zone
Can't we sink something deep inside . . .
That we can certainly justify . . .

TELL: There's bugger all . . . They've kept outside
And this one's closest, ma'am, and soon
That won't be there much longer . . .
Look, if we don't hit it now
We'll have to sink them in their ports
And claim we heard them start their engines
And posed a threat to our Task Force!
And how do you know that they
Won't turn . . . How do you know it ain't
One big bluff . . . they calm us down
And then one night ka-blam and blast
And British lads are feeding sharks.

MAGGOT: Those last words indeed touched my heart
Of course my woman's soul trembled a jot
At thoughts of bloody bodies
All unseamed and torn apart
And widowed mothers clutching their
Now fatherless sons and daughters
Must admit since our wombs carry flesh
And blood and watch the shoot become a plant
Must admit that for a moment I did hesitate
Forgot that I was iron, instead a mum
Worried when child is late . . .
What's the time?

WOODY: It's one o'clock

MAGGOT: (Recovering) Then give the order . . . Let it be swift.
Anyway those bastards started it
Let them now take the consequence . . .

CHORUS: Now cast your minds o'er wind-swept choppy seas
　　　　Where ships lay waiting rocking to and fro
　　　　A great armada, armed with might and men
　　　　Who wait, alert, primed ready to unleash
　　　　The power that is awesome coiled within
　　　　Imagine now the crew. Some sleeping, some awake
　　　　Their radar scanning thunderous clouds,
　　　　Some writing letters home to their sweethearts
　　　　And others still deciphering strange codes
　　　　Which spell the fate of those who live or die,
　　　　Some playing cards, some singing old pop songs
　　　　While others dream of clutching their warm wives
　　　　And in those cloudy seconds between sleep and wake
　　　　Imagine they will turn around and hold their mate.
　　　　For some, alas, this night will be their last
　　　　Their young unfinished lives will be reclaimed
　　　　Within the freezing sea, their unknown graves.

The Conqueror

COMMAND: Up periscope . . . OK, we see them clear
　　　　Action station . . . all at high alert
　　　　It's nearly fifteen hundred hours, Sunday May the Second.
　　　　That's nearly seven o'clock back home
　　　　Opening time in all the pubs
　　　　We'd wander down and have a pint
　　　　Maybe play a game of darts or two
　　　　I've got her in my sights, ten thousand tons
　　　　Of steel, at least one thousand Argy men
　　　　Just slowly ploughing up the sea
　　　　A steady speed of ten to thirteen knots,
　　　　Like some old carthorse pulling reins of foam
　　　　But at her side two dangerous chaperons
　　　　Ready to destroy with claws
　　　　That reach into the sky some twenty miles
　　　　Seek out your heart and then like bloodhounds
　　　　Hold your course until they taste your meat.

SAILOR: They're only blokes like us . . . don't fire . . .
    Not fire one off . . . like in cold blood . . .
    Not warn 'em first and fire a warning shot?
    Like shift over, boys, you're getting close
    It's not the Second World War . . . is it?
COMMAND: We're now four thousand yards away from her
    Portside and steering the same course
    A wicked sea and choppy waves
    Some four or five metres high and fog,
    Standby and fire one off . . . OK . . .
    We'll use Mark-8 torpedoes, they're safe
    Dependable, and should get there on the day.
SAILOR: The wind's now blowing fifty knots
    Across the raging, icy sea . . .
    To put a man alive in that
    Would quietly send him first to sleep
    A few more minutes he might live
    Dreaming in his icy bed
    Until the cold has drained his heart
    And death sucks out his last breath.
COMMAND: Fire one. Forty-three seconds it should take.
SAILOR: God . . . Let them not feel any pain . . . !
    Oh Jesus Christ . . .

(Silence of forty seconds. A sea of anxious faces. One
face in pain. Will it hit?)

COMMAND: . . . A hit! . . .

(Total cheering . . . back-slapping . . . One man still frozen
in his agony . . . Sounds die out, just the faces
moving in celebration. Slow fade.)

CHORUS: The first torpedo pierced the ship like
    It was made of butter – sunk right through
    Then tore inward and upward through

Four steel thick decks . . . It spun its deadly
Groove . . . It sunk itself into its guts
And ripped its soul apart . . . The old ship
Then simply turned around and died . . .
The lights went out . . . just silence . . .

(Darkness . . .)

Dead men were everywhere, in bits.
A piece of arm and here a leg . . .
Upon the deck a figure covered in burning oil
All black and running as the heat roasted
His flesh. Three hundred and thirty sailors died at
    once . . .
The others dragged their shredded flesh
To rafts to face the icy sea, thirty-six hours more
Or less . . . The conscripts, boys of eighteen years
Stayed disciplined and kept their nerve
Each one ready to sacrifice himself to
Help an ally or a wounded friend. At
Seventeen O one just one hour more. The *Belgrano*
Sank stern first beneath the waves.
SAILOR: The dead men did not pay the price
Of peace, for others died in the selfsame
Way, when two days later in revenge
Our ships were sunk, and many died
Or were simply burned alive. . . .
SAILOR: Somebody threw the first stone
When the *Belgrano* was going home.

(On screen the following image: 'I would do it again' . . .
Margaret Thatcher. Blackout.)

MASSAGE

CHARACTERS

DAD
MUM
VARIOUS CLIENTS

AUTHOR'S NOTE

Massage is just another investigation into one of those delightful phenomena of the British way of life along with Wimpy bars, Boots the Chemist, the corner pub, Chinese take-away, chicken tandoori and the newspaper shop, all vying for attention in your average street and round the corner the latest, although not so new, Massage Parlour where your average bloke goes and gets what is endearingly called 'relief', being a simple wank aided by some viscous lubricant. 'Relief' is a choice epithet to describe the British way of sex as if the male had a painful itch or wound and needed some medical aid. The play is a bit of fun with the concept of the massage parlour as the sanctuary for men who come tormented and distraught and are sent away renewed by the dextrous hands of the woman who then reveals herself as a truly liberated female, having to deal with what would appear to be almost a subspecies of the human race, the male. Her role is the stronger of the two since she wields the power and is the possessor of the means of the relief!

No holds are barred in this sexual comedy since I wished to write something erotic, or what may be considered obscene, as an exercise in the aesthetics of this counter-culture. In the end, by freeing language, I felt that the play ceased to be a dirty play since it is open and reveals itself without deviousness or guile . . .

Massage was first performed at the Odyssey Theatre in Los Angeles in February 1997.

DAD:	Barry Philips
MUM:	Steven Berkoff
VARIOUS CLIENTS:	Barry Philips

Director:	Steven Berkoff
Producers:	Ron Sossi and Beth Hogan
Set design:	Don Llewelyn
Lighting design:	John Verd Cook
Costume design:	Roslyn Moore

SET DESCRIPTION

The stage is divided into two areas. Stage left is the 'home' area represented by a small round table and two chairs. Further downstage are an armchair and lamp. These are small islands of domestic sanctuary that can be lit and isolated from the rest. A series of screens separates areas or defines them. Stage right is a massage table tapered slightly to a perspective. On the SR screen is a shelf for the various bottles of unguents needed for the work of the masseuse. Running upstage at right angles and making the back wall is a screen painted with symbols of Great Britain. The screen needs to be backlit so as to produce a silhouette of the large erect penis of an eager client who appears later in the play. A final screen becomes the dividing wall of the two areas. Maureen or 'MUM' enters through the upstage screen and begins her speech, her theme music accompanying her. The actions relating to the sexual activities are mimed with relish and clothes are kept on.

In Massage Parlour

MUM: So many years have passed since first I found a way to
honest toil by doing what I like, that is to squeeze those
miles of cock that sausage-like have passed between these
walls / so many cocks / some small / some large / some tall
and thin have strutted and have heaved their silver pearls
upon this well- worn slab / they stand up to attention,
ready and alert and pass themselves to me, in trust that I
will shed their load and send them out into the world all
light and fresh / and ready now to face the thing in semi-
detached bliss / with me their fantasies are fulfilled / I am
the shepherdess who tends the sheep / and milks the cows,
for that is how it seems / squeeze out the nectar and the
pain / I'll rent my hand and voice / my subtle touch to their
world- weary aching ends of flesh / just aided by the finest
oil / I'll baste their swollen joints, caress and soothe, tickle
and pinch and faster now and faster doth my hand like a
pneumatic pump explore the riches down below and bore
and drill until the hit. The target / bull's eye whoosh / the
spray ascends like showers on an April morn / some
Kleenex doth remove the clues then off they go these noble
and most gallant men of England / to return to their dull
wives with sour miens / their nagging and unwholesome
shrill / who frame their dried-up lips into a ring of woe and
pour the doldrum, poison and demands of married life /
that rings and contracts they believe have given them /
(*A bowler hatted City gent enters*)
GENT: Oh woe is me let me escape and be soft putty in your
hands / I cast myself like Ulysses when he, the sirens' filthy
sound did drive him total mad / give me a massage, Sherry,
if that's your name and make it topless now as well.
MUM: For topless as you know another tenner must be paid /
plus tenner for relief / oil or powder / the choice is yours /
or take the total lot / be bold / invest another ten and I will
shed my briefs / those gossamer sweet drawers and shall
arise like Venus striding forth / as naked as the day / you'll

have me quivering there as succulent as Aphrodite and
guileful as the sphinx / my hands will touch you like you
never knew / you'll writhe like quicksilver between my flesh
/ I am the virtuoso of the wank but lest you should be
tempted and ten pounds more at that / there is a treat in
store which I reserve for only those I like / the special crest
of all the rest / the summit and the peak to make your very
bones cry out and shriek /

GENT: Pray gentle nymph / thou sweet and foul / thou noxious
temptress in these cells of red / tell me thou devil what
treasure might I avail myself without being cleaned of all
my pence and save a buck or two / so that my kids in
private school might feed and not face hunger by my
lustful greed /

MUM: Fear not kind sir nor seek high favours at low cost with
sentimental guile / with chatter of the hardship and the face
of little kids to float all pinched and hungry before my
gentle woman's eyes / I know these cool male tricks to
make a score with chicks with cheap words forged in heat
and lust, and not be paid the price for my soft woman's
paradise / the cost is high / if you cannot afford then stay at
home with tv on and pine / watch your old mate undress to
bed / and as your eyes do scan that worn-out wreck / those
gnarled legs and arse spread out to bust and think, yuk, no
sweet thrill but only wasted life ahead /

GENT: Oh honest whore / those words that trickle from your
oral, smart and lash me with the stings of truth / I pay
much more to feed the shriek at home whose constant
open mouth *keeps* wolf at door / plus two fat bonny brats
which tho' I love, between the three of them, they suck the
life from out my craw.

MUM: What does she do for you? Does she caress you like I do?
Does she anoint your prick with oil that's precious and
perfumed in musk to make it glisten like a rain-lashed oak
or carved by Michelangelo all swollen / knotted and thick
proud with mushroom head glutted in blood / the rich red
ruby racing rampant to the crest / transporting lust to the

nerve centre of it all / the emperor of the body / the stalwart
rising beast / the hungry eyeless mouth / the snake about to
spit / straining at the leash above two mighty balls rich and
filled / those oysters primed and ready to give up their
dewy pearls / I, me my woman's sting / my soft electric
thing I fantasize in you such hard-ons as you never knew
you had / I live to make you glad / that god shoved on your
end this whisper shred of flesh / this morsel / this toy that
the more you eat / the more it grows in solid hunky meat /

GENT: (*Dawning*) Aah! So there's the treat!
MUM: A mouthful of deep throat
You'll be a dog in heat
(*She takes it out and performs it.* GENT *is satisfied and* MUM *is
paid. He 'dresses' and exits. Music.*)

Domestic Bliss

(*Improvisation begins with*)
DAD: (*Reading paper*) 'Ere Maureen, look at this.
MUM: (*Offstage*) What?
DAD: What's in the paper . . .
MUM: What's in the paper?
DAD: Come and look. I can't believe it!
MUM: Believe what?
DAD: This - this 'ere.
MUM: What there?
DAD: What's written here in the paper.
MUM: So tell me!
DAD: It's amazing.
MUM: What is?
DAD: This. Come here. It makes you laugh!
MUM: I'm busy doing your breakfast.
DAD: 'Ere look at this.
MUM: Can't! I'm making your tea and doing your toast, I'm
      scrambling your egg.
DAD: Cor! It's incredible!
MUM: Well, tell me!

DAD: Read it!

MUM: I can't! I'm making the tea and de-fleaing the cat, I'm changing the nappies and cooking your eggs and frying your bacon and making the toast and washing your knickers!

DAD: Oh, so you're busy then?!

MUM: (*Enters with apron and teapot*) Well, what is it then?

DAD: Simple-minded jerks and fuckwits / mouths agape and crutch on fire / wiggle arse and love you's dripping out their stupid lips / while rock and rolling down the grotty disco / dressed like freaks that from your worst of nightmares grew to living flesh and blood / but there the semblance ends / for they to us are like to chalk and cheese / to life and death / from wholesome *Homo sapiens* to thing that from a womb wast nuked and came out like the devil had distributed his evil seed within / they follow the dull parade of clones / the dyed and painted saboteurs of all that's holy / the wreck of our permissive state zapped out on grass and smack / and I don't mean a romp in Epping Forest with your favourite tart for a taste of slap and tickle but the shit they shove into their empty skulls / so roomy that it needs the constant kick of noxious dope to prove that to itself it's still alive.

MUM: More tea, Joe?

DAD: Yeah, pour out the nectar sweet balm and elixir / the tonic for our dried-up British throats / the balm that greets our tired morning eyes / when rising from our stinking pits in Balham, Kent or Palmers Green / prepare ourselves for one more day of shirk and strike / the brown and steaming stew doth reinvigorate our will / stiffens our pride and puts the sparkle back in our jaundiced eyes / that magic brew / that simple British leaf / that greets us late at night before thick slumber wraps us up / a fag just puffed before / put out the light put out your light / oh! the bubble gurgles and it glob glob globules out the old brown pot / that heart-rending and happy sight / old browny on the table top / the pride of England / ne'er feel the stroke of bitter loss or

strife while cuppas will be there to dull the razor's edge /
and as I say farewell to this fair state / let my last taste of
England be / a nice old brown and sweetened cup of tea /
(*drinks*)
Bleedin' hell mate . . . it's bloody cold!
(DAD *moves to his armchair*)
MUM: You shouldn't talk so much.

Job Satisfaction

MUM: Last night I had a busy time I tossed off seven was
fucked by three / and gave head to ten more / so tired but
satisfied with work / my old man in armchair all well and
truly smug at home, in bliss with kids the shiny offspring of
our connubial lust, tho' lately his once almighty hard-on
has hit the dust / which to tell true is no small relief to a girl
who is engaged all day in giving same at work called 'on
the game' / tho' game it hardly is / more like a slog to get
through the assembly line of dirty dogs.

Legal Whoring

MUM: So you who scorn and look askance / you opened up
your legs when first you saw your mystery as capital / and
turned yourself into a painted bait to catch the slippery eel
/ my cunt and woman's touch it's true I sell but you would
not give all until you were well provided for! You ensnared
your men and threw your golden lasso in the air / but first
you saw the lucre in the bank / the sexual capitalist would
tease and goad / say not now darling, later on / would pout
and be all coy in lacy frills / glossy lips and French perfume
in rolling hills / would lie in wait tarantula to catch your
prey / and milk him slowly / that's your way.
You lived in quilted eiderdowns and china sets / a
bedroom spare for passing friends / and drink your
wheatgrass every day to keep those nasty cancer cells from
chewing you away / and sweat your tits off in the gym to

stop the cellulite from creeping in / a dog called Captain
runs amok among the old man's shirts and sox / you so
faithfully daily wash / you lucky bitch / for treasure lines
your flock-lined walls / your tasteless three-piece suite in
lounge and rocking chair for the old man / a ton of babies'
things to wash which stink / au pair bungs it in wash
machine / a friend who visits twice a week / oh super
darling . . .ain't she sweet / your baby's cute / she's only
two / Samantha . . . oh how lovely / shit! She pissed all
over my best suit / the garden's coming on this year / we're
growing pansies and freesias dear / you playing bridge this
afternoon / oh no, today the kids come home from school /
I love that white brocade / the curtains look so fresh and
frothy / don't Captain! Get out into the garden / Samantha!
Don't you give the dog a hard-on / leave him dear / yes, I
know it's pink / oh shit, the cat's shit in the sink / brr! brr!
Hello ma, yes I'm ok I just don't know what to cook today
/ he's getting bored / what shall I make / I know he works
hard . . . 'Evening dear' . . . a peck and then the gin
appears / nice day darling . . . 'not too bad' . . .I'm bored
to death / it's just like dad and mum when I was young /
the same desireless dreary death and boredom dandruff
and bad breath / is this the life / is this for me / you chose it
dear / you held the key / to puss in bank and made him pay
if he was to unlock your safe / you wannit then you work
and say / my pussy's sold not given away a ring a house a
signed contract / he sweats and every day he will regret /
he's bored / tough tits mister / pay you wretch / she's
whored her arse to you you git / you loved it once / you're
bored right now / too bad pal / you're stuck to the cow you
wanna scram? It'll cost you dear / she'll suck your money
better than she ever ate the thing that got you into trouble
mate! She'll drain you dry / she's good at it / she's just a
high-class whore you git / she steals from men and makes
them pay whenever she give puss away / she does it legal
like and smiles in church while ma and pa cry like two
jerks.

(MUM *returns to kitchen*)
DAD: Where's my bloody tea, Maureen?
MUM: Yeah, comin' up, don't jump out y' bloody pram.
(*MUM goes to stove*)

Home

DAD: (*Seated in downstage left armchair with his pipe*)
  What can I say as I relax in this armchair, this soft womb /
  the triumph of my years of slog / and view upon the
  coloured screen the wonders of the human race / and as
  the old bird dishes up the magic of her *cordon bleu* I slosh it
  down with half a pint to take away the taste of mush / my
  cock sits all quiet, comfortable and small at peace and
  smiling in his sable sack / digesting pleasure from the
  afternoon when like a tiger sprung he from his slack and
  concertina'ed shell to march forth into action . . . all pell-
  mell / there is a little place I go to tell the truth / a massage
  parlour on the edge of town where birds perform a little
  light relief for men that carry unwanted horn / the old bird
  she's as good as gold I can't complain but her box don't
  hold no mystery for me / I love her what can I do but when
  nature calls I just have to unload my balls / so I pay a visit
  oh once a month to keep the equipment free from rust /
  this tart she sucked me like a good 'un just to tell you
  straight / my life felt like the source of it was drawn and slid
  along the tunnel of love, my prick / it was the rocket ship
  that made its vertical ascent and soared upwards to heaven
  / my piece of red-hot rocket stood alert on pad / fuelled up
  for scorching lift-off / octane blast / all tight and proud /
  press that magic switch / the button that would send us
  spitting into space / would send the plume all white and
  shining into orbit / at last as if my flesh was inside out and
  raw / as if a fruit was peeled exposing succulently its juicy
  meat / I felt the tremor start like acres down and deep /
  within the inferno where the ache is dim, deep down in the
  abyss where chasms stretch and mountains crack / where

rocks begin to seethe and boil / and lava bakes just aching
to escape and pour into the air its bottled boiling snakes of
white-hot lust / so there I was / it cost a bundle / topless,
bottomless too / I had the lot / the works / the oil and
French or gobble at the end / straining at the leash /
buttocks compressed almost to billiard balls / I turned
myself inside out / and then like mount Vesuvius started to
spout /

MUM: More tea, Joe?

DAD: But hush, here comes the thing from whom I hide the
best part of my sting . . .
Yeah, throw some in and bung us too some holy ghost that
I might then anoint with perfumed marmalade the crusty
bread and wash it down with magic rosy lee . . . nice cuppa
tea . . .

(*Double speed mime of joyful domestic eating scene to music*)

The British Way of Life

DAD: Food for the British worker bred from the holy lineal
strain / the Viking and the Dane have put the good old
British rich blood in our veins / we fought and smashed the
filthy Hun / painted the world red from coast to coast /
from Zanzibar to Taj Mahal / the pukka sahib was master
there / we taught the darkies who's the boss / erased the
aboriginal and tossed the black man back into his shanty
town to make South Africa a jewelled crown / we showed
the Pakis how to play a game of cricket the English way the
world we made a safer place for Christians and our wives
to saunter in / and showed them Jesus, taught them sin /
then watched the millions come pouring in / and I mean
pounds not bleeding wogs / not filthy Krauts or dirty Frogs
/ but good hard British notes / a pound was worth a pound
in them good days / nowadays inflation runs so fast / you're
running like diarrhoea flows out your arse / in case you shit
your wages out before you've time to buy a snout / before
you said hey! twenty smokes it's up again / before you've

time to nosh your grub, that's why mum and me we wolf it
down whenever we go into town / in case the waiter comes
on strong and says hey mate your steak's gone up / it's one
quid more than when you stepped inside the door . . .
Cor, in olden days an Indian was just a darkie in a big
wigwam / but nowadays the high street chimes with names
like Taj Mahal and Tandoori / Eastern Star and Bengali /
the mob have come across to sink the nation in a stink of
pancake rolls and popadoms / hot curries that can make
you shit from Islington to Oxford Street / they've come
across to seek revenge and take this island back with them /
they'll stuff us full of curry that one day just one almighty
fart will blow away this septic isle / we'll float in oceans like
some almighty turd you sometimes see bobbing its little
head in the wine-dark sea / whole streets and boroughs
pound to the sound of drums and cassette decks the size of
tanks that they carry on their shoulder like a little kid you'd
give a ride / they look like blackened Martians skating
down with earphone stuck around their frizzy crown / it's
dangerous now to step outside / in your own manor lest
you collide with King Kong doing fifty miles an hour /
bung us another cuppa Maureen.
MUM: Ok, but then I've got to get to work.
(*kisses him on cheek*)
DAD: Don't work too hard.
MUM: Nah.
DAD: Ta da.
MUM: Ta da

The Whore's Story or One's Story

MUM: I've scanned the western world for cock that gallops at a
    lifted frock / we know it fades / 'tis temporary / that's why
    we add the touch of lie / with cream and powder / pout in
    pink / coyly resist in satin and stink of *eau de pong* behind
    the ears / and make them think we're little dears / small
    pussies cradled in white pants as soft as marshmallows and

tame those red-hot monsters out for game / but cock must
be attached to rocks which sparkle / rock-hard stocks and
shares in bank / and no small wanker out to use us for his
selfish gain / our box is assets / truly stored we are the
sexual overlords / the sexual capitalists of the world / so
whore and housewife are the same / they both go out to
work for loot / the one in hard cash for short time / the
other will wait until what's yours is mine. So *come to me*,
come to *me*, you men of rock whose thighs are weighted
down with balls so heavy under-used and bored / come to
me at massage house / and let my hand play out a tune /
that on your flute will make you swoon / and if you want
the topless too / and bottomless as well, just one score
more will buy the sight that men would die for / rot in hell
even to glimpse / the shining tips and ornaments / those
swelling vales and creamy sponge of silky breasts and as I
plunge your cock into my mouth, my tongue will round its
head enfurl and part my standing legs for you to plunge
your hungry hands into / I'll squirm and wiggle, pulse and
twist / I'll bite your steaming bulging prick / I'll take it deep
down far inside my throat / I'll chew it softly tender, stroke
with spit the smouldering shaft and lick the vein in the
underhalf, running my tongue along the ridge / dip the tip
into the Cyclops eye / while far below you crush and scoop
my creamy bits / my holy fruit my pomegranates / ripe raw
figs, your fingers squeeze my slit and dig / dig down, dig
deep dig far as if to rip the fruit from off its branch / and
then I squeeze your thickened shaft caress your swollen
balls and sense the pulse begin to start / the heavy blood-
swelled prick grows to its final ramrod juicy stick / the
spunk begins to rise / my mouth goes faster faster now / the
knob inflates its crest like some huge flower opened up /
your fingers still like snakes dart in and out my silky satin
mouse / oh yes the flood hot thick and white bursts
through the tunnel in fiery wet hot sticky spouts / in
creamy gooey spurts / the gates break / the flood aches
through / in waves of warm wet silvery glue / oh comey

gurgle gulp and slurp / swallow vast vats of semen down
and lick it clean / while up above your face serene just like
now the moon was free from clouds / and smiled with silly
cheesy grin / meanwhile I felt it shrink again and small like
going back into its cocoon / he gets up, dresses and y-
fronts he puts on / he reckons he's had a tasty one / I send
him out into the world all nice for wifey / his wife would
hate to do the things I do / would say I'm just a dirty whore
/ but her old man comes back for more /

Transactions

MAN *enters massage parlour*

MUM: Hello ducky / seen the menu?
      Hand relief . . .ten pounds

MAN: Oh yeah.

MUM: Topless relief. Fifteen pounds.

MAN: Oh yeah.

MUM: Top and bottomless, twenty pounds

MAN: Oh yeah.

MUM: French twenty-five and full French thirty.

MAN: Oh yeah.

MUM: Spanish thirty and Greek forty

MAN: Oh yeah.

MUM: Greek and French forty-five

MAN: Oh yeah

MUM: All-in fifty.

MAN: Oh yeah.

MUM: Reverse, Greek and French fifty five.

MAN: Mmm.

MUM: Reverse, Greek, French and Spanish, plus bondage
      seventy.

MAN: Mmm . . . what's Spanish?

MUM: Between the boobs, dear.

MAN: And excuse me, but Greek?

MUM: Anal love, love.

MAN: What's French then?

MUM: Oral.

MAN: And full French?

MUM: Oral and cum in the mouth, dear.

MAN: I see.

MUM: All right, dear . . . what would you like?

MAN: Tell you what . . . I'd like a touch of Spanish and a slice of Greek and then spring into a double reverse with a piece of French easin' off into a whisper of bondage / a grab of relief and relax into bottomless sex whip out into Greek and ending in a full French at the end.

MUM: I can't do that, can't go from Greek to French / I can go from French to Greek or you could have a two-girl bottomless-topless hand relief into bondage. A bit of tv French and whip down into Greek finishing up at Athens.

MAN: Ok. I'll have that. How much?

MUM: A hundred pounds all-in but I'll do it for fifty ok?

MAN: Ok.

MAN: (*In upstage room, behind screen*)
I paid my gelt and went into a dark red room / my flies were bursting in anticipation and I sunk into my reveries as I undid my pants / I stood in my knickers with my great sausage squashed tight and making it stiffer, I looked in the mirror and thought it quite nice as I heard muzak trickling through the flock-lined walls / there was Kleenex in the waste bin, I unpeeled my pants and out it sprang like a hoop or like a greyhound sniffing around for meat and wondering what to do . . .

(*From behind screen his silhouette is seen with a giant phallus. The actor can merely carry it in his hand and make it twitch*)

Whore's Life

MUM: Do you think I like my cunt used like a sink / a vile cesspit / a bin of stink / a crock of rotting sperm-choked drain / repository for all the pain of man who stumbles in with breath of rot and yellow grin /

(*Drunken Scotsman enters*)

MUM: His alcoholic brain in nerve-torn shreds / the last bits in the basement of his mind

SCOT: Give us a fuck, hen! (*he undresses and crawls on table*)

MUM: He sees a picture in the shit-heap room he occupies of tits and panties black / stockings held up by straps and open thighs and arse to clutch / he sees the morbid tattered pictures in his head when boredom, drunken conscious stunned only a walking thing that lives to eat and fuck and sometimes shit / a thing that staggers out at night with mates dead equal in thick leer and hate of women, soft things, animals and tears / and fears only that his dick his filthy smegma tip won't stand up when his money's out.

SCOT: (*vomits*) Oh! Sorry hen.

MUM: His heaving bloated corpse / his rotten evil smell / this junk of man / this piece of hell / still tries to get it up / still farts and burps /

SCOT: Oh, fuck it hen, I canny get stiff.. I think I boozed too much, oh shit . . . it's gone again, hang about tell me some filthy stories to make it stiff and sprout.

MUM: I tell him about whips and frightened teenagers well bound with leather straps / legs spread with downy dewy thatch / whose tears flood down and beg and cry / yet burn between their virgin mounds / for fingers, tongues and hard thick pricks to pound / she moans oh no! soft rosebud tits / small even slits he pulls apart / stares inside the flower's heart / its stamens and its pollen exposed to the lurid eye / then whip the soft pink creature make her squeal / her small tight arsehole makes you thrill / bend her over like an animal / examine all her sacred bits / explore those parts that once forbid and secret in the sanctuary of the shy / your cock grows hard by weaker creature's pain / the more it hurts the greater is your gain / you are now hero / conqueror and proud / your cock grows rampant hot and stiff the magic elixir for dick is kicking others / so hit and pinch / slap hard and whip / her eyes they open wide and beg no more but this is sweet for you and then the thick

hard shaft slides in the juicy glue and howl and scream cry
/ oh god these sounds are paradise while far below the
furnace is ablaze / your filthy dick's on fire now and shoots
its scummy load along the trail / and shrivel slurp and slop
/ wipe off /

SCOT: That's great hen, thanks a lot.

(*he staggers out*)

MUM: You and your filth you gather up / open the door and
into the night's old womb you 're swallowed up to join the
throng of human filth that teems along the gutter swill /

SCOT: (*Waiting in parlour*) So there I was / waiting in my rose-
hued room with cock as white and hard as marble / when I
thought of all the lips and eyes and tits and thighs and
sighs and hands clenched in the back row / and shy to
touch the crushy blouse whose swollen promontory housed
within the stiffened bra the marshmallow and squeezy tits
with orbs so pink and delicate that sneaked out when your
hand would clutch the melting snow and nipples sweet
would peep between your fingers / saw her knickers when
in armchair's squelchy throne her knees so high my eyes
would dive down to those svelte and mossy thighs / the
inside of those legs / whose stockings clasped like lizards'
skins and fire glowing in the grate / would wonder as I
glimpsed the ivory veil / that masked the heavy squelchy
mass of sticky schoolboy dream / the pouring lovesick
ecstasy / the juicy runny fruit / the cocky cunt / the figgy
rasp of hissy snaky pungent hole / I would so calmly lift the
gentle dress and wait for her to stop my filth caress / just
wanted now so much my hand to glide right up to where
the heat and scent and fantasy collide and knees and
squeeze and higher yet and no, her hand has censored
nothing. Still I slide now each new inch my itch-hard
hungry fingers scale the slope, another pulse of blood
pours in my prick to service what it hopes will be a fast
insertion into ecstasy / above the tongues twist round and
now one sucks and now one rolls the pink wet carpet out /
she nibbles tip of tongue and close tight eyes whose lashes

like thin spiders' legs crawl out her sweet mince pies and
still / yet still within the thunderstroke of drum pound
heart / my hand scales the warm soft silk and creamy leg
until just at the top of stocking felt the flesh the narrow
channel separating leg from crutch it was a pearly bridge I
scanned / oh sweet the heavy pound of blood / my heart
withstands the heavy thump / the furious flow / I kiss the
harder, flooding mouth and lips with all the flesh my face
can separate from skull as if by some osmosis we conjoined
or rocks whose atoms smashed into each other's grip and
now for all time were fixed / and so her lips and mine were
tight entwined who knows where hers began or where did
mine / and then the arched embrace / her head pulled back
/ my hand / rings her cotton waist / the other like a filthy
snake / dress now gathered up in folds like ripples on a
stone-pierced lake / so my hand was there along the
slippery vale / towards the honey of her soul / and soon so
soon I'd feel my fingers sense the pertinent and thin silky
ridge / and yes I'm holding harder yes I'm near / my heart
is flood in blood so red-hot current thick and then / her
crutch seemed almost now to lose itself to me and slide
towards my hand / my hand becomes my soul / my hunger,
my antennae to my lusts and greedy musts / my hand
becomes a stomach / starved and hunger struck / until my
fingers were in touch with velvet ambrosia and prick-
hungry lust / my hand then knew that gold was there and
waiting to be mined / a sparrow settled in my hand / and
then my dream and ecstasy was in my palm / my fingers
became snakes burrowing beneath the gauze / did lift the
veil so tight and yet just room enough / I pulled it back as if
peeling a skin and felt my fingers like hot knives into butter
sink / and so my fingers sank deep down and drank like
sponges parched and gasping for her touch of soft
underbellies of squids or persimmons that break and crush
open when ripe and squirt the too sweet juice into your
bite /

MUM: (*Enters*) Hello, love . . . day-dreaming?

MASSAGE

(*Mime massage to music,* MAN *lies on stomach*)
    Ok, turn over.
(MAN *lies on back, continue mime of massage*)
    I do not ask for guts hung down in tresses bobbing in the
bubbly seas / I like my pricks hung stiff like some upright
and young spring rose / not withered in a heap / cut off by
missile bullet or knife / you who squeal at this and yet
condone the rats that chew upon your babies' limbs / the
rats that carry plague of hate / hate walks in petticoats and
skirts just as easily as khaki blood- stained pants / hate
stems from thick black bile that's boiled in witches' stew /
round the cauldron we will go / in the poisoned entrails
throw / throw in frustration / dried-up cunt that for a score
of years was parched / and withered prick that died unused
crushed between pinstripe and office seat / balls hung like
prunes or mouldy figs / throw in that too / and too
repression's smelly breath to season it / and then mean
withered fingers that never knew the soft caress / no never
felt the sweetened ache of sex / no never sweetened soft
pulpy parts / throw in the pot small wizened eyes that have
the hate of basilisks / that hate the naked sight of god's
pure fruit / the living flesh / pop in those fishy eyes and stir
until it's thick and rich / then add now the viper's tongue /
the bitter lashing whip of scorn / prejudice intolerance and
greed to make this rot concoction into a rancid paste /
tongue that ne'er knew peaceful balm of love or sounds to
pour oil on the troubled seas / tongue that drinks from
casks of wrath and spews out drivel shit and waste / with
words so vile like sink and shoot to kill / attack revenge /
tongue that consigns young and brilliant boys to drown in
blood and burning oil / if everyman's your son and brother
/ father too / how could you make your pot of evil stew you
crock of filth / if only you knew how lust's sweet balm
could calm and make the temple that you occupy god-
filled / but you never knew / numb withered eyeless / senses
buried in hard crusts of scarry tissue / living at the edge of
life / the barest light from deadened batteries / so throw in

all to make this soup of death / a mass of tangled limbs
tossed in the bloody foam-flecked sea / my son and yours
sinking down deep in gore / were it yours / were it yours /
you filthy evil coward rot-gutted insult to a whore /
(MAN *lies prone on table then slowly exits left*)

The Nature of Dirt

DAD: Oh that made a nice change from all the filth outpouring
from my filthy gob / let's rather cast my mind to other
realms / like strolling down a country lane and picking
bluebells in velvet woods and feel the wind caress my brain /
see fairies dancing on a brook where sunlight hits the
rippling waves / should like to hike down endless roads /
where summer paints a golden haze / nor feel the end will
ever come / like those hot youthful endless days / so strolling
through the blackberries and scratch my knees on thorny
pricks and clutching Wordsworth tenderly I lay beside a
tickling brook / I felt the grass caress my neck / saw mighty
branches float and sway / as if by Indian eunuchs they were
fanned to brush the blowflies from my face / I lay and
thought tho' half asleep I heard the wind whisper sweet
things / saw dancing pair of butterflies dissolve like
snowflakes in the sky / an aching slumber fell and gently
folded me in its spell / I sank like stardust in the sea / or like
a pebble thrown eagerly by some small urchin / hits the wave
so hard and shatters crystal spray then slowly it sinks away /
so sank I 'neath the sound of bells from distant steeple / odd
squawks / the ripple of a brook would talk and distantly in
summer haze some thrilling laughter blazed a path to my
hideaway / yet through the deep veil of my doze heard sweet
young schoolgirls far away rejoice in schoolwork's end of
day / the bells I heard chimed four the magic hour that all
children score upon their hearts for years / the teatime four
when all of England stops / forgets their fears lays their
hammer and their chisel down / even the hangman stops /
and says not now my friend / the noose will wait / the

surgeon deep inside the brain to brilliantly remove the
source of pain / he too will nevertheless stop and pause as he
sees the theatre clock strike four

I lay there so contented on my green and silken bed then
realized oh wretch that I will not be there in village teashop
/ sanctuary / or even greasy Alf's cafe / to celebrate with all
mankind / to be the vital link that binds the souls of
England / hold the teacup trembling to my lips / close my
eyes and taste sweet bliss / but this was not to be / so I lay
back letting the slumber dull the ache of quenching that
old taste I had and soon forgot / the voices grew and then
as I was midway through oneiric land like Endymion to
sleep forever on his little grassy bank / deep in my dreams
or so it seemed to me / I saw a vision slowly walk in
schoolgirl tilted hat and thick pigtails / all glowing nubile
and so virile, strong and bursting out their bodies like a
song to nature / their cotton blouses bulged apart and
pearly buttons seemed to pop as if like young spring roses
could not be restrained from opening their petals to
nature's gaze / their brown and tawny thighs like some
great scythe cut through late summer's grass, knee high /
they slashed their way leaving a trace of giggles hung upon
the day / just like the wake rude ships upon the emerald
green do make / so deep within my hypnos cave / my lids
stitched down and fast asleep I dared not try to wake lest
this be just a dream and fast dissolve in glare of day / 'cause
dreams are sweet little things that come to tease you with
the things you dare not do or cannot have / the things you
fantasise about / would love to take into the upper air but
cannot / lest real world squeals do break your bones as they
turn you on the prejudicial wheels / but casting these dull
thoughts aside / now, came upon my ears some cracking
twigs proclaiming this dream's not all mist / I scarcely
breathed knew not if dream or bold reality stunned my
brain / I screwed all my attention to its source like radar
scan and now the sound was caught inside my web was
scrutinised inspected by taut nerves that stretched to catch

the very air caught on the breath / and now sweet thin and piping words hung on my web like fireflies / mere traces / nothing clear but now I hear a sound like 'oh Helen let's sit here' / Helen! so I even knew the name of one . . . the intimate clue, could call the sound and know its magic would resound inside her sweet ear and make her turn her face to where I lay / heart pounding like Tarquin's before Lucrece's rape

So down they sat while I in grass so tall did spy, and heard their giggling sounds add yet more music to the air so thick in warble chirp and wind that whistles through my secret lair / they came to make love to the sun and shed their girly weeds along the bank / oh hot I was and thrilled to view this yet delightful early morning dew / this unripe rose this unpicked fruit / so just as if to catch the warm and rampant sunrays 'tween their thighs she paused, chin cupped in hands as if in clouds of schoolgirls' dreamy thoughts / while down below the bulging sun did play his golden fingers o'er her mound / and my eye did send a ray of light to ensnare in the open air the sight / of her cupid sweetened and unblemished white / her shining schoolgirl flag / which now with idle fingers underwaist she scooped unpeeling like a second skin does from a snake / and up she lifts her smooth curvaceous bum / two full moons rising as the knickers slide down and one leg at a time is eased from silky cotton fantasies of schoolboys' listless classroom dreams / her small soft crest / her tender mouse was clinging on between the marble columns of her house / and then behold she lay down on the green and dewy bank / and then I saw her very flanks unfold reveal the choice part of her thighs / they seemed to glisten in the light fresh haze of summer's bee-droned endless days as a slender tulip or, like a peapod opened fresh or velvet petals of a flower all hungry for the sun's warm shafts to ooze its yellow molten thru' its heart / it opens slowly now to face the trickling hot rays of the sun's embrace / she sighs and murmurs in falsetto rippling flute, 'if only now . . .' and

this I can't believe but heard the words bruise past my ear /
heard them detonate loud and clear with . . . 'if only now I
had a man's silk prick all would be fine / a big and juicy
horn to play with' / 'hmmm' her friend agrees 'a big hard
juicy prick to stick in here . . .' when even now the thought
draws one small tear to weep for joy between my thighs
and from my throat big lusty sighs / I pinched myself in
disbelief is this a fantasy or wicked dream sent by the devil
in cunning jest that has you grasping out for snatch / your
arms around some luscious girl and then just as you're to
drink your fill awake rudely to mum in curls / but no, 'twas
not a dream / they played and frolicked endlessly / thrusting
their fingers like five keen slaves ready to obey her every
whim / they danced and played sweet lusty tunes upon her
soft and aching quim/

'Oh fuck me', one was saying now, 'oh lovely man please
fuck my lovely burning cunt / it's hot and runny dripping
for a big thick slice of horny pan' / their eyes were closed
tight in their trance so self-inflicted by sweet lust / the child
not yet broken in or satisfied by hot young roughs / so
sadly they must fantasize until some young pink prick gives
them their fill / my tool by now was like a greyhound in the
trap bursting to escape and pour its sap upon those open
flowers / whose honey spilled so wastefully on the grass / so
trembling I undid my bursting flies / I was all thumbs but
out it sprang and reared its head / the knob all big and
angry red, ready to spit its load and quench the fire down
below / where those two sweet urchins did moan / so
stealthily and not to fright I crawled through the long grass
to where the sight and smell did draw my swelling beast
and now half swooning in the summer's heat / I could
almost reach out and touch their feet / the air stood still
and hung so heavy in the perfumed auburn summer and
late afternoon while shadows crawled like inky stains / I
crept snake-like upon these maids who writhed like
thrashing waves beneath a storm-lashed sky / I thought 'tis
now / just follow where your cock will thrive / go in and say

'hello! it's good to be alive' / my penis swollen aching to be
let loose / was dragging me like some great stallion when
on its way home will start to canter when it sniffs familiar
roads / so now in twitches jumps and starts / I'm ready,
can't hold back, I'm home at last / when suddenly in that
split second beheld by thousands, insects, moles and birds.
Each keen to see the rite performed that has gone on since
life on earth unfurled / so in that second held in time / all
silent / golden warm and air like wine / so just then / just in
that split second / thighs all tense like springs ready to
pounce / so just then in that same second she awoke and
screamed 'oh fuck Helen here's a dirty bloke' . . . / her
shrieks tore from the air the fine embroidery / that had with
care been sewn / each stitch to lead to the great
masterpiece / and gazed I in sadness as I watched the two
dissolve in dust shook up by rushing schoolgirl feet and
dumbly contemplated my puzzled and now shrinking meat

    My head ablaze decided to avenge the lust that raged
within my groin / so off to local sauna / high street cheam /
the first time that I had to my local been / but now my
caution's thrown about like some great schooner on the
rampant seas that seeks a harbour anywhere just for some
peace/

MUM: Another day of blissful graft / have a nice day love / 'twas
good to see the men of England going home all happy to
their tea / no more will infants feel the bloody kick / nor
mothers nurse a blackened eye since Jack and Albert, Ted
and Fred will be released in cock and head and sit all
peaceful like before the tv set and chortle at the football /
go to bed / a quiet fart under eiderdown, g'night love / up
and down the breadth of royal England from noble prince
to dustman Bill / turn out the light love echoes still, from
voices all content with secret thrill from furtive hour with
their local whore / I've had them all bring in their joints for
basting / from blue blood cock all white and thin /
stuttering as he tries to stick it in to big black darkie whose
protuberance precedes his owner by five mins at least / so

now home to my Joe / but hush there is the bell / I suppose
there's time for one last seminal spill/

    Hello love, haven't seen you before / you're just in time/

DAD: I hope she's nice.

MUM: Oil or powder what's your choice / come sweetheart now
where's your voice / you've gone a little shy / now that's ok
/ relax we'll make it go away/

DAD: (*Aside*) *Ye gods / I dare not look around but the words
emanating from out that gob sound like my old lady / oh ye gods
/ it can't be / shit and piss and throw in arseholes too / she
sounds the same as Maureen does / oh cruel fate to torment me
like this / I am undone oh bollocks cocks and tits/*

MUM: (*Dawning*) *Hold on now, Maureen, but that back with
spotted bum like roses in a field of snow or raisins in some
porridgey scum looks all familiar like my Joe's / that voice was
gruff and tired like Joe once home from a day of selfless graft
he'd flop into armchair and burp all happy then to be indoors
with cup of tea and familiar moan/*

DAD: *Oh canker, oh rash of tosspots but that smell / those hands with
soft and squishy squeeze seem by me to have been seen in other
places like and shall I guess / washing up dishes in our old nest /
oh cock and Arsenal Spurs as well / Bobby Charlton throw in
the lot / I'd trade to get me out of this hell spot.*

MUM: *Oh cock and sausages that turn to snakes oh blast of hell that
now within my gut awakes the serpent gnawing / now undone
the trick has been found out / the tide of money that flowed like
spunk / with ease has now been washed back with acid bite and
cobra's lash/*

DAD: *Oh god / let the floor open up and swallow me / whole like
Jonah was by the mighty whale / and then spat out in some new
place where she could never see my face / my shame inscribed my
habit exposed with trousers down / no teeming hard-on now but
shrunken rose/*

MUM: *Aye, 'tis true / my old man wandered in no doubt informed by
some vile snooping lout some bastard perchance strolling in
informed him that I work in sin or so they call it / those that
sneak off in a secret hour for subtle flick of wrist or hire flower*

*that ignites those parts that other wives fail to reach / they have
informed on me / those dirty beasts/*

DAD: *Hang on, before my shame and guilt take hold as doth a noose
to hang me high / then what's my old lady doing looking spry /
so this is where the filthy whore did dwell / my wife was milking
cocks in this red-lighted stinking pit of hell / oh farewell peace /
oh farewell joy / my wife's dear precious cunt was just for all the
world a thing to use / their toy!*

MUM: (*Deciding to come clean*) Hello love / what you doing here?
/ doth come to spy upon your wife I fear / some nasty turds
have spun some foul and horrid verbs inside your ear / all
right I confess it's true / what next / divorce or shame / so
kick me out / you've caught me on the game/

DAD: (*Aside*) *Thank god she thinks I only came to spy / I did not
know my trouble and strife / my darling wife was in the market
of open flies / but she thinks I came to discover this hornet's nest
/ this darkened hell hole of the pumping wrist / and oh my
precious Maureen's mixed up in this / I'll be an actor . . .*

You filthy slag! you dirty whore / I could not believe of
those that told me what goes on behind this door / my
darling wife has flogged her rose / my flower / my
ornament of joy / my sceptre / my own doughnut / the furry
cunt that's probably seen the cocks of half the town / that's
tossed its shekels into your greasy pockets / oh rage / oh
slimy mildewed canker / lukewarm tea / choirs on telly /
pubs closed at three / the Rolling Stones and Vera Lynn /
oh curses high and foul on thee / take Thatcher Charles
and Princess Di / I curse on thee that whole foul tribe!

MUM: Oh how your words do thrash like whips and cut my
heart and soul to bits / my husband ne'er again will rest his
head / all snoring in our precious bed / who needs the cash
the filthy dough when in the end your karma knows and
hurls it back like hailstones hard and sharp / it tears the veil
perfumed but thin / the stinking lard comes thru' and foul
corruption too / but know my sweet I did it for us both to
line our future with some easy dough / and gave some
comfort on the way / to those who at the end of slog in

factory and pit have no sweet mate to take the ache and
pain from it /

DAD: How foul you toad / you whore / who knows now oh god!
maybe I'm carrying some obnoxious sore / that's slowly
eating away poor me/

MUM: No sweet fear not / their weapons always were well
sheathed / no never was abused I swear / and checked by
doctors / everywhere who vouschsafed my purity and health
/ I could not don't you fear conceal by subterfuge deceit or
stealth some canker that would eat away your health.

MUM: Oh god / oh shatterer of souls / oh blinding light / remove
from me this awful sight / let me escape from seedy pit
where snakes unroll their foul spit and let me suck down
good old high street air which is like nectar or ambrosia
compared to this unwholesome lair/

MUM: Forgive me, Joe / give me a chance / I'll give up / never
more to swing a leg or shake a wrist to make pneumatic
dance / the money, let it rot and stink/

DAD: (*Aside*) *Now hang about / let's not excite our wrath / we're out
the storm, I'm safe in harbour / do not bite the hand that feeds /
the horn of plenty she has tapped . . . or squeezed / why throw it
out/*

   (*To her*) So what's it all about?

MUM: What . . .?

DAD: I mean to say like I can understand . . . / you need a little
more than I / can rustle up in weekly skive/

MUM: No, I will give it up / I swear Joe / I will work in Woolies'
[Woolworths'] or elsewhere / if you will have me back / oh
Joe I'm on the rack / I'll scrub floors / anything to take
away the sting of being just a whore/

DAD: You make a bundle every week.

MUM: I make enough to make our future sweet/

DAD: You'll bring it home and split it you and me.

MUM: You mean to say . . .

DAD: (*Emotional*) Why give up such lucrative pay?

MUM: Oh Joe, you'll be a pimp!

DAD: Who cares / who wants to save and scrimp / now I'm

getting over the first shock / I now admire / no talk of sin /
free enterprise / there's gold in cock / we have to adjust
now to the times / and morals are ok for those who can
afford to be so wise / but us who get screwed every day /
aye there's the rub for who would bear the whips when
there's a fortune to be made in pricks / so doll I say I do
forgive your ways/

MUM: Oh Joe / I'm overcome with joy / we'll be a partnership
you'll see / toys I'll buy that will delight all free from
grubby tax collector's greed / and when our fortune's made
a house in sunny Spain and swim and bake/

DAD: Sounds good to me love / so I do forgive and beg of thee /
since I am here and to tell true am slightly turned on by
your gear / if you would donate free my dear / one of your
samples for a treat / I'm feeling like a dog in heat/

MUM: Oh Joe / it's been some time since you have wished to
dip in mine/

DAD: Must be the atmosphere or role / for now I must confess /
I find you rather more exotic now I see my wife's a whore /

MUM: Oh Joe, you've made me proud / I'll give you what you
ever dreamed / unleash your fantasies to me and I'll give
you the best you'll see / describe the innermost dark secrets
of your soul / your bestial cravings / anything goes!

DAD: Er . . . I tell you what . . .I think I'll have relief today . . .
with topless too, if that's ok?

(*Mime massage*).

(*Blackout*).

LUNCH

CHARACTERS

MAN
WOMAN

AUTHOR'S NOTE

Two people meet on a bench in a park near the sea. It could be anywhere. The man sells the most humiliating item of uselessness that he could find to foist on to the public . . . space. He sells space in one of those cheap magazines that nobody has ever heard of. I did this once. The magazine would put the names of established and famous firms inside their pages to convince the innocent small printers and tradesmen to buy a half page. I trundled round Stoke Newington with the papers and forms in my briefcase. It was a good old life. I lasted one day. So naturally I used this experience to describe my growing awareness of the space in my own life and this profession seemed an apt metaphor for the male who is hollow and tries to give himself to the woman, who quickly realises the void within him but not altogether void. It's filled with the debris of expected performance, vanity, shallowness and sexual exploitation. Through their mutual catharsis the man learns how easy it is to be honest and reveal himself and how painless it is to do so since we are all afraid of revealing some shallowness we are convinced is at the bottom of all our good intentions.

Lunch was first performance on 19 December 1983 at the King's Head, London. The cast was as follows:

MAN	Ian Hastings
WOMAN	Linda Marlowe
Director	Linda Marlowe
Designer	Linda Marlowe

Empty space bathed in a cool white light – faint music being played –
strange discords which italicize the action from time to time. A beach
anywhere. A WOMAN *sits by a table, she is facing the sea, a deserted*
beach café. MAN *enters frame from left to right. He sees her –*
enormous reaction – freezes. He seems unsure whether to come or go.
So just stares.

She senses him behind her – they hover thus for a moment, she
aware, still, eyes chasing from left to right.

He, as if to pounce – stealthy, but still, eyes boring into her – two
animals caught in each other's fear. He edges forward as if casually,
carrying a briefcase.

MAN: (*Aside*) Beautiful, oh she's beautiful – who is she waiting
for – no one for me –? Her neck soft as a baby's thigh – I
could bite valleys out of it. I could . . .

WOMAN: (*Aside*) Turn around . . .? No, that's an invitation –
who is he – throbbing silently as a shadow behind me –
burning holes in my back.

MAN: (*Aside*) To go up to her – gently slide up like a ghost . . .
kiss the nape of her neck – then she'd murmur softly – soft
as bees and offer her mouth to me like a hungry bird.

WOMAN: Poor beast . . . he's dumb . . .

MAN: Hungry bird . . . mouth open . . .

WOMAN: Shy – he wants to – talk – he should . . . (*Turns her
head quickly.*)

MAN: (*Startled*) Right through me she looked . . . straight
through me . . . I didn't exist . . . I was a tree.

WOMAN: He could . . . he should . . . his mouth . . . aches to
speak . . .

MAN: JAWS LOCKED! . . . TONGUE ROOTED INTO MY MOUTH . . .
granite . . . speak now, or remain mute . . . dumbstruck . . .
Dead
(WOMAN *moves as if to leave.*)
No, no not yet! Budge not thy heavenly bum . . . petal-lined,
proud, strutting . . . Not yet . . . Heat-filled bitch of a
thousand juices! Not yet.

WOMAN: Too late . . . too late, soon . . . Quickly!

MAN: Walk past . . . casually sit . . . Speak! Shout!? No, I'll go
away . . . coward . . . Oh, you terrible priapic coward –
cock hard . . . gut soft . . . coward.

WOMAN: I can't say anything . . . can I?

MAN: Too late – too late – the heart aches – the shock would be
too great.

WOMAN: A pity – he was nice.
(*She has begun – so she must go.*)

MAN: What words ensnare? – captivate – enchant – rape – suggest
– amuse – interest – stun . . . (*To her*) Lovely day!

WOMAN: Yes – yes it is really lovely!

MAN: So many lovely days we're having – all at once.

WOMAN: Suddenly . . .

MAN: You would think it could be summer.

WOMAN: You would think so.

MAN: Yes we're lucky.

WOMAN: Certainly we are.

MAN: Do you mind? (*Seat.*)

WOMAN: Please do.
(*They briskly examine each other.*)

Alternate:

MAN: Blue eyes nice – I like
that – fullness in lips, soft
. . . skin smell, legs
crossed, skirt short . . .
darker recesses leading to
the various succubi and
incubi swarming in her
panties, those gardens of
cotton roses, a child
wandering through hot
gardens . . . those smelling
summer times . . . I love
her . . . (*Easy movement.*)

WOMAN: (*Rapid*) Brown eyes
nice – hair dark soft –
hands strong big . . .
worrying thoughts . . .
swimming nose,
eyebrows, teeth, mouth –
avaricous – devouring –
like to be – now – who is
he – what does he – how
does he – bird-like –
hawk-like predator . . .

MAN: The sea is calm today.

WOMAN: I like it like that – the way it churns in – chasing itself
– not boiling or seething . . .

MAN: Dissolve on shingles as if grabbing with large tentacles . . .

WOMAN: A pile of coins – like coins slipping through its fingers as it retreats . . .

MAN: Tentacles not fingers . . .

WOMAN: It moves – a wave moves like a mole under the water . .

MAN: Or a rat under the carpet . . .

WOMAN: A long wave pushes, pushing until it collapses.

MAN: A fatigue of spume – spent froth white spume . . .

WOMAN: A long last gasp, phew!

MAN: Look at the sea! Like several hurdlers . . .

WOMAN: Racing – legs outstretched . . .

MAN: Relay runners, passing baton . . .

WOMAN: OH! Now they're collapsing.

MAN: The other runner is taking it – now he too collapses.

WOMAN: I like the sounds – lik-lak against the shingle.

MAN: He's sliding back into the arms of a dying wave.

WOMAN: They greet with much murmuring . . .

MAN: More a barely audible whisper – not close friends . . .
  (*Pause.*)

WOMAN: I like the hurdler best – I can see that.

MAN: I like watching them race to the finishing line.

WOMAN: The sun's high in the sky – so heavy . . .

MAN: A fine breeze slides across our faces like cobwebs . . .

WOMAN: The sound of the sea is like whispered thunder . . .

MAN: Thin orgasmic little gasps . . .

WOMAN: That rock looks like a huge claw – frozen as if it pounced on what it shouldn't.

MAN: Little wavelets bob and bow at its base.

WOMAN: Unctuous, spittle, boot-licking – toe-cleaning.

MAN: I thought I felt the earth shift.

WOMAN: It's a lovely day.

MAN: I think you're lovely – too. (*Aside*) HER BUTTOCKS ARE SAILING ON TO MY HAND LIKE A TEA CLIPPER ON ITS MAIDEN VOYAGE BOUND FOR HER ANTIPODES.

WOMAN: (*Shyly*) Strange thing to say on a beach – in your shirt and necktie.

MAN: '. . . rich and modest, but asserted by a simple pin.'

WOMAN: 'They will say: "But how his arms and legs are thin!"'

MAN: 'Do I dare
Disturb the universe?'

WOMAN: 'In a minute there is time
For decisions and revisions which a minute will
reverse.'

MAN: My name is Thomas – Tom to you.

WOMAN: Oh, good – you could have been Bert – I'm so glad –
I'm Mary.
(*Silence.*)
You're not on holiday? What do you do?

MAN: (*Aside*) Desperate finger acrobatics . . . cruelly exposed
electric thigh encases, sheathed . . . my birthday present . . .
(*To her*) Selling mostly.

WOMAN: Mostly selling . . .?

MAN: Space – mostly, I sell spaces of space, acres of nothing.

WOMAN: (*Disappointed – only a travelling salesman*) Oh . . . !

MAN: (*Aside*) She said – her face collapsing – rephrasing herself –
adjusting its concaves and shades – refocusing past me . . .
she crosses her legs, quick sound of surfaces abrasing –
signals of soft regions, the promised land . . . Boredom seeps
through – vinegar through milk . . . 'Oh!' – a collapse of the
lungs – expiration of interest.

WOMAN: (*Gentle tolerance*) I'm sorry – I didn't mean to sound
bored.

MAN: (*Quick aside*) She said, sounding bored.

WOMAN: More surprise really at selling nothing – how can you
sell nothing – a salesman sells something – he must do . . .
mustn't he? Something tangible – tactile?

MAN: I'm different, I sell the promise of something – the
intangible mystery of an empty space – pure white virgin,
untouched, waiting for a buyer to claim – to insert his
identity, his wares . . . his amazing declarations . . .

WOMAN: A trade book . . . ! A trade book! You sell space in a
trade book?

MAN: I promise trade in a space book.

WOMAN: How, promise?

MAN: When the book is full – when the white spaces are bought – those infinite columns of expected wealth – I sell the book.

WOMAN: To whom?

MAN: To them – to the clients themselves, the space buyers, so they can gaze at themselves immortalized forever in block letters – electro-type on quarto double-weight.

WOMAN: Lovely!

MAN: Yes . . . when the space is bought we go to press – printing blocks set up, letterpress, text, matter of context, put out first proof, check it . . . supplement the appendix . . . print a duodecimo for special customers then rush it out.

WOMAN: Exciting!

MAN: They open their books greedy yellow fingers . . .

WOMAN: Like fat worms?

MAN: Yes! Search for their spaces to see themselves described forever in cuneiform characters – they like that . . . Cigarette?

WOMAN: Thanks.

MAN: Do you want to buy some space?

WOMAN: Me?

MAN: How many of you are there? Yes, you.

WOMAN: (*Simply – wishing it were otherwise*) I have nothing to sell.

MAN: Hmmm . . .

WOMAN: *Have* I?

MAN: (*More edge*) Hmmm – you could have – find something – everybody's got something – some one thing – even the successful have got something . . .

WOMAN: All I have is a name.

MAN: That's all you need – sell that – have a half-inch single column, just your name in uncial lettering – you'll excite their imaginations – they'll create dream worlds containing their idealized female – suiting every situation . . . you'll fulfil their fantasies, become a mind-real, homogeneous. Flickering through the hardware section they'll come to your name sitting there like an unfulfilled hope . . . the ink of your nomen stinging their pupils – gently grazing them with mesmeric fantasies – they'll know you in a thousand different ways and shapes, hundreds of colours, textures, smells . . .

WOMAN: (*Smiling*) My name will do that?

MAN: Their minds will do that – but your name, your explosive sibilant sigh will ease the first scab off those old love wounds.

WOMAN: I'm not sure – no, that I want those fat-fingered men dividing me up in their nasty abattoirs – taking me to pieces, examining me . . . imagining me . . .

MAN: You'll feel nothing – not even the tick under the skin as imagination catches desire by the tail.

WOMAN: I will, I'll sense . . . things . . . hundreds of little rays eating me up – my name belongs to me . . . I'll sense things – silent buzzes in the air – hovering invisible gnats . . . biting . . .

MAN: (*Quick aside*) Sensitive, sentient being, a mare trapped in a spider's web – a diastole in the heartbeat . . .

WOMAN: Revolting men, fat, wheezing behind desks in dirty offices . . . Ugh!

MAN: Clean mostly – sterile bright, shining world – the men fractured into brackets, parenthetically courteously explaining, or else in italics 'No, thank you . . . we've all the space we need, thank you, you're welcome, thank you . . .' At five o'clock the exodus – they stream out like diarrhoea . . .

WOMAN: You sound like high pressure – hissing from cracked pipes.

MAN: I'm no pressure – I dissolve into fat and slide under the door – staining the concrete stairs on the way down – those thousands of white – dirty – grey concrete stairs that have gnawed my feet away – choked on the dust – fine dust that concrete secretes – the salesman's disease – bang-bang, up the stairs then slither down in a visceral pool of grease dragging nerve endings, plasma and intestines . . . re-form on the pavement – plunge the eyes back in – the shirt has dissolved into my flesh – become an outer skin . . . Recoup in the ABC – salesman's filling station – pump in the hot brown bird vomit – the others are just sludging in, their faces

slapped pure with rejection, the waitress, sliding around the
dead grease – falling apart at the seams, slithers her knotted
varicosity towards me and for a treat smashes some aerated
bread down my throat which dissolves into a dust, white dust
– like concrete dust, atrophying delicate nasal
membranes . . .

WOMAN: Don't you like your work?

MAN: Love it! Every moment, every earth-shattering cosmological
moment of it . . .

WOMAN: Even your dissolving agony?

MAN: That especially – you know the thrill of exploring this
fascinating city – meeting all those interesting people –
several square feet of flesh float up to you – not to you
directly but somewhere adjacent – dabbling in your
circumference . . . polite neatness glazes back at you, and
you shuffling sweaty lump – lift broken, spine snapped,
eyes at twenty-five watt, glint stumpy teeth, not exactly a
smile more a grimace of pain at the halitosis in your breath
escaping between your teeth like pistons . . .

WOMAN: (*Sickened*) I must go – but it's been nice talking to
you. (*She whisks herself past him. He jumps up and pins her
violently against the table.*)

MAN: (*Continuing*) . . . he may even buy some space to escape
your trajectory of rotting plumbing but usually the
protective secretaries have warned him of your arrival –
'He's tied up, in conference' etc. – they nose you crawling
up the stairs – they're ready – alert as vultures . . . willing
you out but wanting to tear you to pieces – behind the
door other creatures are lurking, grey-faced salesmen with
smiles stitched on to their faces hovering like bats waiting
for you to go . . . Trembling lest you take an order . . .
eyes bulging like grapes . . . order books stained with dead
egg yolk the memory of which long since mercifully
obliterated by some tired old intestine . . . so I come here
for an hour to look at the sea, to escape from it – Oh, by
the way, have a sandwich. (*Opens his briefcase.*) They're
really lovely, and you have a choice – Oh come on, they're

beautiful, made with my own hands, which should add to
the excitement . . . Go on please.

(*In persuading her he has spilt sandwich on her lap.*)

WOMAN: Oh dear – I've just had it . . .

MAN: Cleaned? Here let me . . .

WOMAN: No, don't you're making it . . .

MAN: Worse? I'm terribly . . .

WOMAN: Sorry? Never mind – I must be off anyway.

MAN: Better still – have some soup – it's delicious like
Grandma makes it. (*Takes out bottle.*)

WOMAN: (*Rising*) No! Just leave me alone, will you?

MAN: Sit down! I'm not finished. (*Aside*) Tension's up, she's
become an ice lolly in a whirlwind.

WOMAN: I'm late.

MAN: Sit, animal. To heel! What is this, a cabaret? Go? Is that
what you do? Where are your manners – you call the act
and then walk out – what? You can't like the service? The
sandwiches? Me? All three? In that order – I'm not so bad
really, times are hard in the trade but things could be
worse, you could have done far worse, you should see
some of the casualties wandering around here playing
pocket billiards, but as long as you've got a pound in your
pocket, you don't have to ask anyone for nothing as my
mother used to say . . . a shine on your shoes, a nice
cutaway collar on a van Heusen shirt, you can sit in the
Golden Egg, have a nice cup of coffee, a chocolate éclair,
hold your head up and be a gentleman . . .

WOMAN: Goodbye then.

MAN: Aaaa . . . ! Wait.

WOMAN: I'm late . . .

MAN: Please . . .

WOMAN: I don't want any space.

(*He collapses in chair.*)

MAN: What do you want?

WOMAN: Nothing.

(*He walks over and kneels at her feet.*)

MAN: I'm here.

(*He puts his hand over her calves – she does not move – they remain silently.*)

WOMAN: No thanks – but thanks all the same.

(*She attempts to move but he holds her legs firm.*)

MAN: What's that mean?

WOMAN: No – that's what it means.

MAN: (*Imploring*) Two minutes more – I have something to tell you – marvellous wonders!

WOMAN: I've heard it – entertaining it's been – but I must go please – please let me go, please . . .

MAN: Don't you like me?

WOMAN: (*Weary*) Me . . . ? Like you . . . ?! Don't . . . !

MAN: What were you waiting for?

WOMAN: No one – I like sitting here – alone – that's how I like to be sometimes, I just sit here looking at the sea . . .

MAN: You were waiting! Yes, you were – I smelt your heat from across the beach. Your scent hung in the air like a pollen count – it commingled with the salty ozone and fish and sea, lost itself, but my quivering nostril located your particular waves – hound-dog-like sniffed it out, untangled it from the smell of fish and hamburgers fried, candyfloss, fags and dead sharks; located your special delicate whiff and zoned into it like radar. You were twitching for me, for somebody – yes you were – what did you expect, Gregory Peck? Or do you like the drama, the chat? It gives you satisfaction to be chatted to – sense of adventure – dallying with the mad unknown – weird stranger on the beach . . . picked up . . .

(*She attempts to go.*)

No, stay, you don't want to go back to the bare room, vinyl-lined, do you . . . ? Alone – rattling round four walls except for those flying ducks flight-frozen in dust, your frustration banging off them, the walls not the ducks, the street full of couples sliding happily across your windowpane past dead flies (feet saluting heaven) . . . and you pacing around waiting for the phone. So you come here for your adventures – to dispel the agony or share it.

WOMAN: I have a home and a husband and no agony to share –
so let me go!

MAN: Ooh! A husband – but there's not the joy there was, eh
. . .? So you compensate a little – inject the marriage with
a little spice to hold the structure together – I know how
you feel . . . the same body lying next to you night after
night after night – over and over again – it's sickening isn't
it . . . ? Search for the mad adventure of the first or second
time when you clawed each other apart as if you could
discover, as if you could wrench the secrets from that
ticking body – oh the terrible adventure of a first time . . .
Hurtling yourself at that marvellous machinery of joy –
assaulting, exploring its labyrinthine pleasure grounds . . .
Satin-lined, lovely warm corridors, armed with rubber
teeth and special scented sauna rooms and ice-cream
parlours . . . Don't you wake up with that snorting
creature and for a second imagine that he could be –
something – one else . . . All this fantastic energy
burning holes in our stomachs – all this shock tissue dying
from unuse . . . Don't you ever want something else? Yes,
that's why you come here. Here I am for you – here you
are for me . . .

WOMAN: Nothing . . .

(*He walks over and kneels at her feet.*)

MAN: Here I am.

(*He puts his hands over her calves – she does not move – they
remain silently.*)

WOMAN: You're not looking for me – you're looking for *it*! Any
it, like a dog you sniff all the lamp posts . . . panting,
licking anything that comes your way, if it moves, sniff it,
that's you, you salesman of nothing, you canine groper.

MAN: (*Aside*) Calves hard as sculpture, warm as roses . . .

WOMAN: Wherever you drag your failure you leave a penetrable
whiff, a sour old fag smell – a whine, a hum of decaying
dreams and festering ambitions – it lingers in the air like BO.

MAN: (*Aside*) The blood's pumping – veins enlarging – shifting
masses in the flesh stir with life – the shoots begin to move

– the earth aches – the ache enlarges. THE EARTH BEGINS
TO SHIFT!

WOMAN: You demonstrate your wares like rotting garbage –
you woo like a leper – your expressions are the buried side
of a stone, moving with strange fetid life – dark, decayed,
small scraping movements in the earth – odd creatures
black and runny . . . or crawling . . . what the cat paws but
carefully with distaste –
(*He puts his hands round her hips; holding her more and more
tightly – she remains passive.*)

MAN: (*Aside*) Skulls pounding – a rat-tat-tat murder – blood
soaks the brain, lids twitch and pupils dilate, skin stretches
taut inside, everything taut, tight inside, outside – drums
banging lubricious symphonies – trembling cadenzas –
everybody take your partner – follow the rhythm, together –
millions dancing the maniac jerk, the viscous spasm . . .

WOMAN: (*Not moving*) Take your hands away – your grimy,
greedy little fingers – take them . . . *ay-way* . . . every pore
a little hungry sucking nerve-centre drinking sensation . . .
go away . . . your little slimy worms annoy . . .

MAN: I'm going –I'm going – I'm going, I am going . . . soon . . .

WOMAN: Now.

MAN: Soon – you *can* go – yes, you can go . . .

WOMAN: Now.

MAN: Soon, soon, soon – then you *can* go . . .

WOMAN: Now – now let me go – *please* now –

MAN: Soon, *please* soon – go soon – not now – not yet. (*Rising
tone*) Not *now* – not *just* yet – not *so* soon . . .

WOMAN: (*Weakly*) You're defeating me!

MAN: No quarter – burst through . . .
(*Pause, during which she collects her strength for the climax – to
hurt and be hurt. She beats him frantically.*)

WOMAN: Bite me. Bite snake! Bite loathsome! Draw blood –
drink, drain me – you! You are a loathsome beast –
searching and sniffing – your antennae alert as stretched
tendrils – sensing out, sending waves creeping through the
air, crawling stains of blood through laundered sheets . . .

(*He puts his hands round her neck and gently squeezes.*)

MAN: I want to murder you – draw your life out into me . . .

WOMAN: Murder me – you foul joy – you conquered
    repugnance!
    (*Blackout. Music . . . the amplified sound of flowers opening.*
    Their voices could be prerecorded.)

MAN: I tore into her body's haven
    ripped off rose-petalled flesh
    sucked from a host of seething fountains
    her sweet rich sanguine life

WOMAN: She said
    devour me all
    leave not one sliver
    not one small clue of silken down
    with tenderness he tore my heart out

MAN: Then bit into the puzzle of a frown
    imbibed, engulfed, devoured her . . . all!
    even her arms, long white and thin

WOMAN: No fragment left he of me sacred
    no faint opacity of skin
    not one square white unstained by him
    (*End of blackout. When the lights come up their clothes and*
    physical state could suggest a swift fuck.)

MAN: Anyway, so I suppose . . .

WOMAN: What do you mean?

MAN: It was nice . . . yes . . .

WOMAN: Nice . . . ? For who?

MAN: Not you . . . ? Not nice for you . . . you mean?

WOMAN: Like a fire engine, putting out . . .

MAN: A fire? You! A fire, *you*!

WOMAN: You died from exhaustion on the trek – you didn't
    rouse a twitch – or heat a pale flush . . . 'no quarter' 'burst
    through'! You couldn't burst through an ice-cream in a
    heat wave!

MAN: That black hole in your face squares into a tunnel of
    love . . .

WOMAN: You are a dirty little man.

MAN: Crawling words creep out like spiders from your ancient
gob . . .

WOMAN: I do *believe* you dissolve into fat and slither under doors
– you look like something that dissolved and recomposed
with the bits and pieces off the floor – misshapen – lumpen –
that's failure for you – a man who can't sell nothing – or
make *something*!

MAN: Aah! What do you know you lump of fornicatory stew,
dolloping up bits of your overcooked goo . . . what do you
know! Who can linger on that – it . . . it (*Imagines her body
– miming*) falls apart in your hands – fingers don't find
resistance – strong, muscular, cellular resistance of filth-
packed flesh, no they just sink into you – loose masses of
wobbling, like a pack of dirty stories in aspic . . .

WOMAN: You're a real funfair comic – you're the woodlice that
one finds buried in bars telling the dirty stories you'll never
play in – stand in! Understudy!

MAN: Never play in?! I star in my own melodramas, long runs,
you one-night stand you!

WOMAN: I have a husband, I am to him, my husband, a veritable
drama of sensual events . . . that's what I am – a panoply of
exquisite variations . . . To him that's what I am, beside him
you dissolve – you're androgynous, on you it's an ornament!

MAN: Your husband never makes the love to you you think he
makes, but via you he is loving. Whilst you pant together
exchanging your sweat and stink, his imagination's taking
him to dreamland – you're just his launching pad, his
receptacle for his journeys into outer space where his
dollies lie waiting for him – his icy maidens fixed like cold
glittering stars ready to perform wonderful feats of
endurance . . . but wait until their light dies – just wait
until then – because so will you . . . a pack of memories,
marriage . . . other people's . . .

WOMAN: You are a poisonous spider – you really are . . .
poisonous. Yes, you even look like one – a crawling garden
spider, no not garden – the thing that darts out of dirty
cupboards, that you step on . . . FAST – yes, you do . . . My

husband loves me – yes he does – he loves me and soon it will be time to go home and prepare his supper – he comes keenly – lovingly in – expecting little kitchen noises and smells . . . he brings the cold wintry air in with him . . . smelling of train fumes and of Aqua di Selva – all fresh – a rough chin tickling me, his smells reassuring me – all familiar . . . and he loves me – really and hugely LOVES, and I make him his favourite meals his mother once made him and we eat and watch TV – not plays, or quiz shows, serious things, *Man Alive, Panorama* – we discuss them afterwards and he writes long eloquent letters to *The Times* about injustice – but they never publish them . . . He's full of goodness – exudes it like vapour – it clings to the walls of the room – every room . . . it reaches into the grain of the furniture – becomes part of them, part of me, so secure, cocoon-safe . . . six-ten each evening, his tinkling key in the lock, his hat on the stand faintly grease-stained – his himness coming in – hard, masculine himness wrapping the house with blankets of love . . . and just so he comes in the door, he whistles, so as not to alarm me, so I know it's him – not anyone else, but him – not a burglar or a murderer, a little whistle (*whistles three notes*) and if I'm in the kitchen I whistle back so he knows I'm there – not gone – not died – a victim of GBH or gang-bang angels leather-winged – but there in a perpetual way, like he faces me square on, direct and coming to me, always to me . . . even when not facing me he's coming to me, his thoughts, murmurs, hungers, desires, always reaching me and mine him, so our invisible webs are always gripped even miles apart . . . I finish his sentences, he collides with mine, anticipate his wants – I don't need anything else – don't certainly need you . . .

MAN: No – I'm not a whistling Aqua di Selva-ed square-on . . .

WOMAN: No – you're not square-on – you're oblique – you enter from the side – or the back – like an unseen fist – one only sees the shadow before impact, clenched malice – you –

MAN: No, malice clenched I'm not – a caressing angel more like.

WOMAN: A fist – all of you, a fist, to strike – you caress with your fists to be ready – curled ball of furious venom – be anything else, you couldn't.

MAN: I'm not a fist – my hands are soft – they caress – protect DELICATE THINGS . . . Make flowers grow, life appear, make people happy, women giggle, cats purr, dogs wag . . .

WOMAN: Goodbye then finally.

MAN: Goodbye.

WOMAN: Yes, goodbye.

MAN: Goodbye – go on . . . be home for six-ten – don't break your cocoon, soft-silky warm places should be protected – mad, you are, to be doing with me.

WOMAN: I'm sorry.

MAN: What sorry! Sorry that – sorry for . . . ? What?

WOMAN: Sorry – just sorry.

MAN: That's me, yes, oblique, the darting rat in the corner of your eye . . .

WOMAN: (*Encouraged*) Be careful . . . you're . . .

MAN: (*Showing his hand*) No fist – look (*A silence – he and she just look uncertain.* WOMAN *slowly takes one hand in hers.*)

WOMAN: You've uncurled . . .

MAN: The sea's stopped moving, the earth pauses . . . for a moment . . .

WOMAN: The tide has gone far out . . .

MAN: It begins to return, lovely, I think you are . . .

WOMAN: The sea is lovely and you . . .

THE BOW OF ULYSSES

CHARACTERS

MAN
WOMAN

MAN: So.

WOMAN: Yes?

MAN: You took the best years of my life . . . the best . . . my
   productive years . . . the years I could be fruitful . . . the
   years I could have still been ripe enough . . . to attract a
   bird . . . like a fruit on a tree . . . ripe . . . a little overripe
   but still sweet . . . still with some juice left. Some taste left,
   some desire left, if you like. I had that left . . . some resin
   . . . pap, or flavour. I had that all those years . . . ripeness
   and fecundity, and wasted . . . just wasted. Dead. Like a
   fruit fallen to earth, unpicked and rotting . . . ripened and
   split . . . fly-blown . . . pitted with worms. I still could have
   attracted a bird, a beautiful bird . . . an exotic
   multicoloured bird of paradise. Instead I was left to rot . . .
   hanging in the sun . . . rotting, shrivelling even, yes . . . my
   flesh hangs as I decay like wax in the sun . . . it starts to
   fall, hang, loosen, like wax . . . leaving the bone. Under-
   used cells give up their elasticity . . . not driven by the fires
   of passion . . . so they give up. Decay. Atrophy. Lose hold
   of their grip on life . . . lose their grip on the bone . . .
   loosen, fall away . . . held only by threads . . . just threads
   holding my face on my skull . . . but I was vital . . . my
   vitality shone through . . . it lit up a path. I had horn.
   Power. Pulse. And I gave it away . . . or let it decay . . .
   under-used . . . festering. A giant orchid festering . . .
   curling slowly at the edges. Neglected. Yes, uncared for
   . . . gathering dust. Yes, gathering dust like a flower put in
   a darkened hallway of an old house. An old aspidistra
   gathering dust in an old, green, Victorian bowl . . . they
   went those years, went, just dissolved, crumbled away. I
   was used, useful, kept you company. In fact kept you.
   Used I was, like you feed off a cow or ants feed off the
   queen. Is that what they do, I don't know? Something like
   that, like you keep something on which you feed, suck the
   blood, slowly. Just feed on it, but a little at a time so it can
   almost replenish itself . . . just sink your proboscis into my
   flesh and suck. Suck out all the pulp, the mulch, the fruit,

the honey of my life . . . I was a mug . . . a right mug I was
. . . I mean, let's face it . . . I was a complete and utter
nutter. There I was . . . innocent . . . yes innocent, and I
walked into you like I was ready for picking. So I kept you
all these years. Twenty years. A score of years you fed off
my blood until there's nothing left . . . just thin watery
soup. I had some blood left. I could have found what I
really needed, could still have had enough soup left for the
first course. Get the interest going, found a new life,
revitalised the organ . . . send the blood rushing back to
the brain . . . get the engine ticking over . . . the heart
pumping . . . the pulse racing . . . the eyes flushed, moist,
excited, alive, wide, expectant, happy, alert, on edge,
waiting, hoping, soppy, wanting, being wanted, needing,
being needed, holding, being held, hard, tight, crushed,
warm, eye to eye, nose to nose, tongue to tongue, crutch to
crutch, pounding the old boy once more, the paleologist,
the digger, explorer. Could have had, could have, I could,
I should have, but I didn't . . . I was a mug, I was. I admit,
I confess, I was a right mug, a dozy mug. Unbelievable. I
mean it is unbe-fucking-lievable. That I took it, that I
tolerated it . . . I accepted it . . . like I took it for granted,
like this was the way it has to be. This is what you do . . .
this is how you live. This is the way, this is the form, the
habit, the tradition . . . the way of life . . . this is what
happens! Yeah, sure it cools off, it changes, I know it's not
the same as the first night . . . week . . . month or even
year. I know, I'm a realist, I'm not a dreamer, I've got my
head screwed on . . . I meant I don't say let's get divorced
soon as the horn ain't up seven times a week. Of course
there's more, of course, I don't question it, don't even
mention it, it goes without saying that we get close in one
thousand more tangible, important strands of our life but
there has to be some vibe left, eh . . . I mean there ought to
be some light left . . . I mean forget five hundred watt
bulb, let's have sixty watt. Just enough to see by . . . That's
OK . . . that'll cover the cost . . . lay my table . . . don't

want orgiastic nights ten years on . . . 'tsokay, but a little
light on the subject . . . a little electric passing through us,
eh . . . not too much.

WOMAN: I saved your life.

MAN: Wot?

WOMAN: I saved your life.

MAN: My life?

WOMAN: Yes, your life . . .

MAN: You're claiming *you* saved *my* life?

WOMAN: Not claiming, saved your life from the
meaninglessness, the emptiness. I did save your life from
that . . . that's what I did, I can say it because I did it . . .
that's why I say it . . . you were an empty shell when I met
you, empty, vacant, rolling this way and that . . . trying to
fill your emptiness with your dick. Like an ostrich you
buried your dick and you thought you were safe. All
buried, safe, dark and warm. That's why you kept burying
your few inches of dick, you couldn't get in any further.
But you tried to claw your way back into the womb. Tried
to clamber back in with your fingers, tongue and dick, you
crawled in . . . 'Help me . . . Let me in', you'd whine. So I
let you in my heart, *I* let *you* in, you were desperate to find
a sanctuary for your vulnerable needing body . . . so you
knocked on my door. Remember, I was at peace . . . I
was, though not ecstatic, not idyllic, was comparatively at
peace . . . I could deal with *it*! I did deal with *it*. The fact.
The reality. That maybe there is no one to take me from
my isolation. Only men crawling all over me like lizards
crawling up a cliff looking for holes into which they could
bury their angst and what use was that . . . what use since
my body would be taken over. Mine, and yet maybe I'd
gently persuade them after the burying . . . the digging, the
probing, the rummaging around my *body* . . . that there
were other areas in which to explore . . . other rooms up
there . . . higher, where in fact the view is much better and
you see a lot further and maybe one in ten took time to
look around and kick-start their brain cells into action. So I

gave you life . . . I provided something more than you
knew, than you wanted, than you thought you *needed* . . .
than you were aware of, since you men are not aware . . .
are often not aware of what you need and you ask for water
and we give you wine, you beg for scraps and we give you
feasts. You plead for shelter and we give you warmth . . .
we save your lives . . . you came to me that day twenty
years ago . . . on the beach like the usual naked ape . . .
rampant, insecure, wanting yet fearing . . . needing yet
scared, hunting yet a victim, saying please let me look as if
I am saving you. Look grateful, obedient, happy,
overwhelmed, starving, hungry, yearning, wanting to be
rescued, panting unworthy woman so that you might
rescue us with your horn. Don't threaten horn . . . hook us
with the horn like a hungry fish so grateful to be hooked.
Like fishes waiting for the angler to feel real good. So I
made you feel good on the beach twenty years ago . . . I let
you take me because all you needed was scraps . . . potato
peelings, but I gave you . . . caviar . . . all you wanted was
a waste bin for your surplus spunk . . . I gave you a palace.
All you wanted was a place to hide your nakedness . . . I
gave you a sanctuary . . . so I saved your life, yes, I did, I
gave you that while you were pathetic . . . made life whole
again and said, man you are bigger than the size of your
prick . . . you are bigger than six inches, you are a fully
grown man of six feet, but you do the impossible and
squeeze six feet into six inches. You were a dick attached
to a life support system and I put colour in the rest of your
body and mind, since your poor six inches couldn't carry
the weight of a six foot man forever. So you came to me, a
sad shuffling man . . . reduced like a pygmy to six inches
and I looked down at this little creature and took pity on it
and thought, lo and behold, if I touch it with my magic
wand this ugly mushroom will turn into a human being
. . . a prince, and lo and behold when I did . . . you did
. . . you tried, and out popped a human being . . . not all
at once but gradually, slowly colour returned to the rest of

your body and you were regenerated . . . oh God, you
were happy, you were free at last from the constraints of
horn since that's all you had left. You were a company
man. A dead soul swaying on the Piccadilly line each day
popping from Cockfosters to Hammersmith, like a worm
you burrowed your way through London up to sell
advertising space for a magazine that didn't even exist. So
you didn't exist. You were a con-artist, a vacant, empty
shell, or a crab looking for a shell in which to hide. You
were a salesman of nothing, bereft, barely human even, just
answering the call of nature from time to time, just
knowing that you could still just make a reflection in the
mirror, OK turn on the telly and watch your Scuds! Watch
male energy in action. It makes up for your non-action.

MAN: I'm dying for a cuppa. My tongue's hanging out . . .
listening to you I hear the music . . . following you I climb
the mountain. That first time I met you, the very first time
I mean, on the beach, took the day off, couldn't stand it
any more, couldn't take it . . . couldn't take the pain of it,
the utter uselessness and just so happened to be in that
kind of mood, you know, a little reckless, a Pinteresque
kind of mood if you like, like what happens now and does
it matter. Reckless, like I had nothing left to save, no life
left . . . not much and not worth saving, so would risk
rejection. Also it made me a bit more daring . . . like not
caring, like a kind of cool indifference, since my life was
definitely not working, so what the hell . . . I blew my last
bob on my personality by giving you the chat-up technique
and you weren't exactly reluctant . . . you were in your
own way waiting to be saved . . . you were hanging around
that beach with an air of someone who's waiting for her
ship to come in but has a shrewd idea that it won't . . .
kind of fatalistic . . . if it happens it's a bonus but if not,
well . . . I'm getting used to the four walls, thank you. So I
saved you . . . I . . . saved . . . you . . . me. Yes, yours
truly. You were a right case then if you like, you absconded
from the grim emptiness of reality and lived in the twilight

world of fantasy, inventing some geezer who wore aqua de
selva only because you probably had a one night stand with
some amiable bloke who deposited his load like the coal
man and pissed off into the night, disappeared into the
darkness from whence he materialised but left you with his
quaintly old-fashioned, lime-tinted tang of aqua de selva
which hardly anyone sells any more since hardly anyone
wears it, but the pong lasted a lot longer than his coitus
and so you invented some geezer who comes in at six each
night. Well eventually you admitted you made the whole
thing up as a bit of a giggle but then I should have sussed
you out . . . I mean, do I want to get involved with a basket
case who invents geezers who stink of cheap after-shave? I
mean the warning bells should have gone then. Where did
you get that eh, 'the whistle to show he's there?' Another
bit of your identikit Romeo, the sensitive caring soul who
didn't want to alarm thee but that was your dad . . . he
used to do that for your mum . . . so you were looking for
a dad to indulge you, not a man or husband, but a kind of
dad figure who would always forgive you. So I came along,
a right mug, as if I walked into a spider's web and there
you were wearing your vulnerability like a mask . . . save
me . . . rescue me Mr Man from my empty life . . . my
lifeless emptiness but underneath you were stalking your
victim tarantula-like, waiting for muggins to enter . . . and
then I was well wrapped up, well sealed inside your web of
need, helplessness, weakness, flattery, cajoling, save me
from the big bad wolf of loneliness and despair. So I was
stroked, with cobwebs and slowly, slowly you wrapped me
up and before I knew anything I couldn't move because I
was trapped in guilt . . . I was responsible, suddenly,
quickly found myself responsible for a life, for a whole
human being like I was being eaten yet still felt some
inextricable sense of guilt if I didn't allow the tarantula to
make a visit and each day stick its fangs deep inside me
and suck and suck. You say the colour returned to me?
Not from where I stood. I became thinner and paler and

my colour started to fade, you drained the colour from me
because you didn't really want to link forces, like join up,
make a weft and warp, a Box and Cox, a night and day,
male and female. You were the one who wanted still to
own . . . not partner, possess! Not shake, take! You know
what I mean . . . I suddenly, amazingly walked into,
unbeknown, a den of neurotic needs, not Shangri-La or
Sunnyview . . . 'neurotic needs' should be stamped on the
lintels of your doorpost . . . and I mean yes, I could've left,
yes, true, no one forced me . . . that's right, one does have
a will of one's own, right . . . one wasn't exactly manacled
. . . no that's true officer . . . I was a willing party, not
drugged, doped or whipped . . . no, no, no, but you
pressed the right button, the buttons to see if the man
functions . . . pity, yes pride, protection, yes . . . for the
'weaker' sex, the helpless, skirted, feminine, vulnerable . . .
press the buttons and the men leap. How we are needed
. . . the muscle, the balls the defenders of the realm, the
wiles, the tricks, the lace, the scent, the open, wide-eyed
look for daddy . . . and then she wraps us up, we can't help
it, we respond, I do, respond to the stimulus, to the idea
that among both our minus's and neurotic needs we might
have built a temple where we can pray at the altar for the
end of them. So there you were waiting; and insecure
muggins steps into the trap and I couldn't easily leave, not
easily . . . not without a certain terrible, unforgivable,
horrendous pain . . . (the kids have come and gone, they
don't need us any more, not so much, not so much as we
needed them) so we're left at the beginning, only deader,
with no future joy, with no ache in the soul, with no
missing when you're away and with no needs except, 'Can
you work the video recorder, I need you for that, I never
worked all those switches out.' So we exist for each other
as extension switches to machines . . . we, the machine-
workers . . . you work the fax, I work the answerphone,
you work the spin-dryer, I work the alarm system, you
work the digital oven, I work the CD. So we've become

machine minders, needing each other to fix the machines we possess and without each other what may happen is that chaos would come. I'd find that Sky TV stopped our viewing because I didn't renew the membership . . . I'd be driving with no oil in the car . . . I wouldn't know how to unblock the fax machine when it gets jammed . . . this is what holds our life together . . . this is what we eventually and tragically have become for each other. Remote control buttons . . .

WOMAN: You'd collapse if I left . . .

MAN: I said that!

WOMAN: I mean you'd fall to pieces . . .

MAN: I know, I agree, in part I tend to agree . . .

WOMAN: You'd probably turn over and give up the ghost.

MAN: Not quite . . . let's not get carried away.

WOMAN: You're helpless by yourself, helpless and useless.

MAN: Well maybe, so why don't you go so I can test your theory . . .

WOMAN: I'll go, I want to go, you can't imagine how I need to go, just to get out . . . just to smell some sweet fresh air, oh space, oh beloved wonderful empty space, just the loneliness of space, even the pain of it, since the pain can't last . . . not forever. Nature abhors a vacuum, so something else will come into it, into my space but it won't have your face on it! That's a luxury for starters, since I'm tired of being a bucket for you . . . propping up your crippled ego, the poor male shattered ego. You say I trapped you? The male mantra, the whining dirge, like you saved me from a life of spinsterish solitude . . . along comes Mr Right clutching his broken ego like Humpty Dumpty, hoping I'll repair it while we pretend he's brought precious gems . . . we pretend you arsehole, our whole life is pretence, my whole life, even from the bed I subsidised your broken tawdy ego, to make you feel good . . . Mr Feel-Good . . . so you can stride out of the house thinking you're at least half male. I suffered your stinking bloated corpse next to me all these years, pretending,

acting, fantasising, yes, you were right, you prophesied
correctly all those years ago but you became the thing you
accused me of then, being a launching pad for another's
fantasy. You became my launching pad for me to fantasise
about others and my moans were for others while you
gathered them up like winnings . . . but they were never
yours to collect . . . ever . . . not from the first, they
belonged to me, to my dreams of a man you could never
be . . . but even in that, even in that sad tawdry beginning I
tried to find that part of you that was real and even, dare I
say . . . tender, human and tried to connect beneath the
crap, beneath the poisoned ego like a scum of filth on a
dead lake, tried to find some innocence, something
undefiled, hoped that when the poisons are purged away
underneath there has to be something pure. That's what I
hoped for . . . we all hope for, something real,
uncontaminated. So we live on hope, I did . . . hope . . .
bringing all my love to bear on it like a small shoot of life in
a decayed and rotting building. Nursing it . . . bringing
love like sunlight, water, nourishing, caring, willing,
wanting, trying and even watching but with you my poor
dear, the poisons had eaten in too deeply. Your earth's too
polluted, the shoots would die . . . starved, neglected by
you while your pathetic ego struggled to be a man in a
world that had spurned you. So you came to me to restore
what others had condemned . . . you were a reject when
you came to me . . . but that didn't matter since all human
beings have a soul . . . what the world rejects is not your
soul . . . it's your crumbling ridiculous ambition . . . your
need to be a man . . . successful, acclaimed . . . Mr Big
Dick. But the world, poor love, shut its doors and you
clambered over me trying to break into *my* world. Crawling
back to mama. To childhood when you didn't have to
break open any door . . . but I didn't care . . . you don't
have to prove yourself to me. A soul is worth more than all
worldly success. You crawled back hoping to at least
conquer something, find somewhere where you could at

least lay claim to something . . . where you might at least
succeed in something . . . you salesman of nothing. At
least God gave you the equipment to prove that what
distinguishes you from us is a piece of flesh, that makes
you, if all else fails . . . necessary. The one thing you have
left when all doors are shut . . . when nobody wants,
needs, requests . . . looks forward, hungers, admires you.
You still at least have, were given for free, not made, built,
developed, but given the one thing that makes you feel . . .
when all else fails . . . when life is a grey blur as you sit
festering on some God-forsaken motorway, sitting with
your undigested breakfast already souring in your guts and
turning to lead, even then, even when the day is a
meaningless shambles of futile gestures and you indeed
shamble home with your face 'slapped puce with rejection'.
But nature endowed you with one thing that was your
own. So when all else fails, you have that which to all
intents and purposes is 'needed' . . . you have one thing
left, one thing which is your own, your life-giving force,
and then you return, you return from the world that has
kicked you from pillar to post and say, 'Here I am
sweetheart' and all the doors that were shut in your face,
for all the eyes that judged you with cold indifferent stares,
for all the contempt the world has as your broken ego peers
nakedly out from your eyes that already have fear and
rejection burned inside them, there would be just one
solitary place left . . . one sanctuary left, in all the world
one tiny, warm, safe, solitary sanctuary in which the door
was open. In which you did not have to fight . . . in which
you would crawl nursing your wounds . . . which you
could claim as your own, in which you could indefatigably
and certainly take for granted as your mother's knee . . . in
which you could crawl back and not be judged and you
spat on it, yes you did. And when I am not here . . . when
there is nowhere left for you to crawl back inside . . . when
there is only space and unpaid bills . . . when there is only
sour milk in the fridge and endless repeats on the movie

channel which would, as you say, be cut off anyway because you rely on me to pay the bills and at the same time be the healer of your poisoned soul. So when you return to your den of dead emptiness you will be free . . . free . . .

MAN: Now . . . oh now you give me freedom, now you give it to me when I have nothing left to give, now you have taken from me everything and stripped the tree bare and so now . . . (*Fading out as the story continues forever.*)

STURM UND DRANG

or

CONFESSIONS OF A CAD!

A Comedy of Manners for Three Performers

CHARACTERS

NICK
SIMON
SASHA

Simon enters room where Nick his friend is standing.

SIMON: She's driving me quite mad Nick, yes, insane!
    I call, I know she's there, her answerphone
    collects my anguished words, my grief, my love,
    that she can play back, have a great old laugh.
    I send flowers, orchids. Moyses Stevens' best,
    (I have an account there now, it does save time
    hunting for your Amex card when they're on the line)
    She says she loves me, swears there's only me,
    when we're together, bliss, Christ! Ecstasy!
    Our tongues entwined, our arms and legs unfurled,
    where does my body end, and hers begin?
    Don't smirk Nick, she's no ordinary girl,
    her line, her form, pure sculpture by Bellini,
    I'm touching some erotic masterpiece, I feel,
    she was short-listed for a cameo, for Fellini!
    And now I've lost my mind drenched with her name . . .
    Sasha, Sasha, Sasha, stop driving me insane!

NICK: You sound like what you need is a stiff drink.
    Scotch and soda is all I've got I think . . .
SIMON: Oh? Fine, sure, super, great, oh just a dash,
    oops! When! Love to get well and truly smashed!
NICK: I'll nip out to the pub and buy some booze,
    but tell me first, how you got so confused.
SIMON: I thought I spied her driving late last night.
    I kept her BMW in my headlights . . .
    as we careered fast down the Fulham Road.
    No doubt she's heading for San Lorenzo,
    a rendezvous, ah-ha I thought, quite crazed,
    I'll leap out, smack her escort in the chops,
    a thousand weird scenarios went through my brain.
    The traffic lights turned red at Beauchamp Place,
    I dashed up to her car like a raging bull,
    'Sorree! wrong bird, thought you were someone else.'
    She looked at me like some demented fool . . .
    So everywhere I see only her face,

like a drug addict whose blood craves opium,
so I cannot exist without the taste
of Sasha, Sasha, my sweet lovely sin!
So help me Nick, you must help me to purge
this mad obsession twisting up my nerves.

NICK: I'll put the kettle on for a start!
(*Mimes filling kettle and both wait until he has done this and lit match.*)
You fool, you know she's just a filthy tart.
You're covered in mist, your eyes are dumb,
your ears are blind and so mislead your heart,
your brains are oozing out each time you cum.
You cannot tell your left foot from your right,
so let my words guide you into the light.

SIMON: By God you're right, I'm so enamoured, mad!
To hold the sweetest, darlingest girl of all,
I'm helpless, melt between her arms and thighs,
her eyes like sirens seem to hypnotise,
her nose like a chocolate truffle, one small bite,
those crimson lips so soft you simply die.
I overdose on kisses, day and night.
Oh! She could melt the peaks of Everest!
Turn Michelangelo's David quite obscene,
could raise the dying for one last embrace
and bring a blush to pale Dracula's cheek.
And then her breath, you know those chill moist dawns
before the burning eye turns livid gold
that second of divine infinity.
When all the world seems poised for one exhale,
the air, so pure, so clear, so very still,
and so her breath, so delicate I deep inhale.
No gardens gave me more rapturous bliss,
and that's only the start, the very top,
the head, the merest perfume of her kiss
and then her voice, speak not of flutes and strings . . .

You think Bach's Brandenberg concertos swing?

Forget Debussy, Fauré, Dukas, Brahms,
ignore the saccharin of Stones or Sting,
imagine more a mistral through wild grass,
a whirling spiral on a heathered heath
or branches shaking their autumnal leaves . . .
as through them comes the sweetest melody.
I switch my answerphone to answerplay
just to drink her message once again . . .
Her voice just sounds to me like whispering waves
crashing against the shoreline of my brain,
I rewind and play the goddamn thing again.

NICK: You're quite mad, quite potty, over the top . . .
You're lost Simon, I fear, completely lost.
What you describe's poetic fantasy
and not a shred, oh no, of cold reality.
You've metamorphosed some poor slut to saint,
you euphemise with words while some use paint.
A middle-aged conceit like liver spots
that fleck the flawless flesh of youth
or eyes that slowly lose their clarity,
do not perceive with usual scrutiny
the woodworm chewing beneath the lacquered face.
Poor thing, your self-esteem begins to sag,
the masculine ego, so macho and proud,
is thrilled, the strumpet makes him feel a lad,
you're sexually obsessed, I must surmise
by teeming succubi that prey at night,
those lubric phantoms feast between your thighs
while you lay helpless, half in paradise . . .

SIMON: Just half in paradise and half in hell,
the bitch torments me yet swears she loves me well.

NICK: She's dancing at the disco half the night,
while you lay writhing for her touch and sight,
she's snorting lines of coke and screwing guys,
you think she's living only for your eyes?

She's using you man, 'cause she knows you're hooked,
withdraw, be smart, don't phone and please cool off!
Then let her do the running, act the cad!
Strong will is needed, don't pick up that phone,
don't dial that number or you will go mad!

SIMON: So easier said than done my clever friend,
the woman threatens to devour me whole.
I have to write to her if I don't phone,
hope that my passion dripping through my text
may turn into a string of precious pearls
that she will gladly wear upon her neck . . .

NICK: Wake up and please de-tox, accelerate
the ancient wit I think you once possessed,
puncture this heavy swollen bag of piss.
Remove the scales that adhere to your sex-drugged eyes,
and see this woman as pussy, tits, and thighs,
not some unreal, ethereal, divine goddess
but human, smelling, farting sack of flesh!
Shaved armpits, curling tongs, war paint and kohl,
perfumes and plastic surgeons, rouge, pomade,
a twenty minute Stairmaster for lard,
she sweats her guts out for you in the gym
and spends your fortune trying to get thin.
Come on, wake up, snap out, pontificate,
what is the mystery of female charms
that's got you dangling by your dong.
Creams, lipstick, nail varnish, panty line,
her winsome painted smiles destroy your spine,
mascara and a splash of eau de pong,
a micro skirt pleated like petalled rose,
tempt you to part those petals, you lusty bee,
but once the poor bee's trapped down deep inside,
she feeds on you a morsel at a time.
She'll suck the marrow from your aching bones
or like a spider wrap you in her web.
You've watched a spider wrapping up its prey
just like a female on a shopping day.

Watch her in Harrods on a spending binge,
the sight's obscene, it's bound to make you cringe
when witnessing your fortune shed
into designer tat that costs an arm and leg.
Just see your tide of treasure going out,
leaving you marooned upon sharp reefs
and called by shipwrecked sailors – bankruptcy.
Your blood and sweat are in your Amex card
that she did beg and plead for with salt tears,
'It's so convenient for the shops' she trills,
then you grow pale when you confront the bills.

Your Amex card becomes her magic wand,
and everything she touches turns quite blonde
except your bank statements which now turn red,
blushing in shame to see their master bled.
And all this for a pair of smoking thighs
that our tormented suitor wants to prise
wide open and between those marble scythes,
bury your head like some carnivorous beast
that in some dank dark forest is at its feast . . .
Yukkee my friend, it's really quite obscene,
to get your rocks off needn't cost a bean!!

SIMON: Cynic, mocker and misogynist,
you who never slept the sleepless night
sweating demons in your lonesome bed,
lest strangers' fingers dipped in your precious till
and helped themselves, their greedy digits thrust
like filthy snakes into your honey pot.
Yes, love creates wild fantasies and dreams
but what of that, I tasted paradise,
that's something rationalists never realise.
You're stuck between *The Times*, *Economist*,
the poetry of your soul is stocks and shares,
your heart ne'er flutters at a well-curved rump
but leaps a beat if British Steel is up.
You never anguished for a sweetheart's call

but sweat in fear when trading starts to fall,
and what's between your legs is not for love
but pissing in the Stock Exchange urinal,
while taking bets with mates on the Cup Final.
Your heart is index-linked and beats more fast
when panicked by a swift descending graph.
A plunging neckline won't excite your blood
but plunging share prices will drive you mad.
Soft lips, perfume and woman's sexy eyes
on you are wasted when you see sterling rise.

NICK: You've got me wrong old boy, quite wrong,
you're so obsessed your brain's gone to your dong,
quite amusing what you have to say,
except you do turn out the old cliché
that only 'artistic types' like you can feel,
terribly patronising, so . . . unreal.
I do like pussy with the best of you,
a neatly bevelled arse makes me incline
to lift my head from the *Financial Times*
which is not the only thing I like that's pink,
there are some other things I like to think.
I love a stocking glimpsed, a skirt rode high,
the electric that can flow 'tween strangers' eyes,
the careless brush of fingers, lingering close,
when my sweet-scented secretary takes notes.
And when I say 'dear sir, refer, and yours truly'
I hear her satin legs uncross like sighs,
then she re-crosses, flashing a shock of thigh.
I'm not immune behind my burdened desk,
the one-eyed monster, yes, begins to rise
as if it wants to burst right through my flies.
Her female odour sneaks around my nose,
tries to torment me with unbridled lust
as it sends sinful pictures to my brain.
I struggle vainly, get back on the train,
Dow Jones and blue chip issues and crashed shares,
when all I want to do is clear,

to fuck until my brain comes out my ears,
so don't think you're the only one who feels.
You're just possessed, obsessed, insane and daft,
I keep my lust well bottled and corked in,
but when I want, I'll slice a piece of arse,
like choose, when and where and how and if . . .
But you're completely lost like some poor dog
'cause love's derailed your sanity and wit,
lust's bold and healthy, quite good for a heart
but please don't lose your marbles for a tart!
SIMON: Go on make fun, be cruel and take the piss.
At least my love, obsession if you will,
enchants her bright young ears, gives her sweet thrills.
She (like every female) loves to be
the sole subject of a man's idolatry,
they love to be adored quite frankly, yes.
Worshipped, idolised, simply revered.
They'd trade their diamonds, pearls and French chateaux,
wardrobes stuffed full with haute couture,
for one true love whose heart they know is pure . . .

NICK: Simon, please, you'll make me want to puke,
your precious darling stinks of Jean Patou
like she was swimming in it every morn,
won't let a drop of Bollinger, my dear,
pass through those chiselled ruby lips
unless it's vintage, preferably fifty four.
Her fingers knuckle-dusted with fine gems
from shopping raids to 'ouch' Mappin and Webb,
gold, amethyst, and I think citrine,
are her preferred choice of daytime rings,
but for the night something a touch risqué,
what better than a piece by Fabergé,
St. Laurent, Chanel, and why not Dior,
the very least allowed to graze her flesh,
since nothing must adorn those precious pores
unless it's *the* horribly expensive best!

She hardly deigns to lift one Gucci'd toe
to step inside a roller with a prince
unless he's dressed in perfect Savile Row,
she might allow Armani at a pinch!
She's playing you along while you drip gold,
you'll act King Midas for a little while,
but once your mines start getting low old chap,
you'll be well-booted out into the cold.

SIMON: OK, let's see, you unctuous, sneery cynic,
I'll prove to you this 'tart' that you dare slur
is not the steaming harlot that you think,
since your experience from which you speak,
describes all women simply as a sink
of pure depravity, plain greed and lust,
from your cold-blooded one-night stands from Tramp
or other night haunts where ex-models lurk
in shadowed corners where the melting flesh
is gathering dust from being back on the shelf.
So siren-like they tempt you to a bed,
the loveless fuck, then lay there like the dead.
You wait for dawn like strangers in the dark,
the fuse that linked you now turned bitter cold
and hope that you won't accidentally fart.
Morning arrives with coffee, slam the door
with lies and promises of 'yes, I'll phone',
you rush into the loo with great relief,
the next door neighbours think a bomb explodes!
Is this the life, is all you want just sex?
Somewhere to dip at night your itchy dick,
my God, I'd like a little more tendresse!

NICK: Sex, my dear boy, is really in the head,
you know it's not so great, the foreplay's best
and when you get your catch inside your bed
then grim reality comes to the test.
Oh God, a touch of garlic on her breath.
OK, avoid the kisses, let's get down to work
and just when you're getting nicely aroused

258

she'll say 'No, not tonight, I've got the curse'.
Of course, a gentleman's got to take her word,
can't *very* well dive down between the sheets
and pull on the communication cord!
Or else, expectancy too high, you fear
that when your hard-on's standing to attention,
it runs away just like a frightened mouse
whenever you try to trap it in a condom.
So through the night you try to coax it out,
ah there it is, quick pounce and get it on,
oh no, it's going, going, going, gone.
Turn over, mwa! and then put on the light,
you snooze a while then have another shot,
you lift a leg and if it works . . . jackpot!!
SIMON: How passionate you are, romantic too,
to use a woman like a human loo!
Somewhere to deposit your excess waste,
it's ghastly, awful, even sounds obscene.
Where I have diamonds you make do with paste.
For you she's just a walking repository
for excess spunk, who shall I phone today?
Your Filofax suffers so much abuse
from nightly clawing through its well-thumbed charts,
each name a number for another tart,
like turn the yellow pages when you've got a fuse.
The names of women are so lyrical,
for you each name's a sordid night in bed . . .
Instead of Sarah, Anabelle or Sue,
just call them slut and filthy whore instead.
'Shall we go out tonight, you filthy bitch'
the prettiest ones are busy so she'll do.
You eat a ghastly pasta, make some chat
at La Famiglia or some trendy zoo,
make the requisite expenditure you think
that allows you to use her as a sink . . .
where you can drain away your foul pollution,
yukkee, what a really sick conclusion!

NICK: You wretched, smug, conceited bore you are
　　　with your ideals, your lofty superiority.
　　　I'm parched, I need a drink, some scotch on ice?
SIMON: A splash of water please, ice spoils the purity.
NICK: You shove the bitches on a pedestal,
　　　that's why they always kick you in the crutch.
SIMON: I'd rather err a touch romantically
　　　than see each woman as a walking fuck.
NICK: They're human too, sometimes they need to screw
　　　just easy, no demands, a big stiff dick.
SIMON: Not the ones I fraternise with mate,
　　　they want a man with passion, soul and wit!
NICK: They crave it, want it, love a zipless fuck,
　　　they're just as predatory as a man,
　　　don't fool yourself that you're the one who hunts,
　　　you're the hunted one, you silly . . . cad!
SIMON: No wonder English women are so bored
　　　and give up their favours to the subtle French,
　　　who suss the best route to a woman's heart
　　　is knowing how to use their instrument.
　　　The tune you seem to play is but two notes . . .
　　　Bang! Bang! Not a very complex air . . .
　　　Good God man, what divine pleasures you miss
　　　by having such a poor unsubtle ear . . .
　　　For me she's like a Chopin's dark nocturne,
　　　at times an organ concerto by Bach,
　　　those crashing waves upon an endless shore.
　　　Or playful, witty, brilliant like Mozart,
　　　or even Stravinsky's most dramatic scores,
　　　when I possess her it's the rites of spring,
　　　with slight touches of Darius Milhaud,
　　　you know just thinking of her makes me sing . . .
NICK: Women can be beasts and love hard core.
SIMON: I hate vulgarity in any form.
NICK: They're bored shitless by far too much respect.
SIMON: Woman is to me the ideal sex.
NICK: They like to grip a tool that's good and thick.

SIMON: When we unite I don't just dip my wick.

NICK: They fantasise and love a juicy screw.

SIMON: And after, the vile post-coital blues?

NICK: They're animals and need to be well stuffed!

SIMON: I love it too, the passion and the storm.

NICK: No, you love rhapsodising, they like it rough . . .

SIMON: You wear your love always beneath your belt . . .

NICK: Yes! Love is sweating, pounding hips, the smell . . .

SIMON: You're like an animal, a beast of prey.

NICK: Yes! Must be fed red meat three times a day!

SIMON: You think that half the human race are whores!

NICK: Yes, blast you! Give me hundreds to explore!

SIMON: You are more desperate than a sleazy drunk!

NICK: If women were wine I'd quaff them by the quart . . .

SIMON: You're insane like a crazy alcoholic . . .

NICK: I like to eat them whole, spit out the pips!

SIMON: Really Nick you're turning quite moronic!

NICK: Wish I could blend them in my mixer for a tonic . . .

SIMON: You're beginning to sound, Nick, just like Monsieur Sade.

NICK: Well, that's a compliment to me, I'm glad.

SIMON: Cruelty, sadism, your taste's so . . . raw.

NICK: That's woman for you, mother, madonna and whore!

BLACKOUT.

Sasha enters. The two are shocked.

SIMON: Sasha darling, sweetheart you look so cute,
    we *were* just singing out your charms.
    Of course you know my friend Nick, I presume?

NICK: Delighted to meet again, we met at Cannes.

SASHA: Oh? Yes! Weren't you there when *Wild at Heart*
    grabbed the Palme d'Or? Oh, Lynch is so smart . . .
    Hello there Simon, mwa! (*kisses*) You smell divine,
    what's that you're wearing, Draka Noir?

SIMON: No, not today darling, it's Vetiver,
    I wear it specially for you my dear.

SASHA: I'm simply shattered, I think I'll collapse . . . (*She sits.*)
SIMON: Scotch and soda?
SASHA: Darling, just a dash!
NICK: You've got some project no doubt, on the boil?
SASHA: Still trying to sell the American rights
  for the book I've optioned, *Mutant Killer Girls*,
  hoping to get a completion clause as well,
  below the line costs are a horrid five mill.
  There's some Arab money coming, they're terribly keen,
  but they're insisting on a star, the same old thing.
  Al Pacino just might do it if he's free,
  since it's a super role that would suit him to a 't'.
  His agent's bound to ask the most gi-normous fee
  unless of course he waived it . . . worked for points,
  and maybe after a percentage of the gross . . .
  Where's my whisky darling? You're an awful host.
  (*He pours it.*)
  Oops, when! . . . Got some ice? Hate it warm as toast!
  (*Silence, mime, drinking, cigs, etc.*)
  Seen the most ghastly movie, a sneak preview,
  about this serial killer who fell in love
  with a hooker, who gave the most marvellous screw,
  so he turned from killer hawk to gentle dove.
  So while he was enamoured of her charms
  she, quite innocent, was protected and safe.
  While the madman went killing, she was free from harm
  as long as his vile body she would satiate.
  He came home from orgies of murder and rape
  and quietly ate dinner and watched tv,
  she was so happy, his sweet adoring mate,
  they decided to marry and live 'ever after' happily.
  One day he returned from his orgy of crime
  with blood-spattered shirt, off went her alarms,
  he invented some story of a drunken bar fight.

  But she read of vile murders in the daily news,
  orgies of killings and the police had few clues

except one poor victim, who before she expired
uttered these words to the police standing by,
that when he performed his unspeakable act
he asked if she loved him – 'Do you love me?' he spat.
The lunatic love talk while he cruelly abused
some poor hooker trembling in bed with this rat,
leering and foul as her body he screwed.
What he spake were the clues but they fell on dead ears,
since no victim lived to reveal the truth.
Nobody came to corroborate those lines,
the victims were rotting in their bed of slime.
Now when she read those incredible words,
she recalled how her husband would moan as he sensed
the tremors within – before the eruption.
'Do you love me?' he said, 'Do you love me?' she heard,
exactly like that, it made her afeared.
She remembered the blood-spattered shirts she had cleaned.
Could my husband be the serial killer?
Could he be the monster, it was too obscene.

The daily news items she swiftly cut out
grew frigid in bed since her fear was now strong.
Her warm lithe young body no longer responds
and his criminal nose sniffed that something was wrong.
One night the foul beast was out stalking his prey,
she decided to phone, her tongue felt like clay.
'Hello – hello – please get me the police,
that serial killer, the beast who slays whores,
'Do you love me?' he says when spraying his spore,
I think he's my husband, he says those same words!'

For her man spat these words as he sweated and heaved.
But, thought she, that couples in passion do cry
sweet love words as lust makes their brains slowly fry.
They don't always mean it but want the sweet sauce
poured over the meat they exchange in the raw,
in the heat, in the burning campaign of their joist,

as friction makes fire between their loins.
But the killer, he grew more cautious and sharp,
he found the news-cuttings in her crocodile bag,
he read his own words that the world knew by heart,
he read what she outlined, he screamed, 'Filthy hag!'
He read 'Do you love me?' 'Do you love me?' it said.
As he stirred up her embers, as he thrust deep and cried,
he knew that she knew . . . of his Jekyll and Hyde.
This must be her last night, for tonight she dies!

She'll die tonight, yes! The whore dies in her bed.
The filthy slut he had worshipped and saved,
like the rest she'll be scraped off the face of the earth
and no one will know as she rots in her grave.
So that night he made love so sweetly and pure
like he was counting her heart's final beats.
And as he reached the ultimate temperature,
he spat out those words, the song of the beast.

'Do you love me?' he screamed, 'Do you love me?' he yelled.
But, the cops were now waiting, they wanted it taped
to see if it matched the victim's last words,
the words that she uttered before her sad fate.
The sounds on the tape would curdle the air
as the state purged its hatred and all its fury,
they would fry him alive in the electric chair.
But suddenly, swiftly as he seized her by the throat,
they panicked and shot his head off with a colt.
He lay there, a trunk just spouting up its life,
his body still in her while his flesh turned to ice.

Like reluctant to leave its soft, warm domain,
like fastened in death to its victim, its prey.
They sweated and heaved, to prise off the corpse,
like pulling an octopus from its rocky sea bed,
continually, continually sprayed,
and beneath his blood, beneath his vile gore,

her blushes were redder, of that I am sure.
Like a dirty street dog that thing wouldn't shift,
eventually they had to saw him off at his dick.
(*Pause as they take it in.*)
Sir Anthony Hopkins was fab as the brute,
he was so damned evil my pubic hairs curled.
Meryl Streep was so brilliant I thought, as the girl
played as a French Jew who was brought up in Wales.

NICK: It sounds simply fab and I really must go,
I'll try to get tickets of course for the premiere,
I know the P.R. I'll get on the phone.
I just hate to go with the public my dear.

SASHA: Oh horrid, nasty, can't hear the bloody film,
with those morons from Chingford stuffing themselves
like pigs in a trough with their buckets of popcorn,
munching away, oh the stench of it all!
It's ghastly when you're squashed with the dreary mob,
the proles and the girlfriends, those thick high-heeled slobs,
and the West End at night's just perfectly horrid,
as the plebs leave their pubs in puddles of vomit!

NICK and SIMON: As the plebs leave their pubs in puddles of
vomit!

SASHA: Next time I'll take skis when I decide to see a play
in Shaftesbury Avenue or Charing Cross Road.
Then I can slide back some of the way
after the pubs have deposited their load . . .

NICK and SIMON: After the pubs have deposited their load . . .

SASHA: You know, in New York, the very worst crime
is to let your dog shit just where it desires.
So mink-coated ladies with smart Gucci bags
can be seen in Park Avenue picking up crap . . .

NICK and SIMON: Can be seen in Park Avenue picking up crap!

SASHA: So! What my plan is for the West End's revival
is to give the yobs' girlfriends free buckets and spades,
so whenever the boyfriend heaves up his Black Label
she's forced by law to scoop it away!

NICK and SIMON: She's forced by law to scoop it away!
SIMON: Darling, such indefatigable gifts you have
    for creating innovative brilliant schemes,
    you're quite an inspiration, you inspire my love,
    I think I feel a knocking on my jeans!
    Just hearing those fluted bell-like notes of yours
    sends thrilling vibrations up and down my spine,
    brilliant rendition *re* the film about the whore,
    got excited when you uttered the killer's awful line!
SIMON and NICK: 'Do you love me?' he said, 'Do you love me?'
SASHA: Stop it! Really, I've had just quite enough!
    Don't wish to be reminded again, thank you.
    I wouldn't mind diving into some chow,
    how's Bibendum sound, but I suppose Orso's would do . . .
NICK: I'll leave you two alone, I was on my way,
    we've had a good natter, OK, Simon, thanks.
    Don't see me out, no, I really can't stay.
    (*aside*) Now be firm and be cool, don't be such a wank!
SIMON: Ya! So all the best, Nick, see you Saturday,
    we've got tickets to the Gershwin, if that's OK,
    oh, can you bear to sit through four hours of Ham?
    We have tickets for that at the dreaded Barbican.
SASHA: Can I come please, oh Ken's such a cutey,
    when it starts getting boring you can wait in the bar,
    come in when the action starts getting real juicy . . .
    They say he is *the* next O . . . liv . . . vi . . . ar!

NICK: OK, we'll do something, I'll bring Isabelle.
SASHA: How is she Nicky, is she feeling quite well?
NICK: The abortion was nasty and a bit of a bore,
    so she's resting up now in the Côte d'Azur.
SASHA: When she comes back we must throw a small do.
NICK: She'd like that I'm sure Sasha, so toodle-loo.
SIMON: Toodle-loo, and thank you for your good words.
NICK: 's nothing, we go back a very long way . . .
    At Oxford you still had your head in a whirl.
SIMON: I remember . . . sent down for sneaking in girls,

    bloody good time though. Aah those were the days!
NICK: We got pissed every night and after got laid,
    learned fuck-all for three years except how to play!
SASHA: Are you two still scheming like two naughty boys
    and what did you mean, what were his 'good words'?
    What are you up to Simon . . . What's your ploy?
    Something in the atmosphere seems rather disturbed.
SIMON: You do have a nose, I grant you that Sasha,
    nothing can escape that quivering nostril.
    We wouldn't talk about you, it's not quite the fashion,
    men don't dissect their partners, it's rather more female.

SASHA: Oh bollocks and jam tarts, you men are all the same,
    women might be Jaguars or BMWs.
    Are we costly to run, does she need a lot of juice,
    I'm getting rather bored with it, I'll have a part-exchange.
SIMON: No Sasha, dearest darling and sweetheart,
    you're damned hard to decipher, so at times
    I ask my old friend Nick for a little advice,
    some verbal air-conditioning to take down the heat . . .
    Another objective from a distant pair of eyes.
    Perched on his pinnacle of self-possession . . .
    his gaze like a lighthouse scans stormy skies
    and gives small-craft warnings of bleak depressions,
    or rocks that lurk beneath the endless deep,
    ready to tear your guts out as you're tossed
    upon the snickering waves, you're battered and bossed
    or like a ball being kicked by endless feet . . .

    Or else from the snarling tempest you are spat
    upon a barren shore, the receding tide
    then breaks your timbers and so down you crash
    with no support, no harbour in which to hide . . .
    So yes, you might then say that we as men
    with women navigate a choppy sea,
    no charts or man or compass can detect
    that sudden squall that leaps out from the deep.

Sometimes there's harbour and soft friendly breeze,
you sail into a calm and delicious sea,
you blow a perfumed kiss into my sail
which gathers it up until it hugely swells.
I could then sail upon your flowing tides
and fearless navigate the oceans of life,
blow your air into my canvas cloth
and I will trap each precious tiny drop . . .

It takes our two forces linked and fused
to create the precious brilliant spark
that ignites the engines for our lifetime cruise,
oh Sasha, I feel the fibrillations of my heart.
So don't be rock, reef, tempest, storm or hail
but be a wave that softly carries me.
I'll set up my surf board on your foaming crest
and ride you swiftly to true happiness . . .
(*He holds her in his arms.*)
So Sasha, yes, I asked Nick for a little light
that's all, to see how foolish I have been,
but his light was not quite clear enough
to stop me sinking down into the endless deep . . .!

SASHA: Oh dear, poor Simon, please don't drown for me,
    I'll throw you a life raft instantly my sweet.

SIMON: So sorry dear Nick, we've been rather rude.
    Do forgive us, we just got carried away,
    forgot you were there – became quite obsessed,
    so we'll catch up, shall we, on Saturday?

NICK: Do you want me to go? I mean it's time
    we exchanged so many precious snaps,
    the regurgitating of those old memoirs,
    the sentimental dribble of old chaps,
    who, chewing the fruits of past conquests,
    hope a filament of taste will trickle down,
    a slender waft of memory will persist
    and awake the perfume of some lost gown
    she wore that deep blue velvet night of love.

(You know) the way a single note can strike a chord,
a distant chord of memory,
an odour trapped inside a faded page
brings back the years like it was yesterday,
read it with trembling fingers, drink that wine
that matures, the more your cask of flesh declines.
So Sasha when two men with pasts, both loves and pain,
try to restore some equilibrium,
they might reveal their warts and sores and scars
that each may then offer the healing balm,
since friends possess the scrutinising eye,
they know, can circumnavigate the fleshly world
like satellites they see the moon's dark side.

SIMON: I do appreciate your wise advice,
so forgive me Nick if now I might be bold,
your moon is very dark my ancient friend,
if I am to digest your sordid codes.
The theories of the erotic untermensch
he passed to me like they were the dead sea scrolls,
precious and preserved from ancient times.
Or handed down by Moses to his tribe,
obey or else, this is the way of flesh,
this is his church and where he goes to pray,
not to the holy ghost for his redemption,
but to Priapus, god of strong erections.
The sensualist is like a ripe peach that decays,
then like a fallen fruit, worm-threaded there you lay,
and what the worms don't want the ants will take away.

SASHA: Darling don't be a jelly baby pet.
It's just a little fascinating to get
a wide angled view of the male world,
a panoramic shot with all the flaws,
and then zoom in, close-up on those greasy pores!

NICK (*now wooing Sasha*): Yes peer into the craters and the rifts,
the chancres and the pustulating boils,
the slick of lava bubbling on the crust.
While deep within, the molten furnace glows,

and each new conquest tossed into the stoves
becomes the fuel, the spark, the flame, the meat
that lifts the temperature to raging heights,
that keeps the locomotive on the tracks,
fulfils its speed, its pulse, its furious heat.

SASHA: Thank you Nick, it's so exciting, tell me more.
I never thought that men were so in awe.
It's thrilling, scintillating, sparkling, sweet,
to think that pussy is still men's favourite meat!

NICK: It certainly is a favourite dish of mine,
uniquely guaranteed to lose you weight,
best taken with a glass of vintage wine,
and what a wide variety of tastes!

SASHA: Exciting, enervating, makes you thrill
to be taken on a joy ride to the male world,
investigate the tunnels deep within
the sewers of man's filthy brain, his sins!
Oh scrumptious, wicked and yet so absurd,
as I get glimpses of how males view birds!
The jump-cuts in the video of his mind.
If I could slice his brain and peep inside,
the way you do a tree to see its age,
each ring another year has come and died.
For Nick each year is measured out in spurts
or casual lays, the notches on his belt go round his waist,
but like our ancient Saturn he'll need more rings
to register each boring compulsive fling . . .

NICK: But still I have a space left there for you!

SASHA: Oh God, don't wish to be part of your zoo,
nor join the seedy throng that's on your tape,
nor give you memories so you may prolong
your hard-on when you're sitting all alone
and find your fist's your only one true mate.
No mister, please don't count on me to be
another sordid picture in your rogues gallery.

SIMON: Sasha, brilliant, gosh to hear you speak
is thunder, lightning and your wit's succinct.

You put the bastard in his place, you scored,
when I was palpitating words, his sword
just cut them right in two, the way you'd slice
a pear, whatever I said, slash! His blade
divided it in twain, my brain was reeling.
But you, silver tongued and clever, so street-wise,
disintegrate in one fell swoop this man
of snow who melts before your scorching wit.
Getting a little hot for you, eh Nick?
Around the collar, met your match old chap?
Except her match strikes on your worn-out rap,
that camouflage or verbiage that you wear
is showing holes and rents, a touch threadbare,
if I may be allowed to put the boot in when you're down!

NICK: Oh aren't we getting ever so slightly bold?
The lover's been allowed to come out of the cold.
Yes, put the boot in, go on, have a go,
when all I did was siphon out your fucking woe,
that drained the very life blood out of you,
as if some loathsome leeches of self-doubt
were fastened greedily to the victim's throat.
I poured salt of reason on those slugs
till, bleeding they withdrew from the assault.
The bitter acid of my tongue did burn
and then you found your heart did tick again,
pumping with pride, renewed now with fresh gore,
that once those creatures sucked so nice and free.
You were a bank from which they could withdraw,
or rather rob with ease, instead of guns.
They held up mirrors of your flaws.

SASHA: Nick, sounds just like the devil's got your balls,
just 'cause poor Simon's not a warrior.
Not Kirk Douglas in *Spartacus* or better still,
the intrepid hero Harrison Ford leaping chasms,
a damsel in one arm fainting with orgasms.
Or James Bond standing in the centre of the world,
while entwined round his ankles, nubile girls

ascend the marble calves and inch by inch
they hoist themselves until, like kittens, feast
upon the milk of fame and suck it dry.
So Simon please don't be what you are not,
I like my heroes sensitive and shy,
not over-confident, 'must get it right' . . .
When they line up, the first take of the day
and boldly get it on the nose on 'action!'
Yeah 'great' let's shoot just one more for 'protection'.
They hit the chalk mark every time like pros
but never light the screen up not like those
who take their time to get it absolutely right.
The way you gently sip some vintage wine,
tasting, rolling it around your buds
until you've extracted the very vine
that grapes did come from, the sunbaked earth
that nourished and gave your nectar birth.
Slowly, carefully and with gentle touch,
the gardener cultivates and prunes his branch.
So Simon, be a gardener, plough your fields
with love and carefully sow your seeds,
not scatter them senselessly upon the wind.
Then you can watch and cultivate the blooms,
or else be a merchant of dire misery,
the devil, Nick, whose idea of a gentleman
is one who deigns to pay the clinic fees
to extirpate the results of his seed!
Recuperate in Aspen's fresh white snow,
while deep inside their souls are black as coal.

NICK: No not Aspen my dear but Côte d'Azur,
however your meaning still is very clear.
I'm not sure I admire the way you talk.
So don't judge me, you flaming tart,
who plays men like they were a pack of cards.
Let's try and get a jack, a king or ace
or better still a joker like poor Si.
The fool sits by his answerphone and cries

while you, you cunning bitch, have to decide
which card you'd like to turn up for tonight.
There's plenty of them out there in your pack,
and you, the card sharp, deals beneath the deck.
Yes, I believe that cheating's your best game
and with Simon it's like taking money from a babe.
Don't criticise me you greedy fawning bitch.
The visually challenged use a stick
to navigate the potholes of the world.
You use your 'crutch' instead to get you filthy rich.
Betrayal, taking husbands from their wives,
destroying households, ruining future lives . . .

SIMON: Stop! I just won't hear this any more.
You've gone too far this time Nick, find the door.
(*Nick exits.*)

SASHA: No, let him stew and bubble and spit,
like a mean and dirty gremlin's fit,
he'll explode any second, let him seethe.
The death rattle of the macho is what you hear.

SIMON: When he's caught out in his nefarious deed,
like stinking Dracula caught right in the act,
who fears his game is up, then spike his heart
with some honest observations from a 'tart'.

SASHA: Then all you do is cut off his vile head
and stuff a clove of garlic there instead.